SOVIET MILITARY POWER 1986

CONTENTS

PREFACE

With its introduction in 1981, *Soviet Military Power* gained immediate public attention and was recognized as a detailed, frank, and authoritative report on developments within the military forces of the USSR. It provided information not made available by the Soviets themselves. Subsequent editions have detailed ongoing Soviet military developments in keeping with the belief that informed and free people everywhere can best judge the merits of the policies and programs their governments have designed to meet the Soviet challenge—a challenge faced by all free nations.

Unlike citizens of the Soviet Union, peoples of democratic nations can exercise their right to question the decisions made by their governments. Decisionmaking within the USSR, however, is not subject to public scrutiny or debate. The Soviet leadership can devote a large percentage of the national income to defense programs—a cost no Western nation is willing to pay nor need incur in times of peace. The benefits that accrue to the Soviet military cannot be overlooked or ignored, and they must be examined in the light of their implications for the security of the Free World. In order to make possible a full and precise assessment of the Soviet challenge, both now and during the next several years, this edition of *Soviet Military Power* provides information on trends in the Soviet military.

With the initial deployment of mobile SS-25 intercontinental ballistic missiles to operational ICBM regiments in 1985, the Soviet Union confronted the world with further proof of its intensive drive for offensive military weapons capable of underwriting its political objectives against the West. Deployment of the SS-25 violates SALT II, and the manner in which it has been based violates SALT I.

The new, highly survivable, road-mobile, fifth-generation SS-25s entered service as the deployment of the USSR's highly accurate, fourth-generation, silo-based SS-18 Mod 4 ICBM program was reaching completion. At the same time, test firings of the fifth-generation, rail-mobile SS-X-24 ICBM continued. Preparations were also underway for test flights of three future ICBMs being developed to build on the capabilities of the fourth and fifth generations. By the mid-1990s, nearly all of the USSR's currently deployed strategic nuclear attack forces—ICBMs, SLBMs, and manned strategic bombers—will have been replaced by more advanced strategic nuclear weapons systems.

Paralleling the offensive strategic developments of 1985, the Soviet Union pressed forward with advanced strategic defense systems. Construction continued on new over-the-horizon radars and large phased-array radars capable of tracking greater numbers of targets with increased accuracy. Two new classes of silo-based ABM interceptor missiles in the Moscow ABM system were in advanced stages of testing. More important, advanced research continued on the components that are necessary to achieve a rapidly deployable nationwide ABM system. In 1985, the USSR continued to work on advanced strategic defense technology programs focused on the development of high-energy lasers, kinetic energy weapons, radio frequency weapons, and particle beam weapons. These programs have already produced developmental ground-based lasers capable of interfering with satellites. By the late 1980s, the USSR may well advance to the testing of lasers for targeting ballistic missiles in flight.

Over the past five years, successive editions of *Soviet Military Power* have charted the continuing growth and modernization of the USSR's Armed Forces across the entire spectrum of the Strategic Rocket Forces, Ground Forces, the Air Forces, the Navy, and the Air Defense Forces.

- During this half-decade, Soviet ground forces have been enlarged, and the concept for using a powerful ground force corps, almost twice the size of tank divisions, is being evaluated for conducting large-scale, high-speed operations.

- Main battle tanks of the T-64, T-72, and T-80 series have been entering the Soviet operational inventory of some 52,600 tanks at a rate of 2,300 a year.

- Since 1981, the USSR has produced some 3,800 new fighter and interceptor aircraft for its air forces and 47 new major surface combatants for its expanding naval forces.

- The number of deployed, mobile SS-20 launchers, with missiles carrying 3 MIRV warheads, has almost doubled from 250 in 1981 to 441 in 1985—representing an increase from 750 to 1,323 nuclear warheads—with more warheads available on refire missiles, ready for delivery against targets in Europe, the Middle East, and Asia at ranges up to 5,000 kilometers.

Looking to the future, Moscow shows no indication of reducing the percentage of resources dedicated to the Soviet Armed Forces; the industrial capacity devoted to continued force modernization; research and development, as well as the theft of Western technology, required for new generations of weapons systems; the commitment to improved readiness, mobility, and sustainability to support Soviet forces; and the continued projection of power beyond Soviet borders. Indeed, by each of these measures, Soviet military power continues to grow.

Within the past year:

- The Soviets, in addition to deploying the SS-25, have continued testing the SS-X-24 rail-mobile ICBM.

- The fourth TYPHOON and the third DELTA IV-Class strategic ballistic missile submarines were launched, adding to the number of longer range, more capable MIRVed SLBMs in the USSR's submarine force. Additional units are under construction. A still newer class of strategic ballistic missile submarine is likely to enter the force in the early 1990s.

- Additional units of the new supersonic manned strategic BLACKJACK bomber have emerged to participate in advanced flight-testing of this new bomber, which will carry the 3,000-kilometer-range, nuclear-armed AS-15 cruise missile. At the same time, additional new BEAR H strategic bombers have been produced, with some 40 bombers now carrying the AS-15 cruise missile.

- Increased deployment of the strategic air-launched cruise missile has been accompanied by advanced testing of the sea-launched and ground-launched variants of this missile. Over the next ten years, the Soviets are likely to deploy 2,000 to 3,000 of these nuclear-armed cruise missiles, thereby achieving an entirely new dimension of multidirectional offensive strategic nuclear capability.

- With the continuing deployment of the SA-10 surface-to-air missile and the advanced stage of development of the SA-X-12 SAM system, the USSR has continued to build toward the nationwide deployment of advanced systems not only with air defense capabilities against manned bombers but also with some capabilities against cruise missiles and some types of ballistic missiles.

- The Soviet Navy's new 65,000-ton aircraft carrier, which has half again the displacement and aircraft carrying capacity of the KIEV-Class carriers, has been launched and is being fitted out in preparation for its first sea trials in the late 1980s.

- Both of the USSR's new generation of space-launched vehicles are moving forward with successful test flights of the new medium-lift booster that will carry the manned space plane into orbit. Concurrently, testing is underway for the heavy-lift booster designed to send aloft the USSR's space shuttle as well as space station payloads in excess of 100 tons.

- The Mach-2, all-weather, air-superiority Su-27/FLANKER fighter/interceptor has become operational, joining the MiG-29/FULCRUM in the new generation of highly advanced Soviet combat aircraft.

Each year Moscow has received thousands of pieces of Western equipment and many tens of thousands of unclassified, classified, and proprietary documents as part of its campaign to acquire Free World technology by legal and illegal means. Virtually every Soviet military research project—well over 4,000 each year in the late 1970s and over 5,000 in the early 1980s—benefits from these documents. Some key Soviet armaments and equipment are based at least partly on technology acquired from the Free World. Examples are the look-down/shoot-down capability of the new Su-27/FLANKER and MiG-29/FULCRUM fighter/interceptors, the new heavy-lift Mi-26/HALO helicopter, and the roll-on/roll-off capability of Soviet merchant ships that support naval operations. The assimilation of Free World technology is so pervasive that the United States and other Free World nations have, in effect, been subsidizing the Soviet military buildup. Acknowledging this vulnerability, Free World nations have been working together to counter Soviet attempts to acquire Western technology.

Soviet Military Power 1986 provides a current, authoritative assessment of Soviet global, theater, and conventional force developments, of the doctrine guiding these developments, and of the structure dedicated to supporting the Soviet Armed Forces. This year's edition details Soviet noncompliance with arms control agreements and the threat to peace posed by the USSR's role in regional conflicts. Aggression by Soviet troops or their proxies in Afghanistan, Cambodia, Angola, Ethiopia, and Nicaragua cannot be ignored.

Finally, *Soviet Military Power 1986* reports on US policies and programs and those measures we and our allies have undertaken to meet the continuing Soviet challenge. It also outlines the steps being taken to modernize our nuclear deterrent, the capabilities of our conventional forces, and our research efforts within the Strategic Defense Initiative. It is our hope that one day the threat of nuclear mass destruction can be drastically reduced and eventually eliminated. In the pursuit of that goal, we must continue to take the necessary steps to maintain peace and freedom.

Caspar W. Weinberger
Secretary of Defense

March 1986

Chapter I

The Soviet Military

During the past year, the political and military leadership of the Soviet Union experienced several key changes. These changes will not, however, alter the growth and expansion of Soviet nuclear and conventional forces. The Soviets will continue to invest substantially in their military and, by direction of the new leadership, will apply new technologies to improve the efficiency, quality, and capacity of their industrial base and military equipment. The USSR's heavy industry infrastructure, initiated by Stalin in the First Five-Year Plan in 1927 and still operative today, was designed to support the Soviet military. Thus, the military historically has been the major impetus of industrial growth. The introduction of technologically advanced production techniques—some acquired from the Free World—will further enhance the capabilities of the Soviet Armed Forces.

In addition, the USSR will continue to pursue its global ambitions. Soviet foreign policy will remain guided by Lenin's strategy of "peaceful coexistence" (the furtherance of socialist revolution and class struggle with industrialized nations by means short of major war). To alter this course would portend the collapse of Communist ideology and the failure of international socialism. To further national goals, the new leadership will continue to modernize its armed forces, infuse new technologies into the country's military-industrial base,

The Soviet Union's drive to achieve strategic nuclear superiority has led to the deployment of the highly survivable, road-mobile SS-25 ICBM. In strengthening its increasingly more modern nuclear arsenal with the fifth-generation ICBMs, including deployment of the SS-25 and testing of the SS-X-24, the USSR has violated SALT II, which prohibits the introduction of more than one new type of ICBM. The manner of the SS-25's deployment violates SALT I.

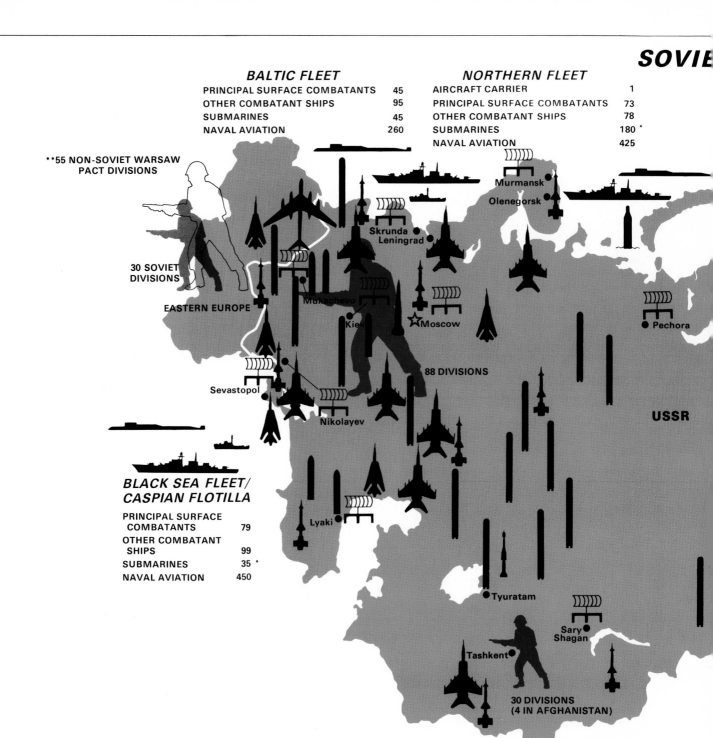

SOVIE[T]

BALTIC FLEET

PRINCIPAL SURFACE COMBATANTS	45
OTHER COMBATANT SHIPS	95
SUBMARINES	45
NAVAL AVIATION	260

NORTHERN FLEET

AIRCRAFT CARRIER	1
PRINCIPAL SURFACE COMBATANTS	73
OTHER COMBATANT SHIPS	78
SUBMARINES	180 *
NAVAL AVIATION	425

**55 NON-SOVIET WARSAW PACT DIVISIONS

30 SOVIET DIVISIONS

EASTERN EUROPE

Murmansk

Olenegorsk

Skrunda

Leningrad

Mukachevo

Kiev

☆Moscow

Pechora

88 DIVISIONS

USSR

Sevastopol

Nikolayev

BLACK SEA FLEET/ CASPIAN FLOTILLA

PRINCIPAL SURFACE COMBATANTS	79
OTHER COMBATANT SHIPS	99
SUBMARINES	35 *
NAVAL AVIATION	450

Lyaki

Tyuratam

Sary Shagan

Tashkent

30 DIVISIONS (4 IN AFGHANISTAN)

The symbols on the map are representational locations and are neither exact nor complete.

NUCLEAR FORCES

ICBMs

SS-11	448
SS-13	60
SS-17	150
SS-18	308
SS-19	360
SS-25	70+

LRINF

SS-4	112
SS-20	441

SLBMs

SS-N-5	39
SS-N-6	304
SS-N-8	292
SS-N-17	12
SS-N-18	224
SS-N-20	80
SS-NX-23	32

BOMBERS

BACKFIRE	270 *
BISON	30
BEAR	150
BADGER	262
BLINDER	135

* Including 125 in Soviet Naval Aviation.
Five BLACKJACK in advanced flight testing.

TACTICAL AIRCRAFT

TACTICAL AIRCRAFT 6,300

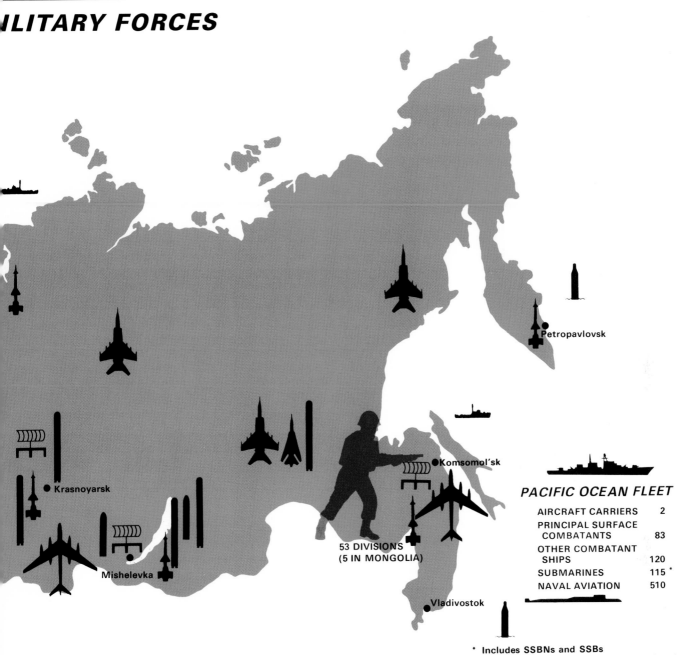

PACIFIC OCEAN FLEET

AIRCRAFT CARRIERS	2
PRINCIPAL SURFACE COMBATANTS	83
OTHER COMBATANT SHIPS	120
SUBMARINES	115 *
NAVAL AVIATION	510

* Includes SSBNs and SSBs
** NSWP Air and Naval Forces not depicted

●Petropavlovsk

●Komsomol'sk

53 DIVISIONS
(5 IN MONGOLIA)

●Krasnoyarsk

Mishelevka

●Vladivostok

GROUND FORCES*

MOTORIZED RIFLE DIVISIONS	142
TANK DIVISIONS	51
AIRBORNE DIVISIONS	7
COASTAL DEFENSE DIVISIONS	1

* Totals exclude 12
mobilization divisions and
2 new Army Corps

STRATEGIC DEFENSE FORCES

ABM RADAR

INTERCEPTORS 1,210

ASAT   SAM** LAUNCHERS 9,000+

ABM LAUNCHERS 100

**In USSR only — does not include Soviet Strategic
SAMs (SA-2/3/5) in Mongolia or with Groups of Forces.

NAVAL FORCES

AIRCRAFT CARRIERS	3
PRINCIPAL SURFACE COMBATANTS	280
OTHER COMBATANT SHIPS	392
COMBATANT CRAFT	745
AUXILIARIES	300
SUBMARINES	375
NAVAL AVIATION	1,645

9   Chapter I The Soviet Military

and pursue the expansion of Soviet influence throughout the Third World.

The Soviet Leadership

Since becoming General Secretary in March 1985, Mikhail Gorbachev has moved rapidly to consolidate his authority and place his personal stamp on Soviet national policy. During his first several months in power, Gorbachev elevated four men to full Politburo status and promoted two others, Defense Minister Sergey Sokolov and the new State Planning Committee Chief Nikolay Talyzin, to candidate Politburo membership. In addition, he placed three of his supporters on the Central Committee Secretariat. Perhaps the most striking example of Gorbachev's political strength was his ouster of one of his main political opponents, Grigoriy Romanov, from both the Politburo and the Secretariat. In addition, five of the eleven Central Committee economic departments have changed hands. The net result has been the emergence of a Party leadership that owes its position and loyalty to the General Secretary.

The swiftness with which the General Secretary has moved on economic issues reflects a sense of urgency to formulate a strategy for stimulating the economy. Current economic growth rates are not high enough to improve both military capabilities and living standards to desired levels while simultaneously ensuring future economic growth. To achieve both program goals, the USSR will have to accelerate lagging economic growth rates. Early indications are the Soviets intend to return to an intensive-growth strategy primarily through improved productivity and new technology.

The policies advocated by Gorbachev to implement the intensive-growth strategy—a shift in investment policy, a speedup in technological advances, a program to increase worker productivity through consumer incentives and stepped-up worker discipline, and increased managerial efficiency through limited decentralization—represent a relatively modest program of economic changes. None of these proposed measures are new, nor do they represent a wholesale restructuring of the Soviet Union's economic system. What is new is Gorbachev's forceful style, his political momentum, his apparent willingness to carry through a limited program of administrative decentral-

ization in the interest of economic efficiency, and his intent to increase investments for industrial machinery.

The Soviet military has a strong, long-term interest in the success of initiatives designed to stimulate the economy. The military stands to benefit if the Soviet industrial base can be modernized and if economic performance can be improved over the long term. If significant economic growth can be achieved, the technological foundation for present and future military programs will be enhanced.

Soviet Doctrine and Strategy

To the Soviets, military doctrine is concerned with the essence, purpose, and character of a possible future war and the preparation of the country and its armed forces for conducting such a war. Military strategy deals with defining the strategic tasks of the armed forces; carrying out measures to prepare the armed forces, the economy, and the population for war; determining potential adversaries; and determining the size and composition of military forces necessary to wage war. The actual practice of preparing the country and its armed forces for war as well as training troops for strategic, operational, and tactical combat is encompassed in Soviet military art—the effective application of national power to achieve political goals.

Soviet military writings state that a future war would be a decisive clash on a global scale between two diametrically opposed socioeconomic systems—socialism and capitalism. The existence of two distinct and opposing camps means that a future world war would be a coalition war. The Soviets believe that an outcome favorable to their interests depends on complete unification of the political, economic, and military forces of all countries within the socialist coalition. To this end, the Soviets have concentrated on developing and implementing a single strategic policy for the entire Warsaw Pact forces. Marshal Kulikov, Commander in Chief (CINC) of the Warsaw Pact, has referred to his command as a unified combat formation.

The Soviet approach to preparing for and actually conducting coalition warfare is governed by the assumption that any coalition, be it military or otherwise, derives its strength from the cohesiveness of its members. Conversely, they argue that when its unity is

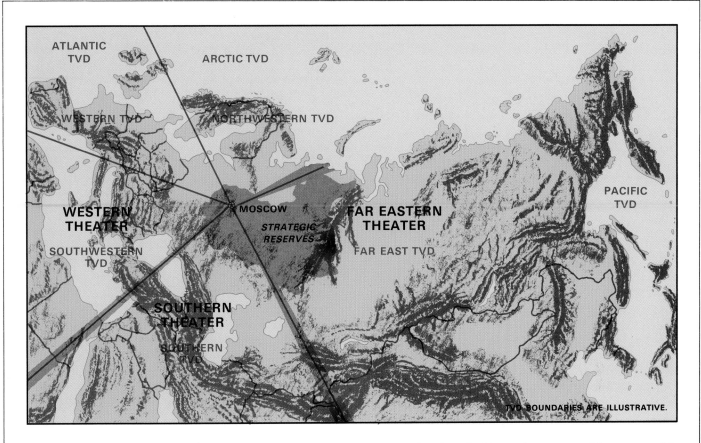

ATLANTIC TVD · ARCTIC TVD · WESTERN TVD · NORTHWESTERN TVD · PACIFIC TVD · WESTERN THEATER · MOSCOW · STRATEGIC RESERVES · FAR EASTERN THEATER · SOUTHWESTERN TVD · FAR EAST TVD · SOUTHERN THEATER · SOUTHERN TVD · TVD BOUNDARIES ARE ILLUSTRATIVE.

threatened or begins to erode for whatever reason, the entire alliance and each member of that alliance is placed at risk. The cohesion of a coalition, from the Soviet perspective, is both its greatest strength and its greatest vulnerability. The Soviets believe that the ability of the Warsaw Pact to function in an effective and cohesive manner is a key factor in the successful prosecution of a future war. In a like manner, they argue that internal contradictions plague the NATO Alliance and tend to undermine its political and military effectiveness and hence are a critical vulnerability.

The Soviets have devoted considerable energy toward building the Warsaw Pact into a strong military alliance while at the same time exploiting NATO's perceived vulnerabilities. This effort reflects Moscow's determination to forge a cohesive coalition based on Soviet military strategy and guided by Soviet policy objectives, regardless of their implications for the sovereign rights of member states. The military principles governing the conduct of coalition warfare constitute a key element in Soviet strategy—a strategy aimed at dividing and destroying an opposing coalition while at the same time maintaining the unity of the Warsaw Pact.

The Soviets believe that a world war could be waged for a period of time with conventional weapons only. Although general nuclear war is not considered inevitable, the Soviets believe it is possible that a conventional war will escalate to a nuclear conflict. Despite the fact that strategic nuclear forces would play the dominant role in such a war, the Soviets recognize the crucial function of combined arms in seizing and occupying ultimate objectives. The Soviets believe that a world war could be relatively brief or could develop into a protracted conflict. Great importance is attached to the initial phase of a war because to a large degree it would determine the course of all subsequent actions. This accounts for the extraordinary attention the Soviets pay to their overall mobilization capability and their perceived requirement for the rapid transition of high-level political-military control organs from a peacetime to a wartime footing in order to take maximum advantage of the initial period of a conflict.

Soviet doctrine envisions a future world war of wide scope waged over vast territories. Such a war would be characterized by an absence of continuous fronts, rapid and sharp changes in the strategic situation, and deep penetrations

11

into rear areas of the forces involved. Forces would rely on mobility to maneuver and wage an intense struggle to seize and maintain the initiative. The Soviets emphasize the primacy of the offensive, stating that military and political objectives are ultimately achieved only through aggressive and continuous offensive actions. Although defensive actions would occasionally be necessary, they would be active and innovative operations undertaken to support nearby offensive operations or to create favorable conditions for resuming the offensive.

The Soviets believe that victory in war is possible only through the combined and coordinated efforts of all services and troop branches. As a result, Soviet military strategy, which views warfare as a series of interdependent large-scale operations, is the same for all the services. The Soviet concept of combined arms warfare specifies that the various services and independent units must be brought together under a single unified commander. This permits the most effective use of all forces and weapons and ensures their united and coordinated employment in achieving overall strategic objectives.

Although the Soviets envision the possibility of three theaters of war—Western, Southern, and Far Eastern—they employ the concept of theaters of military operations (*Teatr Voennykh Deistvii,* abbreviated TVDs) in planning for strategic operations. A European TVD, for example, can be a thousand kilometers in both depth and width. Military assets employed in a TVD vary and are usually determined by political objectives and enemy strength. For the conduct of actions on a strategic scale, plans are formulated for the full spectrum of combat for the entire geographic area encompassed by a TVD.

The TVD organizational concept enables military planners to work out the strategy and tactics to achieve political objectives in the geographic region, taking into consideration the capabilities of the missiles, aircraft, ships, and ground forces at their disposal. While a strategic operation within the various TVDs may be conventional only, nuclear strikes are still planned within the operational concept down to division level.

On a global scale, the Soviets have identified ten continental TVDs and four oceanic TVDs. These are:

● the Western TVD, which includes

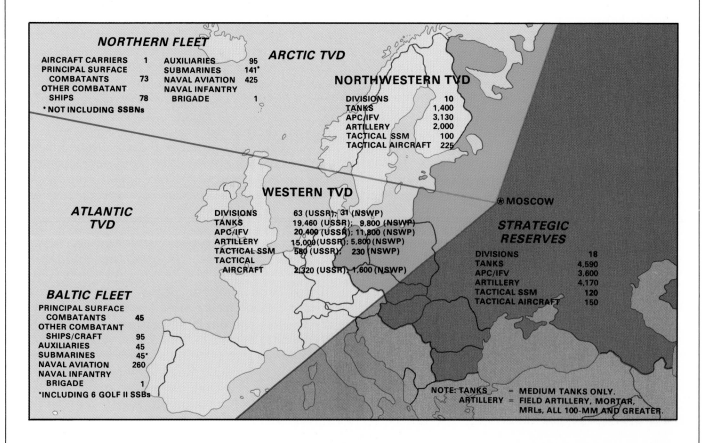

the NATO Central Region, the Baltic approaches, East Germany, Poland, Czechoslovakia, and the western USSR;

- the Northwestern TVD, which covers the Scandinavian Peninsula, Iceland, and the northwestern USSR;

- the Southwestern TVD, which includes the NATO Southern Region, the eastern Mediterranean, Hungary, Romania, Bulgaria, and the southwestern USSR;

- the Southern TVD, which covers Southwest Asia including Afghanistan, Iran, eastern Turkey, the Caucasus, and the Turkestan region of the USSR;

- the Far Eastern TVD, which covers Siberia, the Soviet Far East, Mongolia, China, the Koreas, Japan, and Alaska;

- the North American, South American, African, Australian, and Antarctic TVDs;

- the Arctic Ocean TVD, which covers the Arctic Ocean and the Barents and Norwegian Seas.

- the Atlantic Ocean TVD, which covers the Atlantic Ocean south of the Greenland-Iceland-UK gap;

- the Indian Ocean TVD; and,

- the Pacific Ocean TVD, which includes that ocean as well as the coastal areas of the Soviet Far East.

The contemporary Soviet concept of the theater strategic operation has expanded in scope and complexity. The Soviets now plan for a theater operation to consist of several fronts conducting dynamic, fast-moving operations to seize strategic ground objectives located 600-800 kilometers away. Front offensive opera-

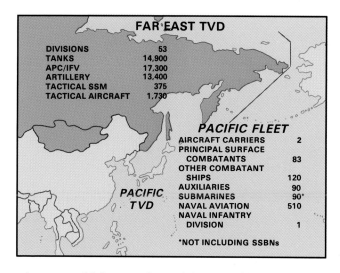

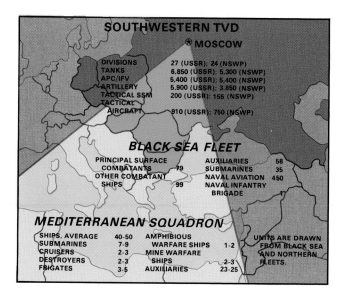

tions would be conducted in coordination with air, antiair, assault (airborne, amphibious, or joint), and naval operations. The air operation would be a massive offensive campaign designed to gain air superiority and disrupt and destroy an enemy's command and control and nuclear capability. Frontal forces would contribute to the air operation by attacking enemy air and air defense facilities with rocket, artillery, and ground forces. In turn, the air operation, by degrading and disrupting enemy command, control, and communication as well as aviation and nuclear capabilities, would create favorable conditions for the fronts to accomplish their objectives quickly.

A theater-wide antiair operation involving tactical and strategic air defense assets coordinated at the theater level would be conducted to defend allied forces from enemy aircraft. In addition, naval forces would operate off coastal flanks to destroy enemy naval forces, secure the coastal flanks of the theater, participate in amphibious operations, and thwart the enemy's attempt to employ amphibious forces.

If the war escalated to the nuclear level, the Soviets could employ nuclear strikes of varying scale and scope. Such actions could involve the coordinated use of ground, Strategic Rocket Forces (SRF), naval, and aviation systems. Nuclear strikes would be exploited by frontal forces taking advantage of shock and disruption.

Specific Soviet aims in a global war would be to:

- defeat NATO forces at any level of conflict, occupy European NATO countries, and use Europe's surviving economic assets to assist Soviet recovery;

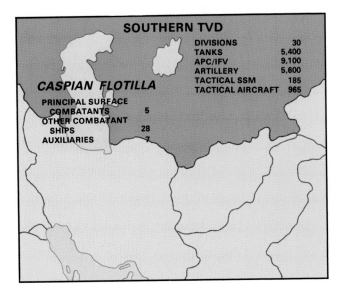

SOUTHERN TVD

DIVISIONS	30
TANKS	5,400
APC/IFV	9,100
ARTILLERY	5,600
TACTICAL SSM	185
TACTICAL AIRCRAFT	965

CASPIAN FLOTILLA

PRINCIPAL SURFACE COMBATANTS	5
OTHER COMBATANT SHIPS	28
AUXILIARIES	7

- neutralize separately China and the United States and its allies by disrupting and destroying their military forces; and
- dominate the post-war world in which socialism would replace capitalism as the basic politico-economic system in all nations.

From an internal viewpoint, the Communist Party of the Soviet Union (CPSU) leadership would seek to maintain its control over the Soviet Government, civilian population, military, police, and internal security organs. Efforts would be made to minimize losses to the Soviet leadership, essential scientific and technical personnel, to the general population, and to the economy. Repair and recovery operations would be organized to deal with war-related damage.

Soviet Armed Forces Structure

Supreme leadership of the USSR's Armed Forces is vested by the Soviet constitution in the CPSU and the highest bodies of the Soviet Government—the Presidium of the Supreme Soviet and the Council of Ministers. Party control of the military, however, is facilitated by the existence of the Defense Council, an organization that is chaired by the CPSU General Secretary and consists of top Party, government, and military leaders. The Defense Council is the most senior decisionmaking body for all aspects of national security policy. It also forms the nucleus of what would be expanded in wartime to the highest Party-state body responsible for establishing unified strategic

leadership of the USSR and providing centralized direction to the national economy and the entire war effort. In this regard, it would perform functions similar to the USSR's World War II State Defense Committee.

Party dominance of the Soviet Armed Forces is assured through its decisionmaking authority. The top Party leadership establishes military doctrine and approves military strategy as developed by the General Staff. The Defense Council, the highest decisionmaking body for all aspects of national security policy, reflects the Party's wishes on all defense, budgetary, organizational, and senior personnel assignment matters. Senior military officers are selected from a Central Committee list, and all major organizational changes in the Soviet military must be approved by the Defense Council.

Direct control and administration of the daily activities of the Soviet Armed Forces is entrusted to the Ministry of Defense (MoD), headed by Marshal of the Soviet Union (MSU) Sergey Sokolov. As Minister of Defense, Sokolov is charged with maintaining the condition and overseeing the development of the armed forces, including officer recruitment and conscription of enlisted personnel; equipping the forces with weapons systems and military materiel; developing military strategy, operational art, and tactics; training the forces; and ensuring high standards of military discipline and political loyalty. Sokolov also is responsible, in coordination with local Soviet government organizations, for the civil defense program.

The Ministry of Defense Collegium functions as a consultative body and policy review board. Chaired by Sokolov, the Collegium discusses and resolves issues connected with the development of the armed forces, their combat and mobilization readiness, and the effectiveness of military and political training. Membership includes the Deputy Ministers of Defense, the Chief of the Main Political Directorate, and other top military leaders.

The Minister of Defense exercises control of the armed forces through First Deputy Ministers and Deputy Ministers of Defense. The First Deputy Ministers are: MSU Sergey Akhromeyev, Chief of the General Staff since September 1984; MSU Viktor Kulikov, Commander in Chief of the Warsaw Pact Forces since 1977; and former CINC of the Ground Forces, Vasiliy Petrov. Five of the eleven Deputy Ministers

Stavka of the Soviet Supreme High Command

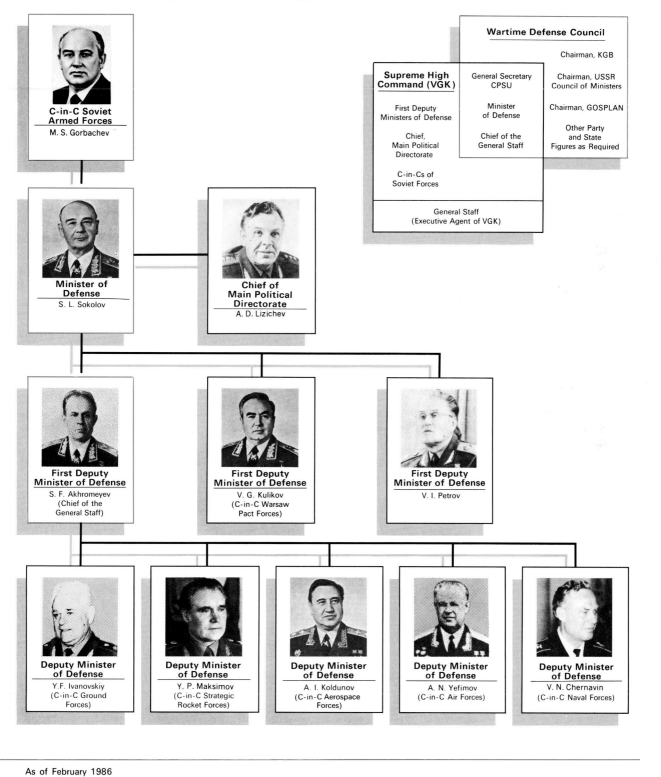

C-in-C Soviet Armed Forces
M. S. Gorbachev

Minister of Defense
S. L. Sokolov

Chief of Main Political Directorate
A. D. Lizichev

First Deputy Minister of Defense
S. F. Akhromeyev
(Chief of the General Staff)

First Deputy Minister of Defense
V. G. Kulikov
(C-in-C Warsaw Pact Forces)

First Deputy Minister of Defense
V. I. Petrov

Deputy Minister of Defense
Y. F. Ivanovskiy
(C-in-C Ground Forces)

Deputy Minister of Defense
Y. P. Maksimov
(C-in-C Strategic Rocket Forces)

Deputy Minister of Defense
A. I. Koldunov
(C-in-C Aerospace Forces)

Deputy Minister of Defense
A. N. Yefimov
(C-in-C Air Forces)

Deputy Minister of Defense
V. N. Chernavin
(C-in-C Naval Forces)

Wartime Defense Council

Supreme High Command (VGK)

First Deputy Ministers of Defense

Chief, Main Political Directorate

C-in-Cs of Soviet Forces

General Secretary CPSU

Minister of Defense

Chief of the General Staff

Chairman, KGB

Chairman, USSR Council of Ministers

Chairman, GOSPLAN

Other Party and State Figures as Required

General Staff (Executive Agent of VGK)

As of February 1986

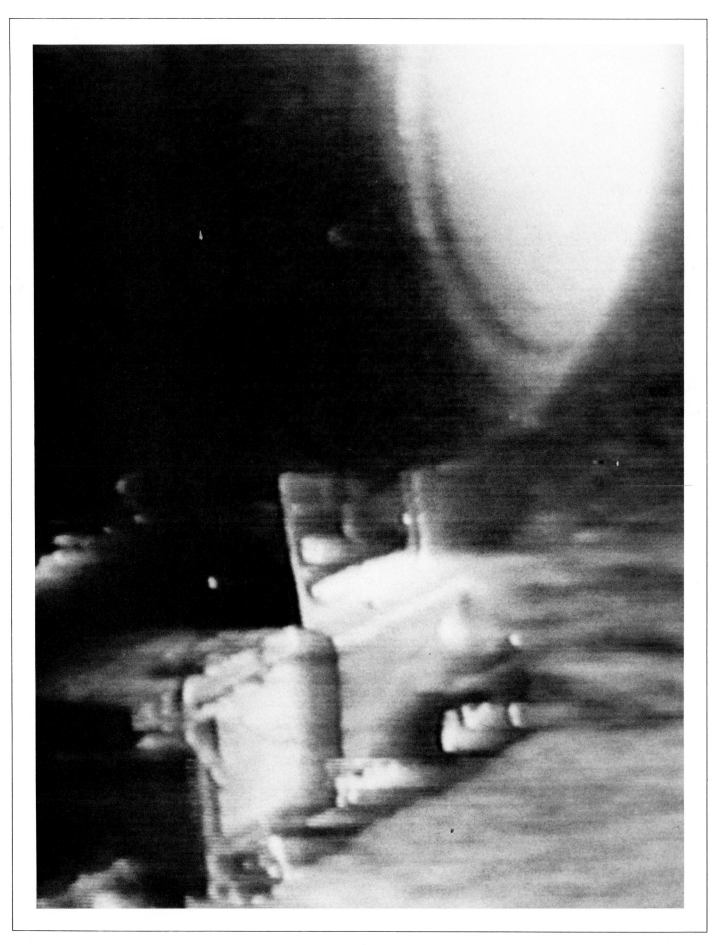

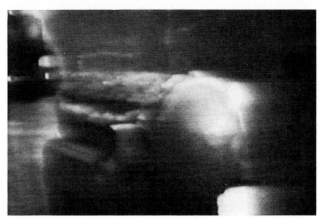

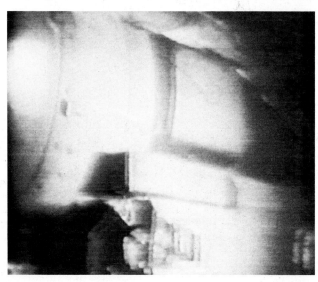

The Soviets' 441 SS-20 LRINF launchers, discussed in the nuclear forces chapter, are a constant reminder of the growing nuclear threat from accurate and survivable mobile missile systems. At top, the SS-20 transporter-erector-launcher is illustrated configured for operational deployment. The photos, at left and above, are of a Soviet SS-20 transporter-erector-launcher used for crew training and familiarization.

Chapter I The Soviet Military

are CINCs of the services—Strategic Rocket Forces, Ground Forces, Navy, Air Defense Forces, and Air Forces.

The five service CINCs are responsible for the peacetime administrative management, including combat and political training of the forces. Operational control of the forces rests with a peacetime structure of the Supreme High Command (*Verkhovnoe Glavnokomandovaniye,* abbreviated VGK) and is administered by the General Staff. The other six Deputy Defense Ministers are in charge of civil defense, rear services, the main inspectorate, construction and billeting, personnel, and armaments.

The most important element in the Soviet Ministry of Defense for peacetime forces management, as well as wartime control of operational formations, is the General Staff headed by Marshal Akhromeyev. As the central military staff organ, the General Staff exercises operational control over the armed forces and is responsible for coordinating the activities of the main staffs of the 5 services, the staffs of the 16 military districts, 4 groups of forces, 4 fleets, rear services, civil defense forces, and the main directorates of the Ministry of Defense.

The General Staff coordinates military planning, advises the Defense Council on matters of military policy, develops military strategy for approval by the Defense Council, and directs functions common to all of the services. The major responsibilities of the General Staff in peacetime are to ensure that military forces reach and sustain a high level of combat readiness and to prepare strategic operation plans in the event of war. During wartime, the General Staff would be the primary organization to implement operational orders of the Supreme High Command.

Territorially, the Soviet Armed Forces located within the USSR are organized into 16 military districts (MDs). An MD is a high-level administrative command element that contains military units up to army level, training institutions, recruitment and mobilization offices or military commissariats, and other military establishments. The primary mission of a military district is to train military units to ensure a high level of combat readiness.

Other important responsibilities include registration and induction of draftees, mobilization, civil defense, and premilitary and reserve training. In the event of war, certain military districts, such as those on the periphery of the USSR, could generate fronts or other operational field forces, either singly or in combination. Soviet units stationed in Eastern Europe are organized into four Groups of Forces located in Poland, East Germany, Czechoslovakia, and Hungary.

Military districts and Groups of Forces are subordinate to the Ministry of Defense. They contain their own organic staff elements responsible for political affairs, personnel administration, training, rear services, construction and billeting, and civil defense. Each MD and Group of Forces command staff has officers who serve as chiefs of their respective service components. Soviet naval forces are assigned to four fleets, all of which have command and staff organizations and relationships similar to those of military districts.

The structure of the Soviet Armed Forces extends to non-Soviet Warsaw Pact forces as well. The Soviet commitment to ensure that the military resources of all Warsaw Pact states will contribute effectively to a war effort is an important element in Moscow's attempt to achieve military superiority. The Warsaw Pact organization has a central role in the military effort of the Bloc states and in the USSR's overall objectives. Because of the importance of that role, the Soviets have made sure that their control is complete and unchallengeable.

Through the subordination of non-Soviet Warsaw Pact forces the Soviets seek to guarantee that the coalition will act as a single body and that the interests of Eastern Europe are the same as those of the USSR. In terms of a wartime strategy, the Soviet objective of dismantling NATO and maintaining the cohesion of the Warsaw Pact is of primary importance. For the East European member states, this means that their particular national interests, especially in time of war, will be subsumed by Soviet-defined policies. From the Soviet perspective, such a consequence would be the inevitable and necessary result of properly preparing to fight and win a coalitional war.

Wartime Command and Control

The Soviets believe in a rapid and efficient transformation of their peacetime national security organization into an operational command capable of successfully achieving all major political and military objectives in the event of general war. To this end, they have established peacetime national security and high-level military organizations that closely approximate the expected wartime structure. These peacetime organizations could shift their activities to wartime operations with minimal disruption and little augmentation in membership. Party and state control would be maintained through the relocation of selected high-level officials to hardened emergency facilities.

In the event of war, the current Defense Council probably would be expanded to include representatives of the highest Party, state, and military leadership. It would function in a manner similar to the World War II State Defense Committee, ensuring centralized political and economic direction of the entire war effort. General Secretary Gorbachev would function as wartime Defense Council Chairman and exercise direct leadership of the Soviet Armed Forces as Supreme Commander in Chief of the VGK and head of its General Headquarters *(Stavka)*.

The Ministry of Defense Collegium would probably provide the foundation for the wartime *Stavka* VGK, which would include, in addition to Gorbachev, the Minister of Defense, the Chief of the General Staff and other First Deputy Ministers of Defense, the Chief of the Main Political Directorate, and the five Armed Forces Commanders in Chief.

The General Staff would serve as operational staff and executive agent for the *Stavka* VGK. Working in conjunction with the main staffs of the five services, the Main Operations Directorate of the General Staff would draft strategic operations plans for consideration by the *Stavka* VGK. Once approved, these plans would be issued to operational commanders as orders of the VGK. This group would ensure timely and precise execution of the VGK military campaign plans by the operational commands.

In order to ensure centralized control of strategic planning and decentralized battle management of the armed forces, the Soviets in wartime would employ intermediate High Commands of Forces in TVDs that would be subordinate to the VGK and would be responsible for directing the efforts of subordinate formations. Commanders for four of the probable TVD High Commands are: Marshal of the Soviet Union N.V. Ogarkov; Army General I.A. Gerasimov; Army General M.M. Zaytsev; and Army General I.M. Tret'yak. In certain circumstances, the VGK might create High Commands for specific strategic directions (that is, a major axis or avenue of attack not already under the control of a High Command in a TVD).

The Soviets also have created an elaborate system of emergency relocation facilities, many of which are hardened and designed to ensure the survival of Party and state control by protecting high-level Party, government, and military leaders. These facilities are equipped with hardened communications equipment and would serve as alternate command and control posts for the top leadership in wartime. In addition, essential personnel of critical industries would be evacuated along with critical machinery out of urban areas and away from immediate battle areas to emergency locations to facilitate their continued operation. All these measures are designed to provide uninterrupted functioning of the various elements of Soviet strategic leadership and the national economy in wartime, including nuclear war.

A wartime coalition command structure also has been created for the quick transformation of the Warsaw Pact into an effective military alliance capable of operating as an extension of the Soviet Armed Forces. Since the late 1970s, the Soviets have introduced and institutionalized measures aimed at modernizing the Warsaw Pact's unified command structure. Integration would be achieved through the complete wartime subordination of the armed forces of the non-Soviet Warsaw Pact countries to the High Commands of Forces in the Western and Southwestern TVDs. These commands provide a key link between the supreme military authority vested in the VGK and the fronts and armies operating within the various TVDs.

In keeping with the Soviet concept of combined arms operations, the TVD commander has at his disposal not only the assets available in the ground forces but also the naval and air assets assigned to the TVD itself. In the case of the Western and Southwestern TVDs, some, if not all, of the armed forces of the non-Soviet Warsaw Pact states operating in these TVDs will be subordinate to the Soviet TVD commands. This subordination reflects Moscow's belief that well-equipped and well-trained Warsaw Pact forces, under Soviet leadership, can defeat any other coalition.

Chapter II

Nuclear Force Operations

The Soviet Union has pressed ahead with the development and deployment of new generations of increasingly capable land, sea, and air forces for nuclear attack. Modernization of the fourth generation of intercontinental ballistic missiles (ICBMs) is essentially complete. In clear violation of the SALT II Treaty, deployment of a fifth-generation ICBM, the SS-25, has begun, and its deployment has been undertaken in a manner that violates SALT I. This highly survivable weapon system represents the world's first operationally deployed road-mobile ICBM. Development continues apace on the SS-X-24, which could be deployed in a rail-mobile version this year.

The Soviets' strategic nuclear-powered ballistic missile submarine (SSBN) force remains the largest in the world. Construction continues on several new TYPHOON-Class SSBNs. The SS-NX-23, the USSR's most capable long-range submarine-launched ballistic missile (SLBM), is nearing operational status. It is deployed on the DELTA IV and probably will be deployed on DELTA III SSBNs.

The USSR currently has three manned intercontinental-capable bombers in development and production—the BEAR H, the BLACKJACK, and the BACKFIRE. Newly built BEAR H bombers are the first launch platform for the long-range AS-15 air-launched cruise missile (ALCM).

Projections for the years ahead are:
- Additional TYPHOON-Class submarines,

The USSR's forces for intercontinental nuclear attack include growing numbers of the new TYPHOON-Class (lower left) and DELTA IV-Class (center, entering tunnel) strategic ballistic missile submarines fitted with new generations of MIRVed missiles with greater range, payload, and accuracy. These submarines may operate from bases where tunnels are being constructed for protection.

BLACKJACK and BEAR H bombers, and SS-X-24 ICBMs, all carrying many more warheads than the systems they are replacing, will be deployed.

- By 1990, if the Soviets continue to maintain over 2,500 missile launchers and heavy bombers and even if they are within the quantitative sublimits of SALT II, the number of deployed warheads will grow to over 12,000.
- Although the Soviets would not necessarily expand their intercontinental attack forces beyond some 12,000 to 13,000 warheads, they clearly have the capability to do so. Based on recent trends, even under SALT, the Soviets could deploy over 15,000 warheads, or by violating SALT, over 20,000 warheads by the mid-1990s.

The modernization and upgrading of these strategic forces have been paralleled by growth and increased capabilities of the Soviets' longer range intermediate-range nuclear force (LRINF) and short-range ballistic missile (SRBM) systems deployed with Soviet combat forces. Significant improvements in nuclear-capable aircraft as well as increases in tactical missiles and nuclear artillery have also occurred.

Nuclear Doctrine and Strategy

Soviet leaders since the 1960s have followed a consistent and relentless policy for the development of forces for nuclear attack. The Soviet leadership recognizes the catastrophic consequences of a general nuclear war. However, Soviet military forces have taken actions and exhibited behavior which indicate that they believe a nuclear war could be fought and won at levels below general nuclear war. The grand strategy of the USSR is to attain its objectives, if possible, by means short of war by exploiting the coercive leverage inherent in superior forces, particularly nuclear forces, to instill fear, to erode the West's collective security arrangements, and to support subversion. Thus, the primary role of Soviet military power is to provide the essential underpinning for the step-by-step extension of Soviet influence and control.

In any nuclear war, Soviet strategy would be to destroy enemy nuclear forces before launch or in flight to their targets, to reconstitute the war base should nuclear weapons reach the Soviet homeland, and to support and sustain combined arms combat in different theaters of military operations. Several overarching strategic wartime missions are:

- to eliminate enemy nuclear-capable forces and related command, control, and communications capabilities;
- to seize and occupy vital areas on the Eurasian landmass; and
- to defend the Soviet state against attack.

These missions would involve:

- disruption and destruction of the enemy's essential command, control, and communications capabilities;
- destruction or neutralization of enemy nuclear forces on the ground or at sea before they could be launched; and
- protection of the Soviet leadership and cadres, military forces, and military and economic assets necessary to sustain the war.

Strategic and theater forces and programs in place or under active development designed to accomplish these objectives include:

- hard-target-capable ICBMs, new submarine-launched ballistic missiles, LRINF ballistic missiles, and land- and sea-based cruise missiles;
- short-range ballistic missiles (SRBMs) and free rocket over ground (FROG) systems deployed with combat troops;
- bombers and ALCMs designed to penetrate US and allied defensive systems;
- large numbers of land attack and antiship cruise missiles on various platforms;
- antisubmarine warfare (ASW) forces to attack Western nuclear-powered ballistic missile submarines;
- air and missile defenses, including early warning satellites and radars, interceptor aircraft, surface-to-air missiles (SAMs), antiballistic missile (ABM) radars and interceptors, and some antiaircraft artillery;
- antisatellite weapons;
- passive defense forces, including civil defense forces and countermeasures troops and equipment devoted to confusing incoming aircraft; and
- hardened facilities numbering in the thousands, command vehicles, and evacuation plans designed to protect Party, military, governmental and industrial staffs, essential workers, and to the extent possible the general population.

Supporting a land war in Eurasia and eliminating the US capacity to fight and support a conflict would require the capability to employ theater and strategic forces over a variety of ranges and the destruction of:

- military-associated command and control facilities and other assets;
- war-supporting industries, arsenals, and major military facilities;
- ports and airfields in the United States and along air and sea routes to European and Asian theaters of war; and
- satellite surveillance sensors, ground-based surveillance sensors, and related communications facilities.

Soviet nuclear forces are designed and personnel are trained to fulfill their missions under all circumstances. Soviet leaders appear to believe that nuclear war might last weeks or even months and have factored this possibility into their force planning. Despite public rhetoric alleging their commitment to no first-use of nuclear weapons, the Soviets have

A launch-under-attack circumstance would place great stress on attack warning systems and launch coordination. To meet the demands of a launch-under-attack contingency, the Soviets have established an elaborate warning system. Satellite, over-the-horizon radar, and early warning systems have been built to provide the Soviet Union with the capability to assess accurately and respond effectively to any nuclear attack. These warning systems could give the Soviets time to launch their nuclear forces very quickly.

Nuclear Forces-Bombers

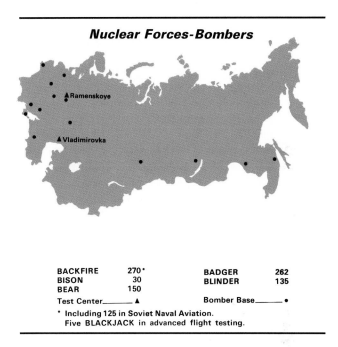

BACKFIRE	270*	BADGER	262
BISON	30	BLINDER	135
BEAR	150		
Test Center ▲		Bomber Base ●	

* Including 125 in Soviet Naval Aviation.
Five BLACKJACK in advanced flight testing.

Nuclear Forces-SLBMs

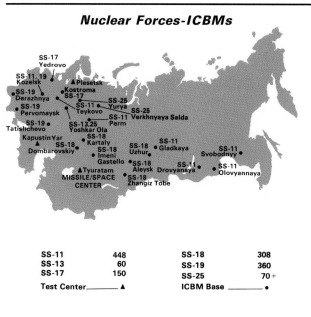

SS-N-5	39	SS-N-18	224
SS-N-6	304	SS-N-20	80
SS-N-8	292	SS-NX-23	32
SS-N-17	12		
Test Center ▲		SLBM/SSBN Port ●	

developed extensive plans either to preempt a nuclear attack or to launch a massive first strike.

The key to a successful preemptive attack would be effective coordination of the strike and accurate intelligence on enemy intentions. Meeting these demands in war requires reliable command, control, and communications under all conditions.

Nuclear Forces-ICBMs

SS-11	448	SS-18	308
SS-13	60	SS-19	360
SS-17	150	SS-25	70+
Test Center ▲		ICBM Base ●	

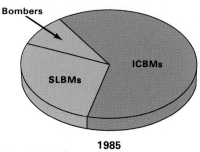

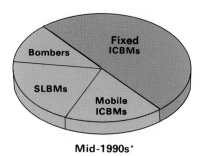

1985

Mid-1990s

*Estimates based on current trends.

Follow-on strikes would require the survival of the command, control, and communications systems as well as the weapons themselves. The Soviets have invested heavily in providing this survivability. The SS-17, SS-18, and SS-19 ICBMs are housed in the world's hardest operational silos. The Soviets are building silos for the new ABM interceptors around Moscow. To increase its survivability, the SS-20 LRINF missile is mobile. The mobile SS-25 ICBM is being deployed; the development of the mobile SS-X-24 continues; and a mobile surface-to-air missile, the SA-X-12, with some capabilities against certain types of ballistic missiles, is almost operational. The launch-control facilities for offensive missiles are housed in very

Base support facilities for the road-mobile SS-25, consisting of launcher garages equipped with sliding roofs, already exist at several bases, with more bases under construction.

hard silos or on off-road vehicles. Communications are redundant and hardened against both blast and electro-magnetic pulse damage. Higher commands have multiple mobile alternate command posts available for their use, including land vehicles, trains, aircraft, and ships. Bombers are assigned dispersal airfields. Ballistic missile submarines could be hidden in caves, submerged in deep fjords just off their piers, or dispersed while being protected by Soviet surface and submarine forces.

The belief that a nuclear war might be protracted has led to the USSR's emphasis on nuclear weapon system survivability and sustainability. For their ICBM, LRINF, SRBM, SLBM, and air defense forces, the Soviets have stocked extra missiles, propellants, and warheads throughout the USSR. Some ICBM silo launchers could be reloaded, and provisions have been made for the decontamination of those launchers. Plans for the survival of necessary equipment and personnel have been developed and practiced. Resupply systems are available to reload SSBNs in protected waters.

Soviet Intercontinental Attack Forces

Intercontinental Ballistic Missiles

The operational Soviet ICBM force consists of some 1,400 silo and mobile launchers, aside from those at test sites. Some 818 of the silo launchers have been rebuilt since 1972; nearly half of these silos have been refurbished since 1979. All 818 silos have been hardened against attack by currently operational US ICBMs. These silos contain the SS-17 Mod 3 (150 silos), the SS-18 Mod 4 (308), and the SS-19 Mod 3 (360), which were the world's most modern de-

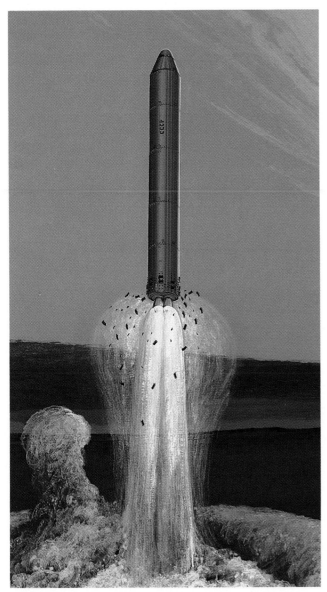

Although the USSR has recently completed the deployment of its fourth-generation ICBMs and has started deploying a fifth generation, even newer ICBMs are in development. The Soviets' new SS-18 follow-on is nearing the flight test stage. When deployed, it is likely to carry at least ten warheads and to have better accuracy and greater throw-weight than its predecessor.

was specifically designed to attack and destroy ICBMs and other hardened targets in the US. The SS-18 Mod 4 force currently deployed has the capability to destroy about 65 to 80 percent of US ICBM silos, using two nuclear warheads against each. Even after this type of attack, over 1,000 SS-18 warheads would be available for further attacks against targets in the US. The SS-19 Mod 3 ICBM, while not identical to the SS-18 in accuracy, has similar capabilities. It could be assigned similar missions and could be used against targets in Eurasia. Although the SS-17 is somewhat less capable than the SS-19, it has similar targeting flexibility.

The remaining Soviet ICBM silos are fitted primarily with the SS-11 Mod 2/3s and SS-13

US *and Soviet* ICBM Launcher and Reentry Vehicle (RV) Deployment 1970-1986

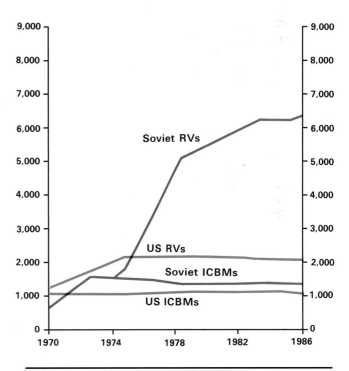

ployed ICBMs until the more modern, mobile SS-25 was deployed.

Each SS-18 and SS-19 ICBM can carry more and larger MIRVs than the Minuteman III, the most modern deployed US ICBM. The SS-18 Mod 4 carries at least ten MIRVs, and the SS-19 Mod 3 carries six, whereas the Minuteman III carries only three. The SS-18 Mod 4

Mod 2s. These ICBMs of older vintage are housed in less-survivable silos and are considerably less capable. Nevertheless, their destructive potential against softer area targets in the United States and Eurasia is significant in terms of many of the Soviet requirements outlined earlier.

The most recent development in the Soviets' operational ICBM force occurred with the deployment of their road-mobile SS-25 missile, in violation of SALT I and SALT II. The SS-25 is approximately the same size as the US Minuteman ICBM. It carries a single reentry vehicle and is being deployed in a road-mobile configuration similar to that of the SS-20. As such, it will be highly survivable with an inherent refire capability. Several bases for the SS-25 are operational, with a total of over 70 launchers deployed. They consist of launcher garages equipped with sliding roofs and several support buildings to house the requisite mobile support equipment.

Within the past year, the Soviets have begun dismantling SS-11 silos in compensation for SS-25 deployments. The Soviets are expected to continue to dismantle SS-11 silos. By the mid-1990s, all SS-11s will probably be deactivated.

Deployment programs for all of the currently operational silo-based Soviet ICBMs are essentially complete. The command, control, and communications system that supports the Soviet ICBM force is modern and highly survivable, and the reliability of the ICBMs themselves is regularly tested by live firings from operational complexes.

Some silo-based ICBMs in the current force that the Soviets decide not to replace with modified or new ICBMs will, in accord with past practice, be refurbished to increase their useful lifetime and reliability. During this process some system modifications also could be made.

Force Developments. Soviet research and development on ICBMs is a dynamic process involving many programs. A modernized version or a new replacement for the liquid-propelled

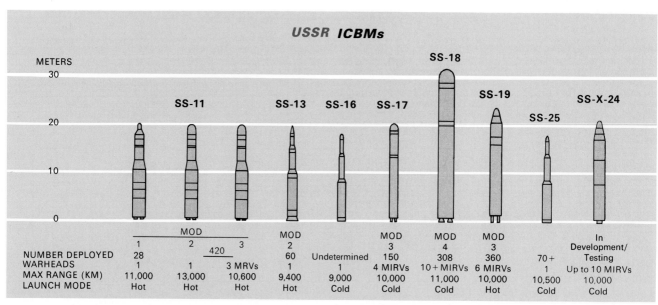

	SS-11 MOD 1	SS-11 MOD 2	SS-11 MOD 3	SS-13 MOD 2	SS-16	SS-17 MOD 3	SS-18 MOD 4	SS-19 MOD 3	SS-25	SS-X-24
NUMBER DEPLOYED	28	420		60	Undetermined	150	308	360	70+	In Development/Testing
WARHEADS	1	1	3 MRVs	1	1	4 MIRVs	10+MIRVs	6 MIRVs	1	Up to 10 MIRVs
MAX RANGE (KM)	11,000	13,000	10,600	9,400	9,000	10,000	11,000	10,000	10,500	10,000
LAUNCH MODE	Hot	Hot	Hot	Hot	Cold	Cold	Cold	Hot	Cold	Cold

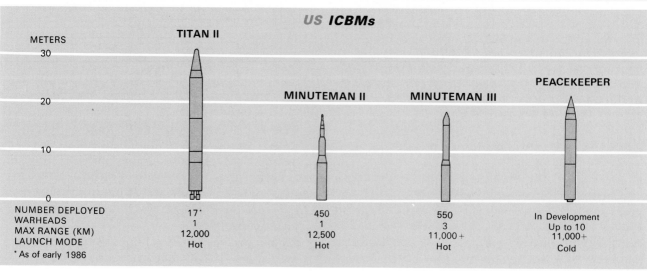

	TITAN II	MINUTEMAN II	MINUTEMAN III	PEACEKEEPER
NUMBER DEPLOYED	17*	450	550	In Development
WARHEADS	1	1	3	Up to 10
MAX RANGE (KM)	12,000	12,500	11,000+	11,000+
LAUNCH MODE	Hot	Hot	Hot	Cold

* As of early 1986

Modernization of Soviet ICBMs
Warhead Mix

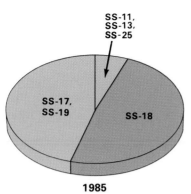

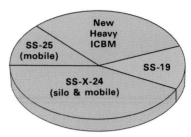

1985

Mid-1990s*

* Estimates based on current trends.

SS-18 is likely to be produced and deployed in existing silos through the end of the century.

The Soviets appear to be planning on new solid-propellant ICBMs to meet many future mission requirements, including a counterforce capability. The Soviets already have two new solid-propellant ICBMs—the small, mobile SS-25 described above, now being deployed, and the SS-X-24. The medium-size SS-X-24 is well along in its flight test program. The SS-X-24 deployment in a rail-mobile mode could begin as early as late 1986. Silo-based deployment could occur later. Early preparations for the deployment of the SS-X-24 are already underway.

Activity at the Soviet ICBM test ranges indicates that two additional new ICBMs are under development. A new ICBM to replace the SS-18 is nearing the flight test stage of develop-

*The rail-mobile **SS-X-24** missile, carrying ten independently targetable warheads, is likely to be deployed as early as late 1986.*

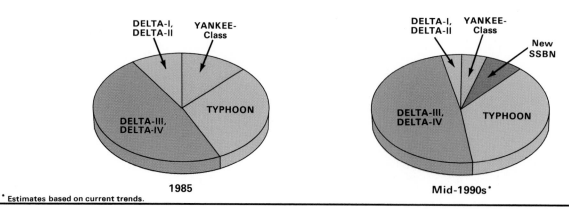

**Modernization of Soviet SLBMs
Warhead Mix**

1985

Mid-1990s*

* Estimates based on current trends.

ment. Additionally, a solid-propellant missile that may be larger than the SS-X-24 will begin flight-testing in the next few years. Both of these missiles are likely to have better accuracy and greater throwweight potential than their predecessors. A third possible development is that a MIRVed version of the SS-25 will be developed later this decade. Such a development would further expand the already large warhead inventory possessed by the Soviets. By the mid-1990s, the Soviet ICBM force will have been almost entirely replaced with new systems, a number of which may violate SALT II constraints.

Submarine-Launched Ballistic Missiles

The Soviets maintain the world's largest ballistic missile submarine force. As of early 1986, the force numbered 62 modern SSBNs carrying 944 SALT-accountable nuclear-tipped missiles. Neither total includes the 13 older GOLF II SSBs with 39 missiles which are currently assigned theater missions. The GOLF III SSB and HOTEL III SSBN are only SALT-accountable for their missile tubes. Twenty SSBNs are fitted with 336 MIRVed submarine-launched ballistic missiles (SLBMs). These 20 units have been built and deployed within the past nine years. Two-thirds of the ballistic missile

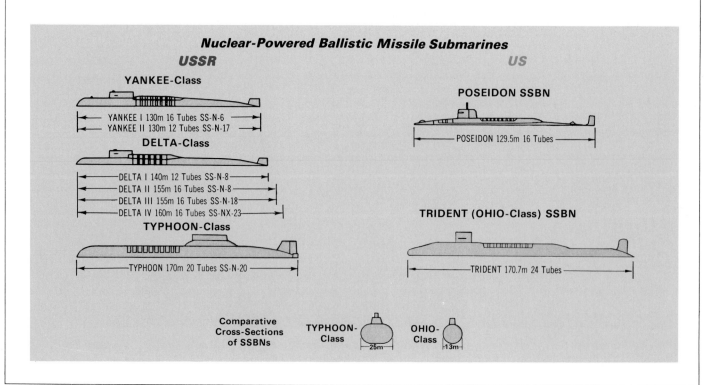

Nuclear-Powered Ballistic Missile Submarines

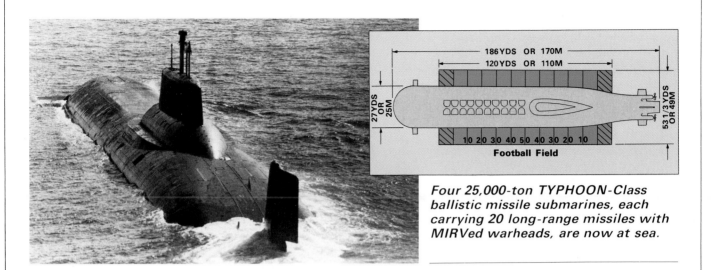

Four 25,000-ton TYPHOON-Class ballistic missile submarines, each carrying 20 long-range missiles with MIRVed warheads, are now at sea.

submarines are fitted with long-range SLBMs, enabling them to patrol in waters close to the Soviet Union. This affords protection from NATO antisubmarine warfare operations. Moreover, the long-range missiles allow the Soviets to fire from home ports and still strike targets in the United States.

Four units of the modern Soviet ballistic missile submarine, the TYPHOON, have already been built. Each TYPHOON carries 20 SS-N-20 solid-propellant MIRVed SLBMs. The TYPHOON is the world's largest submarine, with a displacement a third greater than that of the US Ohio-Class. It can operate under the Arctic Ocean icecap, adding further to the protection afforded by the 8,300-kilometer range of its SS-N-20 SLBMs. Three or four additional TYPHOONs are probably now under construction, and by the early 1990s the Soviets could

have as many as eight of these potent weapons systems in their operational force.

In accordance with the SALT I Interim Agreement, the Soviets have, since 1978, removed 14 YANKEE I units from service as

Modern SSBN Force Levels

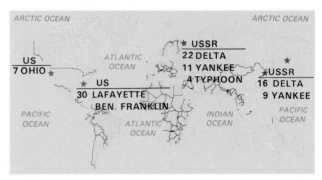

Nuclear Submarine-Launched Ballistic Missiles

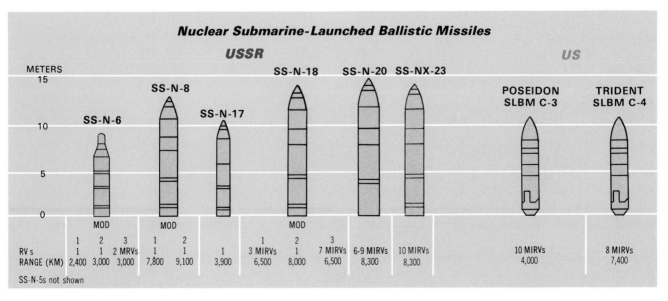

	USSR										US	
	SS-N-6	SS-N-8	SS-N-17	SS-N-18			SS-N-20	SS-NX-23		POSEIDON SLBM C-3	TRIDENT SLBM C-4
	MOD	MOD		MOD							
RVs	1 2 3	1 2	1	1 2 3			6-9 MIRVs	10 MIRVs		10 MIRVs	8 MIRVs
	1 1 2 MRVs	1 1	1	3 MIRVs 1 7 MIRVs							
RANGE (KM)	2,400 3,000 3,000	7,800 9,100	3,900	6,500 8,000 6,500			8,300	8,300		4,000	7,400

SS-N-5s not shown

ballistic missile submarines. These units had to be removed as newer submarines were produced in order for the overall Soviet SSBN force to stay within the 62 modern SSBN/950 SLBM limits established in 1972. These YAN-KEEs, however, have not been scrapped. Some have been reconfigured as attack or long-range cruise missile submarines.

Force Developments. The Soviets have launched three units—two of which are currently accountable under SALT—of a new class of SSBN, the DELTA IV, which will be fitted with the SS-NX-23 SLBM, now being flight-tested. This large, liquid-propelled SLBM will have greater throwweight, carry more warheads, and be more accurate than the SS-N-18 which is currently carried on the DELTA III SSBN. The SS-NX-23 is likely to be deployed on DELTA IIIs as a replacement for the SS-N-18.

The Soviets probably will begin flight-testing a modified version of the SS-N-20. Additionally, based on past Soviet practice, they probably will develop a modified version of the SS-NX-23 before the end of the decade. Both modified

versions of the SS-N-20 and SS-NX-23 are likely to be more accurate than their predecessors and eventually may provide the Soviets with a hard-target capability for SLBMs.

To ensure communications reliability, the Soviets are expected to deploy an extremely low frequency (ELF) communications system that will enable them to contact SSBNs under most operating conditions.

Strategic Aviation

The five air armies subordinate to the

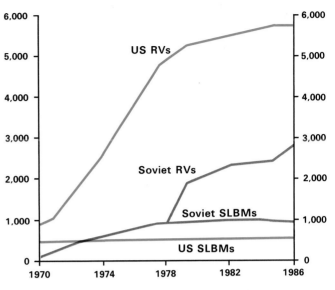

US and Soviet SLBM Launcher and Reentry Vehicle (RV) Deployment 1970-1986

Supreme High Command (VGK) which contain the Soviet strategic bombers and strike aircraft are:

- Smolensk Air Army;
- Legnica Air Army;
- Venitza Air Army;
- Irkutsk Air Army; and
- Moscow Air Army.

The assets of the air armies include some 180 BEAR and BISON bombers, 145 BACK-FIRE bombers, 397 medium-range BLINDER and BADGER bombers, and 450 shorter range FENCER strike aircraft. The Soviets have allocated these aircraft among five air armies to cover specific theaters of military operations (Europe, Asia, and the United States) and yet retain the flexibility to reallocate aircraft as necessary during wartime. This flexibility allows the Soviets to alter the use of their strategic air assets as circumstances require. Soviet Naval Aviation assets include some 125 BACKFIRE and 230 BLINDER and BADGER bombers. Air army BEAR and BISON bombers also could be made available for maritime missions. In addition, the air armies and Soviet Naval Aviation have a total of some 530

Two units of the newest Soviet ballistic missile submarine, the DELTA IV, are now on sea trials.

31   **Chapter II Nuclear Force Operations**

Modernization of Soviet Heavy Bombers
Weapon Mix

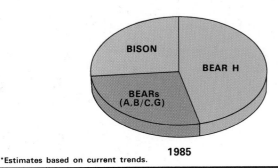

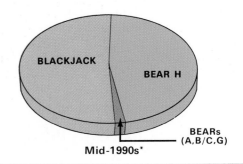

1985

*Estimates based on current trends.

Mid-1990s*

tanker, reconnaissance, and electronic warfare aircraft.

The Soviets are in the process of upgrading their long-range bomber force. The new BEAR H bomber, which carries the AS-15 long-range cruise missile, became operational in 1984. About 40 of these aircraft are now in the inventory. BEAR H bombers have been observed in training flights simulating attacks against the North American continent.

The BEAR H is the first new production of a strike version of the BEAR airframe in over 15 years. Additionally, the Soviets are reconfiguring older BEAR aircraft, which carry the subsonic AS-3 air-to-surface missile (ASM), to carry the newer supersonic AS-4. Several of these reconfigurations, known as BEAR Gs, are operational.

The Soviets have been producing the BACKFIRE, their most modern operational bomber, at a rate of about 30 per year. Several modifications have been made to the aircraft and further modifications are likely to upgrade performance. The BACKFIRE can perform a variety of missions including nuclear strike, conventional attack, antiship strikes, and reconnaissance. Its low-altitude capabilities make it a formidable platform for high-speed military operations. Additionally, the BACKFIRE can be equipped with a probe to permit in-flight refueling to increase its range. This would improve its capabilities against the contiguous United States.

The Soviets have assigned some FENCER strike aircraft to the air armies. The FENCER is a supersonic, variable-geometry-wing, all-weather fighter-bomber that has been in oper-

ation since 1974. Four variants have been produced, the most recent introduced in 1983. The FENCER is still in production, and the number assigned to air armies is likely to increase over the next few years.

Force Developments. The BLACKJACK, a new long-range bomber larger than the US B-1B, is still undergoing flight-testing. The BLACKJACK will be faster than the US B-1B and may have about the same combat radius.

US and Soviet Intercontinental-Capable Bombers[1]

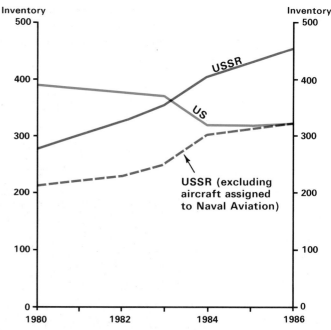

[1] US forces include B-52, FB-111, and B-1B; Soviet forces include BEAR, BISON, and BACKFIRE.

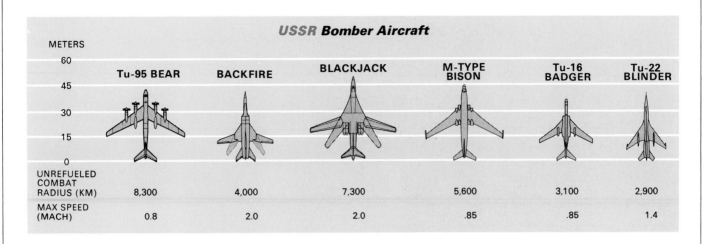

USSR Bomber Aircraft

METERS	Tu-95 BEAR	BACKFIRE	BLACKJACK	M-TYPE BISON	Tu-16 BADGER	Tu-22 BLINDER
UNREFUELED COMBAT RADIUS (KM)	8,300	4,000	7,300	5,600	3,100	2,900
MAX SPEED (MACH)	0.8	2.0	2.0	.85	.85	1.4

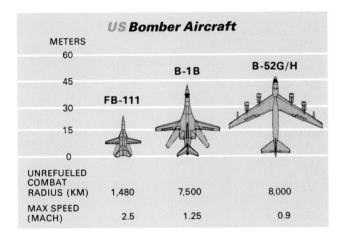

US Bomber Aircraft

METERS	FB-111	B-1B	B-52G/H
UNREFUELED COMBAT RADIUS (KM)	1,480	7,500	8,000
MAX SPEED (MACH)	2.5	1.25	0.9

The new bomber will be capable of carrying cruise missiles, bombs, or a combination of both and could be operational as early as 1988. It probably will be used first to replace the much less capable BEAR A bomber and then the BEAR G bomber.

For several years the Soviet Union has been developing the MIDAS, an aerial-refueling tanker version of the Il-76/CANDID aircraft. When deployed in the near future, the new tanker can be used to support tactical and strategic operations and will expand significantly the ability of the Soviets to conduct longer range missions.

Long-Range Cruise Missiles

The AS-15, a small, air-launched, subsonic, low-altitude cruise missile, became operational in 1984. It is similar in design to the US Tomahawk and has a range of about 3,000 kilometers. It is currently deployed with the BEAR H and is expected to be carried on the BLACKJACK when that aircraft becomes operational. The BEAR H and eventually the BLACKJACK, in combination with the nuclear-armed AS-15, will significantly increase Soviet capabilities for strategic intercontinental air operations.

The Soviets have a sea-launched version and a ground-launched version of the AS-15 under development. The sea-launched variant, the SS-NX-21, is small enough to be fired from standard Soviet torpedo tubes. Possible launch platforms for the SS-NX-21 include three VICTOR classes of nuclear-powered attack submarines (SSNs); the reconfigured YANKEE-Class SSN; and the new AKULA-, MIKE-, and SIERRA-Class SSNs. The SS-NX-21 is expected to become operational soon and could be deployed on submarines off US and allied coasts.

The ground-launched cruise missile variant, the SSC-X-4, will probably become operational this year. Its mission will be to support operations in the Eurasian theater since the Soviets are unlikely to deploy it outside the USSR and its range is too short for intercontinental strikes. The SSC-X-4 is being developed as a mobile system and probably will follow operational procedures similar to the SS-20 LRINF system.

In addition to these variants of the AS-15, a larger cruise missile is under development. This missile, designated the SS-NX-24, will be flight-tested from a specially converted YANKEE-Class nuclear-powered cruise missile attack submarine (SSGN). It could become operational by 1987. A ground-based version of this missile may be developed.

All of these cruise missiles probably will be equipped with nuclear warheads when first deployed and will be capable of attacking hardened targets. These systems could be accurate enough to permit the use of conventional war-

The BEAR H bomber is a launch platform for the 3,000-kilometer-range, nuclear-armed AS-15 cruise missile.

heads, depending on munitions developments and the types of guidance systems incorporated in their designs. With such warheads and guidance, cruise missiles would pose a significant non-nuclear threat to US and Eurasian airfields and nuclear weapons.

US Strategic Nuclear Forces

In measuring and evaluating the continuing improvements being made by the USSR's strategic forces, it is useful to bear in mind the status of US forces, the modernization of which is discussed in Chapter VIII. By mid-1986, US strategic deterrent forces will include:

- 1,000 Minuteman ICBMs;
- 17 Titan ICBMs (the Titan force will be retired by the end of 1987);
- 240 B-52G/H model bombers plus about 23 aircraft undergoing maintenance and modification;
- 56 FB-111 bombers plus some 5 aircraft undergoing maintenance and modification;
- 17 B-1B bombers;
- 480 Poseidon (C-3 and C-4) fleet ballistic missile launchers; and
- 168 Trident fleet ballistic missile launchers.

The historic and continuing objective of US nuclear forces is deterrence of nuclear and ma-

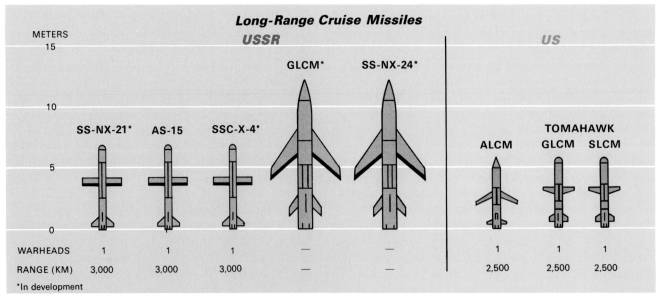

Long-Range Cruise Missiles

	USSR					*US*		
	SS-NX-21*	AS-15	SSC-X-4*	GLCM*	SS-NX-24*	ALCM	TOMAHAWK GLCM	SLCM
WARHEADS	1	1	1	—	—	1	1	1
RANGE (KM)	3,000	3,000	3,000	—	—	2,500	2,500	2,500

*In development

jor conventional aggression against the United States and its allies. This policy has preserved peace for a quarter-century and, in sharp contrast to the Soviet priority accorded nuclear warfighting, is based on the conviction, widely held in the US, that there could be no winners in a nuclear conflict. The United States does not now have a first-strike policy, nor do we plan to acquire a first-strike capability in the future. Rather, US deterrence policy seeks to maintain the situation in which any potential aggressor sees little to gain and much to lose by initiating hostilities against the United States or its allies. In turn, the maintenance of peace through deterrence provides the vital opportunity to pursue the US goal of eliminating nuclear weapons from the arsenals of all states.

Realizing these deterrence objectives requires the development, deployment, and maintenance of strategic forces whose size and characteristics clearly indicate to an opponent that his politico-military objectives cannot be achieved either through the employment of nuclear weapons or through political coercion based on nuclear advantages.

Soviet Non-Strategic Nuclear Forces

Longer Range
Intermediate-Range Nuclear Forces

The Soviets began a vigorous effort to modernize and expand their intermediate-range nuclear force in 1977 with the deployment of the first SS-20 LRINF missiles. Each SS-20 is equipped with three MIRVs, more than doubling the

The Soviets have converted a YANKEE-Class nuclear-powered ballistic missile submarine into a cruise missile attack submarine as the test platform for the large, long-range, nuclear-tipped SS-NX-24 cruise missile. The SS-NX-24 aboard submarines will add yet another dimension to the Soviet strategic threat to the United States in the years ahead.

number of LRINF warheads that existed in 1977 when the SS-20 was first deployed. The SS-20s also have significantly greater range and accuracy and a much shorter reaction time than the missiles they are replacing.

The Soviets have deployed 441 SS-20 launchers at bases west of the Urals and in the Soviet Far East. During 1984, the Soviets began construction of more new bases for the SS-20

than in any other year. Some of this construction was to facilitate the relocation of SS-20 units that had been displaced from their former bases. (These bases are being converted to accommodate the SS-25 mobile ICBM.) In spite of some conversions, real growth was observed in the SS-20 force in 1985.

The mobility of the SS-20 system, unlike the SS-4, allows it to operate under both on- and

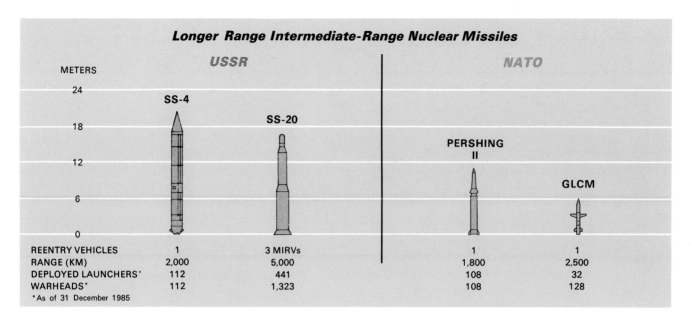

Longer Range Intermediate-Range Nuclear Missiles

	USSR			NATO	
	SS-4	**SS-20**		**PERSHING II**	**GLCM**
REENTRY VEHICLES	1	3 MIRVs		1	1
RANGE (KM)	2,000	5,000		1,800	2,500
DEPLOYED LAUNCHERS*	112	441		108	32
WARHEADS*	112	1,323		108	128

*As of 31 December 1985

off-road conditions. Consequently, the survivability of the SS-20 is greatly enhanced because of the difficulty in detecting and targeting this system when it is field deployed. Further, the SS-20 launcher can be reloaded and refired, and the Soviets stockpile refire missiles.

In addition to the SS-20s, the Soviets still maintain approximately 112 SS-4 LRINF missiles, all of which are located in the western USSR opposite European NATO.

Future Force Development. The Soviets are flight-testing an improved version of the SS-20 which is expected to be more accurate than its predecessor.

The mobile SS-20, in addition to being a more accurate and survivable LRINF missile system, does not require fixed sites to support launches.

Shorter Range Missiles

Current Systems and Force Levels. In 1985, a brigade in the Belorussian Military District became the first operational unit to receive the SS-23 shorter range INF missile. The SS-23, with its 500-kilometer range, represents a marked improvement in range and accuracy over the 300-kilometer SS-1/SCUD B surface-to-surface missile it is now beginning to replace. If the SS-23 follows the same sequence of deployment seen with the SCUD B, the Western Military Districts will receive it first, followed by deployment to the Group of Soviet Forces, Germany.

Each front commander also may have a brigade of 12 to 18 SCALEBOARD missiles available that are more accurate than the older missiles they replaced. Over 70 SCALEBOARD launchers are opposite European NATO and 40 are opposite the Sino-Soviet border. There is a battalion opposite southwest Asia/eastern Turkey, and one brigade is maintained in strategic reserve. Because of their greatly increased accuracy, the new short-range missiles can also be employed effectively with non-nuclear warheads.

In 1984, the Soviets forward-deployed the SCALEBOARD short-range ballistic missile to Eastern Europe. These front-level weapons, which normally accompany Soviet combined arms formations, are now in position to strike deep into Western Europe.

Sea-Based Forces

The Soviets also maintain and operate 13

Chapter II Nuclear Force Operations

GOLF II-Class ballistic missile submarines equipped with 3 SS-N-5 SLBMs each. Six GOLF IIs are based in the Baltic, where they pose a threat to most of Europe, while the remaining seven patrol the Sea of Japan, where they can be employed against targets in the Far East.

Short-Range Nuclear Forces

Current Systems and Force Levels. Soviet armies and fronts have missile brigades equipped with 12 to 18 SS-1C SCUD SRBMs. Over 500 SCUD launchers are located opposite European NATO, and over 100 are opposite the Sino-Soviet border and in the Far East. Additionally, about 75 are opposite southwest Asia and eastern Turkey, with one brigade held in strategic reserve.

The Soviet division commander has a variety of nuclear assets available to him. The most predominant such system at division level is the unguided free rocket over ground (FROG), which is deployed in a battalion of four launchers. The Soviets are replacing FROGs with the more accurate, longer range SS-21s in some divisions opposite NATO. There are now 500 FROG and SS-21 launchers opposite NATO.

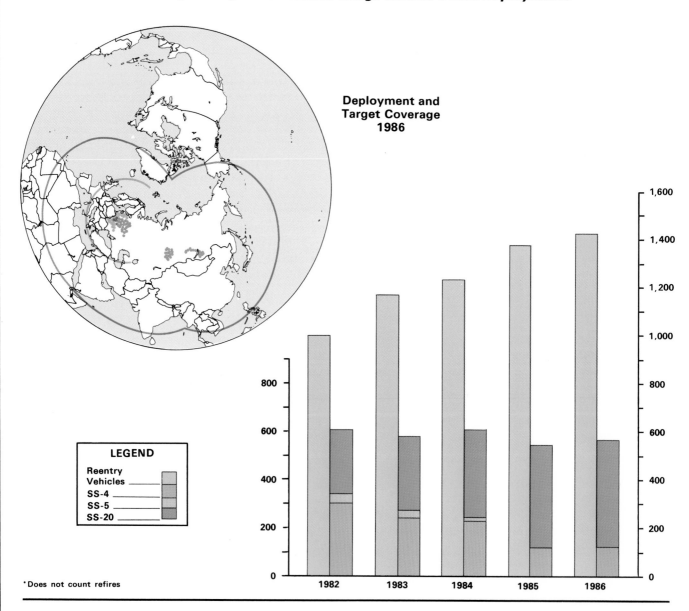

Soviet Longer Range Intermediate-Range Nuclear Force Deployments*

Deployment and Target Coverage 1986

LEGEND
Reentry Vehicles
SS-4
SS-5
SS-20

*Does not count refires

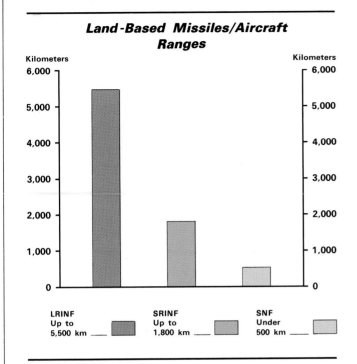

Land-Based Missiles/Aircraft Ranges

Kilometers   Kilometers

LRINF
Up to
5,500 km
SRINF
Up to
1,800 km
SNF
Under
500 km

Another 215 FROG launchers are opposite the Sino-Soviet border and in the Far East; about 100 are opposite southwest Asia and eastern Turkey; and about 75 are in strategic reserve.

Front commanders also have available nuclear-capable artillery tubes. Three new self-propelled, nuclear-capable artillery pieces are being added to the inventory: a 152-mm gun, a 203-mm self-propelled gun, and a 240-mm self-propelled mortar. When fully deployed, the total number of these new nuclear-capable artillery tubes plus older 152-mm howitzers that are also capable of firing nuclear rounds will exceed 10,000.

Force Developments. As in all other nuclear attack forces, the Soviets probably will continue to seek ways to improve the capabilities of their tactical missiles and nuclear artillery. These improvements will be accomplished through incremental modernization of existing systems as well as through the introduction of entirely new systems.

The Soviets probably will continue to seek improvements for their short-range ballistic missile force. Advancements in warhead capabilities, accuracy, and reliability are expected. Combined arms commanders would then have enhanced non-nuclear targeting options and more flexible and survivable SRBMs. These systems will be capable of delivering nuclear, chemical, or conventional warheads closer to the forward edge of the battle area and at greater depths within the military theater of operations.

US Non-Strategic Nuclear Forces

Longer Range Intermediate-Range Nuclear Forces

The initial deployment of Pershing IIs and ground-launched cruise missiles (GLCMs) began in Europe in late 1983. According to the agreed schedule, the number of US LRINF missiles deployed in Europe on 31 December 1985 totaled 236 missiles on 140 launchers. These consist of 108 Pershing II missiles on 108 launchers and 128 GLCMs on 32 launchers. The deployment of US Pershing II and ground-launched cruise missiles responds to the Soviet LRINF missile threat to NATO.

Shorter Range Intermediate-Range Nuclear Forces

With the removal of US Pershing Is and the Soviet SS-23s replacing SCUDs in Europe, the Soviet Union will maintain its substantial numerical superiority in shorter range non-strategic nuclear missiles while improving the qualitative characteristics of its forces. The USSR also has a significant numerical advantage in SRINF aircraft and is reducing the qualitative advantage NATO has enjoyed. This is occurring despite NATO's SRINF aircraft modernization program, in which older aircraft are being replaced by the F-16 and Tornado.

Short-Range Nuclear Forces

Short-range nuclear forces (SNF) consist of tube artillery and missiles of much shorter range than INF. The United States' SNF is made up of Lance tactical missiles and nuclear artillery. Although SNF artillery traditionally has been an area of NATO advantage, the balance has shifted dramatically in favor of the Soviets in recent years. The Soviets also have achieved parity in overall numbers of SNF missiles.

Chapter III

Strategic Defense and Space Operations

Over the last 25 years, the Soviets have increased their active and passive defenses in a clear and determined attempt to blunt the effect of any attack on the Soviet Union. The USSR has major passive defense programs, including civil defense and structural hardening, designed to protect important assets from attack. It also has extensive active defense systems which utilize weapons systems to protect national territory, military forces, or key assets. Soviet developments in the area of active defenses fall into three major categories: air defense; ballistic missile defense based on current technologies; and research and development on advanced defenses against ballistic missiles.

Important recent activities in the Soviet Strategic Defense Program (SSDP) include:

- upgrading and expanding the world's only operational ABM system around Moscow;
- construction of the Krasnoyarsk ballistic missile detection and tracking radar, which violates the 1972 ABM Treaty;
- extensive research into advanced technologies for defense against ballistic missiles, including laser weapons, particle beam weapons, and kinetic energy weapons;
- maintaining the world's only operational antisatellite (ASAT) system;

The Soviet Strategic Defense Program is involved in extensive research on advanced technologies for defense against ballistic missiles, including work on particle beam weapons, kinetic energy weapons, and laser weapons. The USSR already has ground-based lasers, conceptually illustrated here, capable of interfering with some US satellites and could have prototypes for ground-based lasers for defense against ballistic missiles by the late 1980s.

- modernizing their strategic air defense forces; and
- improving passive defenses by maintaining deep bunkers and blast shelters for key personnel and enhancing the survivability of some offensive systems through mobility and hardening.

Evidence of the importance the Soviets attach to defensive damage limitation can be traced to the beginning of the nuclear age. The National Air Defense Forces became an independent service in the late 1950s and since 1959 have generally ranked third in precedence within the Soviet Armed Forces, following the Strategic Rocket Forces and the Ground Forces.

By the mid-1960s, two new mission areas— ASAT operations and ABM defense—were added to the National Air Defense mission. As a result, Soviet strategic defense against ballistic missiles includes the world's only operational ABM system and a large and expanding research and development program. In addition, the Soviets have the world's only operational antisatellite system, which has the capability to destroy critical US and other satellites in low-earth orbit.

The Soviet emphasis on the necessity of research on ballistic missile defense was demonstrated in 1972 by then-Minister of Defense Grechko shortly after the signing of the ABM Treaty. Speaking to the Soviet Presidium, he said that the Treaty "places no limitations whatsoever on the conducting of research and experimental work directed towards solving the problem of defending the country from nuclear missile strikes."

The Soviet emphasis on strategic defense is firmly grounded in Soviet military doctrine and strategy. In the event of nuclear war, Soviet offensive forces are to:
- destroy or disrupt enemy nuclear-associated command, control, and communications; and
- destroy or neutralize as many of the enemy's nuclear weapons as possible on the ground or at sea before they are launched.

Soviet defensive forces, lending greater credibility to offensive forces, are to:
- intercept and destroy surviving weapons —aircraft and missiles—before they reach their targets; and
- protect the Party, the state, military

forces, industrial infrastructure, and the essential working population with active and passive measures against those weapons that survive attacks by Soviet offensive forces.

In pursuit of these goals, the USSR places considerable stress on the need for effective strategic defenses as well as offensive forces. In the Soviet view, the USSR could best achieve its aims in a nuclear war if it attacks first, destroying much of the US and allied capability for retaliation. Defensive measures, both active and passive, would in turn prevent those enemy forces that survived a Soviet first strike from destroying targets in the USSR.

In *Military Strategy*—originally published in 1962—Marshal V.D. Sokolovskiy defined the aim of Soviet strategic defenses in this way: "They have the task of creating an invincible system for the defense of the entire country.... While, in the last war, it was sufficient to destroy 15-20 percent of the attacking air operation, now it is necessary to assure, essentially, 100 percent destruction of all attacking airplanes and missiles." Soviet defensive force developments over the past 25 years demonstrate that the strategy articulated by Sokolovskiy still applies.

Ballistic Missile Defense

The world's only operational ABM system is maintained around Moscow. In 1978, the Sovi-

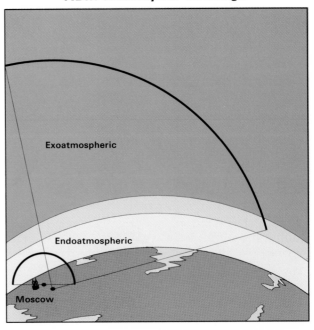

ABM Interceptor Coverage

Exoatmospheric

Endoatmospheric

Moscow

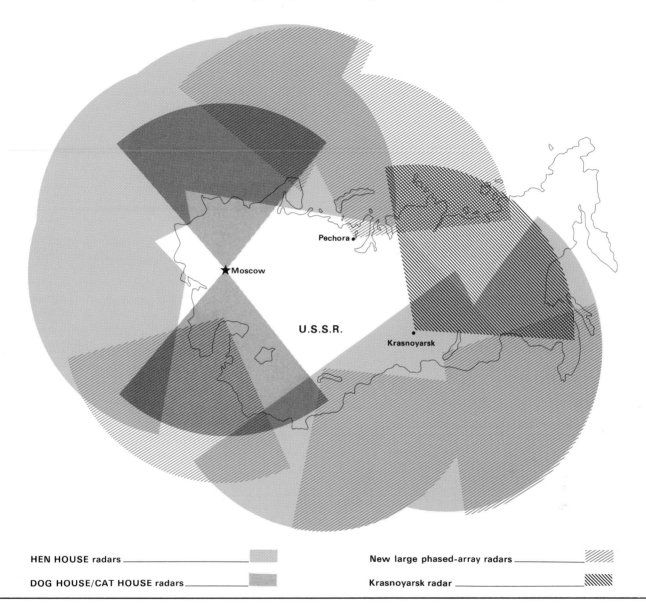

HEN HOUSE radars _____

DOG HOUSE/CAT HOUSE radars _____

New large phased-array radars _____

Krasnoyarsk radar _____

ets began to upgrade and expand that system to the limit allowed by the 1972 ABM Treaty. The original single-layer Moscow ABM system included 64 reloadable above-ground launchers at 4 complexes and DOG HOUSE and CAT HOUSE battle management radars south of Moscow. Each complex consisted of TRY ADD tracking and guidance radars and GALOSH exoatmospheric interceptors (nuclear-armed, ground-based missiles designed to intercept warheads in space shortly before they reenter the Earth's atmosphere).

When completed, the modernized Moscow ABM system will be a two-layer defense composed of silo-based, long-range, modified GALOSH interceptors; silo-based GAZELLE high-acceleration endoatmospheric interceptors designed to engage targets within the atmosphere; associated engagement, guidance and battle management radar systems; and a new large radar at Pushkino designed to control ABM engagements. The silo-based launchers may be reloadable. The new system will have the 100 ABM launchers permitted by the ABM Treaty and could be fully operational by 1987.

The Soviet system for detection and tracking

43   Chapter III Strategic Defense and Space Operations

of ballistic missile attack consists of a launch-detection satellite network, over-the-horizon radars, and a series of large phased-array radars.

The current launch-detection satellite network can provide about 30 minutes warning after any US ICBM launch and can determine the general origin of the missile. Two over-the-horizon radars directed at the US ICBM fields also could give the same 30 minutes warning.

The next operational layer of ballistic missile detection consists of 11 large HEN HOUSE ballistic missile early warning radars at 6 locations on the periphery of the USSR. These radars can distinguish the size of an attack, confirm the warning from the satellite and over-the-horizon radar systems, and provide target-tracking data in support of antiballistic missile forces. The capability of these radars has been improved since the signing of the ABM Treaty.

The Soviets are now constructing a network

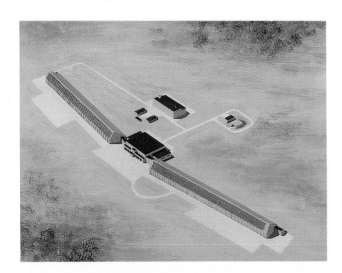

The 11 large HEN HOUSE ballistic missile early warning radars, top left, at 6 locations on the periphery of the USSR, provide warning and target-tracking data in support of the Soviet ABM system. The DOG HOUSE radar, top right, provides battle management for the antiballistic missile interceptors around Moscow. The Soviet Union is violating the ABM Treaty through the siting, orientation, and capability of the large phased-array, ballistic missile detection and tracking radar at Krasnoyarsk, bottom left. The receiver and transmitter of the large phased-array, ballistic missile detection and tracking radar at Pechora are shown at bottom right. The design of the Krasnoyarsk radar is essentially identical to that of the Pechora radar. Unlike the Pechora radar, however, the Krasnoyarsk radar does not meet the ABM Treaty requirement that early warning radars be located on the periphery of the Soviet Union and be oriented outward.

of six new large phased-array radars that can track more ballistic missiles with greater accuracy than the existing HEN HOUSE network. Five of these radars duplicate or supplement the coverage of the HEN HOUSE network, but with greatly enhanced capability. The sixth, under construction near Krasnoyarsk in Siberia, closes the final gap in the Soviet early warning radar coverage against ballistic missile attack. Together, the six new large phased-array radars form an arc of coverage from the Kola Peninsula in the northwest Soviet Union, around Siberia, to the Caucasus in the southwest.

The United States is now constructing new ballistic missile early warning radars, known as PAVE PAWS, that are located on the periphery of our territory and oriented outward. These radars are much less capable than Soviet large phased-array radars. Both the US and the USSR, in signing the ABM Treaty, recognized the need for ballistic missile early warning radars. At the same time, they recognized that ballistic missile early warning radars can detect and track warheads at great distances and therefore have a significant antiballistic missile potential. Such an ABM capability would play an important role in a nationwide ABM defense, which the treaty was designed to prevent. As a result, the US and the Soviet Union agreed that future ballistic missile early warning radars must be located on a nation's periphery and be oriented outward. In that way, the desirable and legitimate goal of early warning could be advanced while minimizing the danger that an effective nationwide battle management network could result.

The Krasnoyarsk radar is designed for ballistic missile detection and tracking, including ballistic missile early warning. It violates the 1972 ABM Treaty as it is not located within a 150-kilometer radius of the national capital (Moscow) as required of ABM radars, nor is it located on the periphery of the Soviet Union and pointed outward as required for early warning radars. It is 3,700 kilometers from Moscow and is situated some 750 kilometers from the nearest border—Mongolia. Moreover, it is oriented not toward that border, but across approximately 4,000 kilometers of Soviet territory to the northeast.

The Soviet Union has claimed that the Krasnoyarsk radar is designed for space tracking, rather than ballistic missile early warning, and therefore does not violate the ABM Treaty. Its design, however, is not suited for a space-tracking role, and the radar would, in any event, contribute little to the existing Soviet space-tracking network. Indeed, the design of the Krasnoyarsk radar is essentially identical to that of other radars that are known—and acknowledged by the Soviets—to be for ballistic missile detection and tracking, including ballistic missile early warning.

The growing Soviet network of large phased-array, ballistic missile detection and tracking radars, of which the Krasnoyarsk radar is a part, is of particular concern when linked with other Soviet ABM efforts. Such radars take years to construct and their existence might allow the Soviet Union to move rather quickly to construct a nationwide ABM defense if it chooses to do so.

The Soviets also are developing components of a new ABM system that would allow them to construct individual ABM sites in a matter of months rather than the years that are required for more traditional ABM systems. Soviet activities in this regard potentially violate the ABM Treaty's prohibition on the development of a mobile land-based ABM system or components. We estimate that by using these components the Soviets could by the early 1990s quickly deploy an ABM system to strengthen the defenses of Moscow and defend key targets in the western USSR and east of the Urals.

In addition, the Soviets have probably violated the prohibition on testing surface-to-air missile (SAM) components in an ABM mode by conducting tests involving the use of SAM air defense radars in ABM-related testing activities. Moreover, the SA-10 and SA-X-12 SAM systems may have the potential to intercept some types of strategic ballistic missiles.

Taken together, all of the Soviet Union's ABM and ABM-related activities are more significant—and more ominous—than any one considered individually. Cumulatively, they suggest that the USSR may be preparing to deploy rapidly an ABM defense of its national territory, contrary to the provisions of the ABM Treaty.

Advanced ABM Technologies

In the late 1960s, in line with its longstanding emphasis on strategic defense, the Soviet Union initiated a substantial research program into advanced technologies, some of which are applicable for defense against ballistic missiles. That program covers many of the same technologies involved in the US Strategic Defense Initiative but represents a far greater investment of plant space, capital, and manpower.

Laser Weapons

The USSR's laser program is much larger than US efforts and involves over 10,000 scientists and engineers and more than a half-dozen major research and development facilities and test ranges. Much of this research takes place at the Sary Shagan Missile Test Center where the Soviets also conduct traditional ABM research. Facilities there are estimated to have several lasers for air defense, lasers capable of damaging some components of satellites in orbit, and a laser that could be used in feasibility testing for ballistic missile defense applications. A laser weapons program of the magnitude of the Soviet Union's effort would cost roughly $1 billion per year in the United States.

The Soviets are conducting research on three types of gas lasers considered promising for weapons applications—the gas-dynamic laser, the electric discharge laser, and the chemical laser. Soviet achievements in this area, in terms of output power, have been impressive. The Soviets also are aware of the military potential of visible and very short wave-length lasers. They are investigating excimer, free-electron, and x-ray lasers and have been developing argon-ion lasers for over a decade.

The Soviets appear generally capable of supplying the prime power, energy storage, and auxiliary components needed for most laser and other directed-energy weapons. They have developed a rocket-driven magnetohydrodynamic generator which produces over 15 megawatts of electrical power—a device that has no counterpart in the West. The Soviets may also have the capability to develop the optical systems necessary for laser weapons to track and attack their targets. They produced a 1.2-meter segmented mirror for an astrophysical telescope in 1978 and claimed that this was

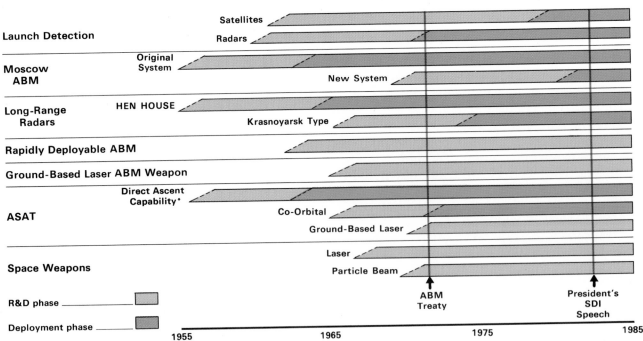

Soviet ABM/Space Defense Programs

Soviet programs for ABM and Space Defense, which include advanced technologies and space-based weapons, were in place prior to the 1972 ABM Treaty and have continued to expand in scope and size. During the same time period, US ABM/Space Defense research has been limited in scope as well as the level of effort in terms of resources invested.

*Potential capability of the Moscow ABM system.

Coverage of Ballistic Missile Detection and Tracking Systems

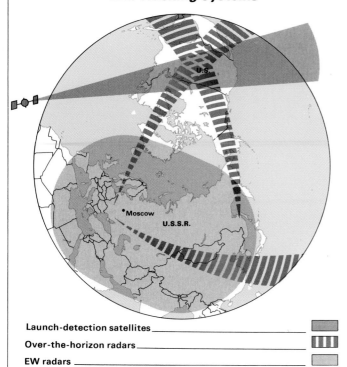

Launch-detection satellites _____

Over-the-horizon radars _____

EW radars _____

weapons are likely to lead to ground-based deployments in the early 1990s and naval deployments in the mid-1990s.

Particle Beam Weapons

Since the late 1960s, the Soviets have been involved in research to explore the feasibility of space-based weapons that would use particle beams. We estimate that they may be able to test a prototype particle beam weapon intended to disrupt the electronics of satellites in the 1990s. A weapon designed to destroy satellites could follow later. A weapon capable of physically destroying missile boosters or warheads probably would require several additional years of research and development.

Soviet efforts in particle beams, and particularly ion sources and radio frequency quadrapole accelerators for particle beams, are very impressive. In fact, much of the US understanding of how particle beams could be made into practical defensive weapons is based on Soviet work conducted in the late 1960s and early 1970s.

Radio Frequency Weapons

The USSR has conducted research in the use of strong radio frequency signals that have the potential to interfere with or destroy critical electronic components of ballistic missile warheads or satellites. The Soviets could test a ground-based radio frequency weapon capable of damaging satellites in the 1990s.

Kinetic Energy Weapons

The Soviets also have a variety of research programs underway in the area of kinetic energy weapons, using the high-speed collision of a small mass with the target as the kill mechanism. In the 1960s, the USSR developed an experimental "gun" that could shoot streams of particles of a heavy metal such as tungsten or molybdenum at speeds of nearly 25 kilometers per second in air and over 60 kilometers per second in a vacuum.

Long-range, space-based kinetic energy systems for defense against ballistic missiles probably could not be developed until the mid-1990s or even later. The USSR could, however, deploy in the near-term a short-range, space-based system useful for satellite or space station defense or for close-in attack by a maneuvering satellite. Soviet capabilities in guidance and control systems probably are ad-

a prototype for a 25-meter mirror. A large mirror is considered necessary for a space-based laser weapon.

Unlike the US, the USSR has now progressed in some cases beyond technology research. It already has ground-based lasers that have a limited capability to attack US satellites and could have prototype space-based antisatellite laser weapons by the end of the decade. The Soviets could have prototypes for ground-based lasers for defense against ballistic missiles by the late 1980s and could begin testing components for a large-scale deployment system in the early 1990s.

The remaining difficulties in fielding an operational system will require more development time. An operational ground-based laser for defense against ballistic missiles probably could not be deployed until the late 1990s or after the year 2000. If technology developments prove successful, the Soviets may deploy operational space-based antisatellite lasers in the mid-to-late 1990s and might be able to deploy space-based laser systems for defense against ballistic missiles after the year 2000. The Soviets' efforts to develop high-energy air defense laser

The USSR's operational antisatellite interceptor designed to destroy space targets with a multi-pellet blast is launched from the Tyuratam Space Complex, where two launch pads and storage for additional interceptors and launch vehicles are available.

equate for effective kinetic energy weapons for use against some objects in space.

Computer and Sensor Technology

Advanced technology weapons programs—including potential advanced defenses against ballistic missiles and ASATs—are dependent on remote sensor and computer technologies, areas in which the West currently leads the Soviet Union. The Soviets, therefore, are devoting considerable resources to acquiring Western know-how and improving their abili-

ties and expertise in these technologies. An important part of that effort involves the increasing exploitation of open and clandestine access to Western technology. For example, the Soviets have long been engaged in a well-funded effort to purchase illegally US high-technology computers, test and calibration equipment, and sensors through third parties.

Antisatellite Operations

The USSR has had for more than a dozen years the world's only operational antisatellite system, which is launched into the same orbit as its target satellite and, when it gets close enough, destroys the satellite by exploding a conventional warhead. Given the complexity of launch, target tracking, and radar-guided intercept, the Soviet ASAT system is far from primitive. Soviet ASAT tests have been largely successful, indicating an operational system fully capable of performing its mission. In addition, the nuclear-armed GALOSH ABM

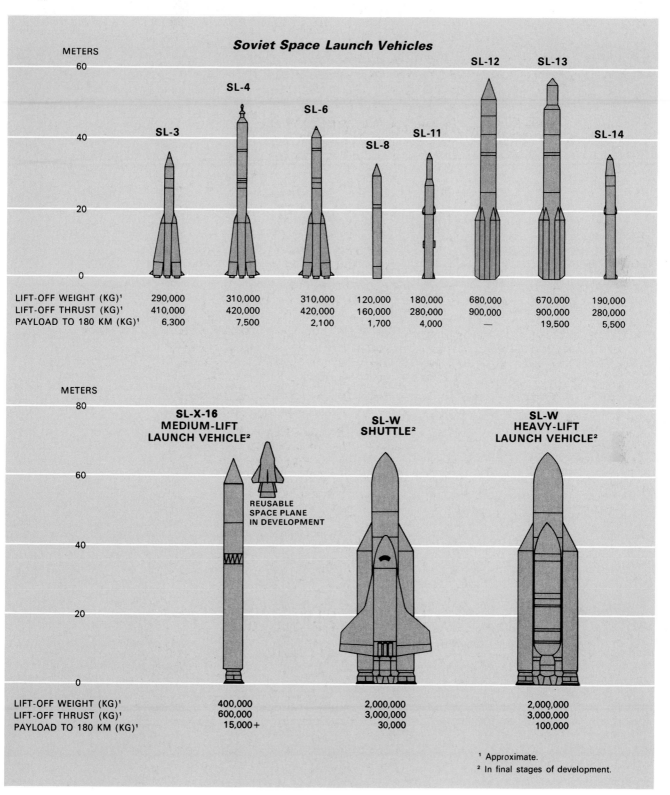

Soviet Space Launch Vehicles

	SL-3	SL-4	SL-6	SL-8	SL-11	SL-12	SL-13	SL-14
LIFT-OFF WEIGHT (KG)¹	290,000	310,000	310,000	120,000	180,000	680,000	670,000	190,000
LIFT-OFF THRUST (KG)¹	410,000	420,000	420,000	160,000	280,000	900,000	900,000	280,000
PAYLOAD TO 180 KM (KG)¹	6,300	7,500	2,100	1,700	4,000	—	19,500	5,500

	SL-X-16 MEDIUM-LIFT LAUNCH VEHICLE²	SL-W SHUTTLE²	SL-W HEAVY-LIFT LAUNCH VEHICLE²
LIFT-OFF WEIGHT (KG)¹	400,000	2,000,000	2,000,000
LIFT-OFF THRUST (KG)¹	600,000	3,000,000	3,000,000
PAYLOAD TO 180 KM (KG)¹	15,000+	30,000	100,000

REUSABLE SPACE PLANE IN DEVELOPMENT

¹ Approximate.
² In final stages of development.

interceptor deployed around Moscow has an inherent ASAT capability, and Soviet ground-based lasers may be able to damage some components of satellites. Furthermore, as noted previously, the Soviets are engaged in research and, in some cases, development of weapons which ultimately may serve as ballistic missile defense systems but probably will first provide ASAT capabilities.

Operations in Space

The Soviets operate several space systems that support both military and civil users. These include manned spacecraft, reconnaissance and surveillance vehicles, new space boosters, and a variety of other support systems. The Soviets have made progress in their space plane and space shuttle programs, with the first flight of a Soviet shuttle expected in late 1986 or 1987.

The primary focus of Soviet space operations is military, as evidenced by the fact that at least 70 percent of Soviet space launches are purely military in nature and support both offensive and defensive operations. The USSR attempts to mask the true nature of most of its space programs by declaring that launches are "scientific," usually without providing details on what kind of "scientific" mission is being conducted. The results of these "scientific" missions are rarely published or even disclosed.

Military Support from Space

The Soviets are increasing their efforts to develop and deploy space systems to support military operations. They now operate several space-based reconnaissance and surveillance systems, two of which have no US counterpart. The latter are the nuclear-powered Radar Ocean Reconnaissance Satellite (RORSAT) and the Electronic Intelligence

As part of its efforts to militarize space, the USSR has pressed forward with an active research and development program, centered at Tyuratam, to deploy increasingly capable space-based reconnaissance and surveillance satellites as well as space-based military communications systems. Soviet achievements in manned space operations are typified by their continued use of the SALYUT-7 space station and development of their soon-to-be-tested space shuttle, seen here mated to the heavy-lift launch vehicle.

Ocean Reconnaissance Satellite (EORSAT), both of which are used to locate and target naval forces. Two RORSATs were launched in August 1985 in time to support a Soviet naval exercise in September. This was not the first time RORSAT launchings have taken place prior to military exercises.

The Soviet satellite reconnaissance program has matured and has incorporated significant enhancements. The Soviets have improved their satellite imagery reconnaissance capability and are gradually improving their space-based electronic intelligence assets as well. They have demonstrated great versatility and flexibility in launching and maintaining several surveillance systems in orbit and are capable of redirecting them for worldwide missions as situations dictate.

The Soviets continue to operate an extensive network of satellites for missile launch detection and attack warning missions. For a number of years, the USSR has had the capability to monitor US ICBM fields.

The Soviets have also pressed ahead with the development and deployment of a global navigation satellite system known as GLONASS. When fully developed, this system will provide three-dimensional (latitude, longitude, and altitude) positioning data.

New Launch Systems

Soviet Military Power 1985 reported two new space launch vehicles under development, a heavy-lift system and a medium-lift system. Launch pad compatibility testing has continued on the heavy-lift vehicle, a Saturn V-Class booster, and the Soviets have flight-tested the Titan III-Class medium-lift vehicle.

The heavy-lift booster system apparently will be used to launch the Soviet shuttle orbiter, a craft similar to the US space shuttle orbiter. This launch system will also be able to carry very heavy payloads of about 100,000 kilograms, enabling the Soviets to assemble very large modular space stations in orbit. This type of system could also be instrumental in the launch of other heavy payloads, such as directed-energy ASAT and ballistic missile defense weapons.

The medium-lift booster may be used to launch the Soviet space plane, which is a different program from the space shuttle. This small, manned craft could be used for real-time reconnaissance missions, satellite repair and main-

tenance, crew transport, space station defense, and enemy satellite inspection or destruction.

When these new launch systems become operational, the Soviets will have ten different types of expendable launch vehicles and two reusable manned space vehicles. These systems will give the Soviets a versatile and redundant capability to conduct and augment military operations in space. In addition, the Soviets would have a distinct advantage during times of crises or hostilities because of the launch surge capability provided by their large number of launch vehicles.

Manned Operations

In early 1985, the Soviets experienced trouble with their SALYUT-7 space station that resulted in failure of its electrical system. They announced in March it had fulfilled its mission and was being "mothballed." In June, however, two cosmonauts were launched from Tyuratam aboard SOYUZ T-13. Using manual rendezvous procedures, the cosmonauts succeeded in docking with the inactive station. Efforts to revive the space station commenced, and within two weeks the crew was operating the station normally and was probably conducting military-related experiments. This repair mission provided valuable experience in space station maintenance that will contribute greatly to Soviet efforts to achieve a significant, per-

US and Soviet **Space Launches**

manent manned presence in near-Earth orbit.

Last September, the Soviets conducted the first space station crew rotation in the history of manned space flight when SOYUZ T-14 delivered three additional cosmonauts to SALYUT-7. One T-13 cosmonaut and one T-14 cosmonaut subsequently deorbited on SOYUZ T-13. Crew rotation will become commonplace when the Soviets deploy their first large modular space station, which is likely to be launched in the late 1980s. The Soviets took a major step toward this capability with the launch of an advanced SALYUT station with six docking ports in early 1986.

Further progress toward a deployment of a new station was demonstrated by COSMOS-1686, which docked with SALYUT-7 in early October 1985. Such modules have a high-capacity cargo transport capability and could be outfitted as reconnaissance platforms, nuclear power "substations," or laboratories for various types of research and experimentation.

These modules will serve as interchangeable components of future large modular space stations, and each is capable of autonomous operation. Once deployed, this space station will provide the Soviets with a manned space-based military capability for missions such as reconnaissance, command and control, ASAT, and ballistic missile defense support operations as well as satellite maintenance and repair. Such space stations will probably be serviced and supported by the Soviet shuttle and space plane.

The Soviets have realized that men in space can significantly contribute to military operations. Soviet cosmonauts aboard a space station in low-earth orbit can observe large areas of the Earth's surface and transmit real-time information to military forces below. From the altitude at which SALYUT operates, much of the Earth's surface can be seen with great clarity. If supported with optics, a cosmonaut could make out details such as airfields, port facilities, major transportation routes, and ships at sea.

Passive Defenses

In the more traditional areas of strategic defense, Soviet military doctrine calls for passive and active defenses to act in conjunction to ensure wartime survival. Physical hardening of military assets to make them more resistant to attack is an important passive defense tech-

nique. The USSR has hardened its ICBM silos, launch facilities, and key command and control centers to an unprecedented degree. Much of the current US retaliatory force would be ineffective against these hardened targets.

Soviet leaders and managers at all levels of the government and Communist Party are provided hardened alternate command posts located well away from urban centers—in addition to many deep bunkers and blast shelters in Soviet cities. This comprehensive and redundant system, patterned after a similar system designed for the Soviet Armed Forces, provides more than 1,500 hardened alternate facilities for more than 175,000 key Party and government personnel throughout the USSR. In contrast, the US passive defense effort is far smaller and more limited; it is in no way comparable to the comprehensive Soviet program.

Elaborate plans also have been made for the full mobilization of the national economy in support of the war effort. Reserves of vital materials are maintained, many in hardened underground structures. Redundant industrial facilities are in active production. Industrial and other economic facilities have been equipped with blast shelters for the work force, and detailed procedures have been developed for the relocation of selected production capabilities. By planning for the survival of the essential work force, the Soviets hope to reconstitute vital production programs using those industrial components that could be redirected or salvaged after an attack.

In addition, the USSR has greatly emphasized mobility as a means of enhancing the survivability of military assets. The SS-20 and SS-25 missiles, for example, are mobile. Rail-mobile deployment of the SS-X-24 is expected soon. The Soviets are also developing an extensive network of mobile command, control, and communications facilities.

Air Defense

The Soviet Union has since the 1950s invested enormous resources in a wide array of strategic air defense weapons systems. Taken together, the Soviet strategic air defense network is a potent and increasingly capable force which would attempt to limit the retaliatory capability of our strategic bombers and cruise missiles. With the emergence of the Soviet cruise missile and the enhanced bomber threat to the United States, the US has under-

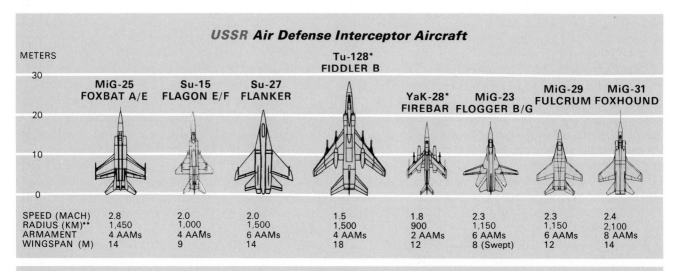

USSR Air Defense Interceptor Aircraft

	MiG-25 FOXBAT A/E	Su-15 FLAGON E/F	Su-27 FLANKER	Tu-128* FIDDLER B	YaK-28* FIREBAR	MiG-23 FLOGGER B/G	MiG-29 FULCRUM	MiG-31 FOXHOUND
SPEED (MACH)	2.8	2.0	2.0	1.5	1.8	2.3	2.3	2.4
RADIUS (KM)**	1,450	1,000	1,500	1,500	900	1,150	1,150	2,100
ARMAMENT	4 AAMs	4 AAMs	6 AAMs	4 AAMs	2 AAMs	6 AAMs	6 AAMs	8 AAMs
WINGSPAN (M)	14	9	14	18	12	8 (Swept)	12	14

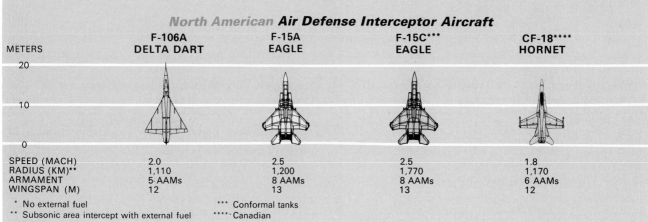

North American Air Defense Interceptor Aircraft

	F-106A DELTA DART	F-15A EAGLE	F-15C*** EAGLE	CF-18**** HORNET
SPEED (MACH)	2.0	2.5	2.5	1.8
RADIUS (KM)**	1,110	1,200	1,770	1,170
ARMAMENT	5 AAMs	8 AAMs	8 AAMs	6 AAMs
WINGSPAN (M)	12	13	13	12

* No external fuel   *** Conformal tanks
** Subsonic area intercept with external fuel   **** Canadian

taken measures to improve its air defense capabilities.

The Soviets have deployed numerous strategic air defense systems with capabilities against aircraft flying at medium and high altitudes. They are now in the midst of a major program to improve their capabilities against aircraft and cruise missiles flying at low altitudes. That effort includes partial integration of strategic and tactical air defense assets, the upgrading of early warning and surveillance capabilities, the deployment of more efficient data transmission systems, and the development and initial deployment of new aircraft, associated air-to-air missiles, surface-to-air missiles (SAMs), and airborne warning and control system (AWACS) aircraft.

Currently, the Soviets have more than 9,000 strategic SAM launchers, over 4,600 tactical SAM launchers, and some 10,000 air defense radars. More than 1,200 Air Defense Forces interceptor aircraft are dedicated to strategic defense. An additional 2,800 interceptors as-signed to Soviet Air Forces (SAF) will be drawn upon for strategic defense missions. Collectively, these assets present a formidable defense barrier against any attack.

The most capable Soviet air defense interceptor aircraft, the MiG-31/FOXHOUND, has a look-down/shoot-down and multiple-target engagement capability. More than 100 FOXHOUNDs are now operationally deployed at several locations from the Arkhangelsk area in the northwestern USSR to the Far East Military District. Two new fighter interceptors, the Su-27/FLANKER and the MiG-29/FULCRUM, also have look-down/shoot-down capabilities and are designed to be highly maneuverable in air-to-air combat. The look-down/shoot-down capability was acquired from the US through espionage. The Soviets have deployed over 100 MiG-29/FULCRUM aircraft to operational units and have recently begun to deploy the Su-27/FLANKER. These three aircraft are equipped with two new air-to-air missiles—the long-range AA-9 (for the FOXHOUND) and the medium-range AA-10 (for the FULCRUM and FLANKER)—that can be used against low-flying targets.

The USSR is also deploying the MAINSTAY AWACS aircraft, which will improve substantially Soviet capabilities for early warning and air combat command and control, especially against low-flying aircraft. The MIDAS, a tanker variant of the Il-76/CANDID which should be operational soon, will significantly increase the endurance of the new air defense aircraft, particularly the MAINSTAY and some of the new fighters—if an air refueling capability for them is incorporated.

The Soviets maintain the world's most extensive early warning system for air defense. It is composed of a widespread network of ground-based radars linked operationally with those of their Warsaw Pact allies. As previously noted, more than 10,000 air surveillance radars of various types provide virtually complete cover-

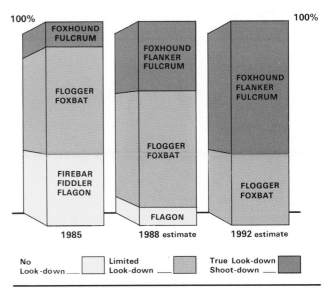

Interceptor Aircraft Radar Capability

age at medium-to-high altitudes over the USSR and, in some areas, well beyond the Soviet Union's borders. Three over-the-horizon radars for ballistic missile detection could provide additional warning of the approach of high-flying aircraft.

The USSR also has an active research and development program to improve its air surveillance network. In 1983, it began to deploy two new types of air surveillance radars which will enhance Soviet capabilities for air defense, electronic warfare, and early warning of cruise

The new generation of all-weather air defense interceptors equipped with a true look-down/shoot-down radar includes the MiG-29/FULCRUM, armed with the AA-10 missile, top left, and the MiG-31/FOXHOUND, armed with the AA-9 missile, above.

The mobile version of the SA-10 SAM is in the process of being deployed.

missile and bomber attacks. The Soviets are also continuing to deploy improved air surveillance data systems that can rapidly pass data from outlying radars through the air surveillance network to ground-controlled intercept sites and SAM command posts.

Soviet strategic surface-to-air missiles provide low-to-high-altitude barrier, area, and terminal defenses under all weather conditions. Five systems are now operational: the SA-1, SA-2, and SA-3, and the more capable SA-5 and SA-10. The recent Soviet air defense reorganization permits more efficient integration of strategic and tactical SAM systems. Although most tactical SAMs have a shorter range than their strategic counterparts, many have better capabilities against targets flying at low altitudes.

The surface-to-air missiles of the SA-X-12 air defense system are designed to counter high-performance aircraft at all altitudes, will also have a capability against tactical ballistic missiles, and may have the potential to engage some types of strategic ballistic missiles.

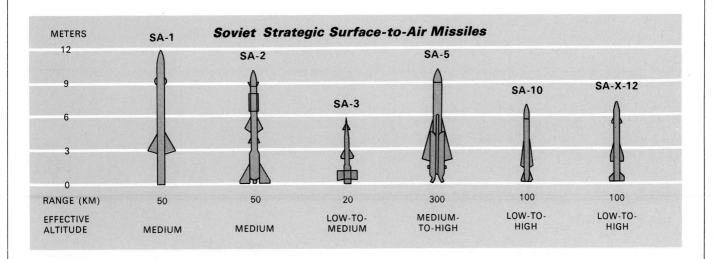

Soviet Strategic Surface-to-Air Missiles

	SA-1	SA-2	SA-3	SA-5	SA-10	SA-X-12
RANGE (KM)	50	50	20	300	100	100
EFFECTIVE ALTITUDE	MEDIUM	MEDIUM	LOW-TO-MEDIUM	MEDIUM-TO-HIGH	LOW-TO-HIGH	LOW-TO-HIGH

Soviet Strategic SAM Air Defense Barrier Illustrated from Fixed Sites*

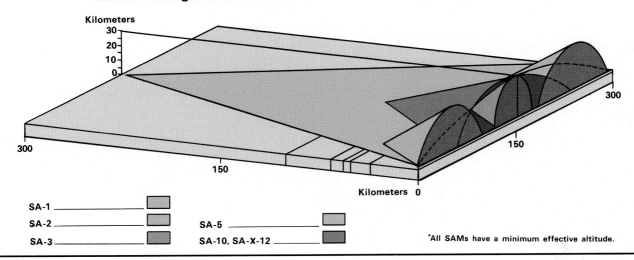

SA-1 _____ ▢
SA-2 _____ ▢   SA-5 _____ ▢
SA-3 _____ ▢   SA-10, SA-X-12 _____ ▢

*All SAMs have a minimum effective altitude.

Over the years the Soviets have continued to deploy the long-range SA-5 and have repeatedly modified this system. Further deployment and upgrading are probable to enhance the SA-5's capability to work in conjunction with low-altitude systems like the SA-10.

The SA-10 has some capability against low-altitude targets with small radar cross-sections, such as cruise missiles. The first SA-10 site was operational in 1980. Over 60 sites are now operational, and work is progressing on at least another 30. More than half of these sites are located near Moscow; this emphasis on Moscow and the patterns noted for the other SA-10 sites suggest a first priority on terminal defense of command and control, military, and key industrial complexes.

In keeping with their drive toward mobility as a means of weapons survival, the Soviets are in the process of deploying a mobile version of the SA-10. This mobile version could be used to support Soviet theater forces and to permit periodic changes in the location of SA-10 sites within the USSR to counter US retaliatory forces more effectively.

The Soviets are also flight-testing another important mobile SAM system, the SA-X-12, which is capable of intercepting aircraft at all altitudes as well as cruise missiles and short-range ballistic missiles. As previously noted, the SA-10 and SA-X-12 may have the potential to intercept some types of strategic ballistic missiles as well. This is a serious development because these systems are expected to be deployed widely throughout the Soviet Union in the 1980s. They could, if properly supported, add significant point-target defense coverage to a nationwide Soviet ABM deployment.

Chapter IV

Soviet Forces for Theater Operations

Control of theater operations rests with the Soviet Supreme High Command (VGK). Major elements of all five of the USSR's branches of the armed forces (ground, naval, air, air defense, and Strategic Rocket Forces) would be devoted to theater warfare. A large component of these forces would be retained immediately under the control of the VGK to be employed or allocated at its discretion. These elements include strategic aviation air armies, SS-4 and SS-20 units of the Strategic Rocket Forces, airborne forces, military transport aviation, a large strategic reserve of ground forces (primarily units stationed in the interior military districts of the USSR), and an extensive logistic support structure.

A High Command of Forces in the TVD would have primary responsibility for conducting the theater strategic operation. Under its control would be several fronts, a naval fleet (if applicable), strategic air defense elements in the TVD, and any strategic air army and airborne elements allocated by the VGK.

The front is the basic combined arms component of theater forces responsible for land operations. The closest NATO equivalent would be an army group with organic tactical aviation. A front consists of several combined arms

The USSR maintains the world's largest stockpile of chemical warfare agents. Virtually all Soviet conventional weapons systems—mortars, artillery pieces, helicopters such as these Mi-24/HINDs, aircraft, and long-range tactical missiles—can deliver chemical munitions in the forward battle zone and against rear areas. Furthermore, Soviet research institutes are engaged in developing new chemical agents with even greater lethality and are investigating binary weapons systems that would reduce the hazards associated with handling and storage.

and tank armies, a large assigned aviation element called the Air Forces of the Front, and an extensive support structure including several surface-to-air missile (SAM) brigades, an artillery division, and several surface-to-surface missile (SSM) brigades. Armies have a combined arms structure similar to a front, with three to five tank or motorized rifle divisions constituting their basic maneuver elements. A tank army has a preponderance of tank divisions while a combined arms army has a preponderance of motorized rifle divisions.

Theater Warfare Capabilities

A command system that will ensure effective control of diverse operations is essential to the conduct of theater strategic operations. The Soviets have made a significant investment in the control structure of their various TVDs, including the construction of several hundred hardened, bunkered command posts and communications centers; the creation of an extensive communications system in peacetime; and the establishment of numerous, well-equipped mobile signal and headquarters support units. In wartime, the Soviets would field a robust and survivable command system featuring numerous hardened, fixed, and mobile command posts; a dense communications network providing redundant channels between command posts; and extensive camouflage, concealment, and deception.

In 1985, the Soviets began activating peacetime High Commands within the TVDs with high-ranking officers appointed as permanent commanders in chief (CINCs). This increased the readiness of Soviet forces by moving the peacetime command structure much closer to the wartime mode. Marshal Ogarkov, the former Chief of the Soviet General Staff, is believed to have been appointed head of the crucial Western TVD oriented against NATO's Central Region.

The Soviets are increasing the speed and effectiveness of their command, control, and communications (C^3) system by introducing numerous computer systems and other automated aids. Commanders and staffs are being assisted in rapid decisionmaking by computerized combat models resulting from a large military operations research effort. The Soviets have also employed the results of numerous Western operations research efforts published in open-source journals.

Planned TVD Operations

As expressed in their literature, the Soviets believe that the Western TVD would be the scene of the decisive conflict between NATO and the Warsaw Pact. Accordingly, they have deployed a very large force there that includes their best equipped and most ready units. Soviet ground forces in the theater have the most modern tanks, infantry fighting vehicles, and self-propelled artillery in the Soviet inventory. Moreover, air forces in the TVD comprise over 37 percent of all the Soviet tactical aviation assets.

Within the Western TVD, deep-interdiction attacks against NATO airfields and other deep targets would be conducted by FENCER aircraft as well as almost 400 Strategic Aviation BACKFIRE B/C, BLINDER, and BADGER G medium bombers stationed in the western Soviet Union. Force capabilities will continue to improve as additional BACKFIREs replace older BADGERs.

The combined Baltic Fleet, consisting of the Soviet Baltic Fleet plus the East German and Polish navies, has a substantial force of principal surface combatants and relatively large numbers of missile-capable minor combatants. The Polish and East German navies are particularly strong in amphibious warfare and would contribute substantially to Soviet amphibious operations in the Baltic.

The Soviets envision a complex theater strategic operation involving a rapid advance across West Germany, Denmark, and the low countries to immediate objectives on the French border, the North Sea coast, and the Danish straits. This advance would be made possible by a massive air operation to paralyze NATO's air, air defense, theater nuclear, and command and control capabilities and by an amphibious operation to secure the Danish straits. Continued operations across France would then be conducted after immediate strategic objectives are attained. The Soviets would hope to win a quick victory through speed and surprise in this theater before NATO could fully mobilize or bring in reinforcements.

Operations in the Northwest and the Southwest TVDs are considered secondary to the decisive operations in the Western Theater in Soviet plans. The Northwestern TVD contains Soviet Northern Fleet bases with numerous strategic submarines. Soviet theater operations would be conducted to protect the

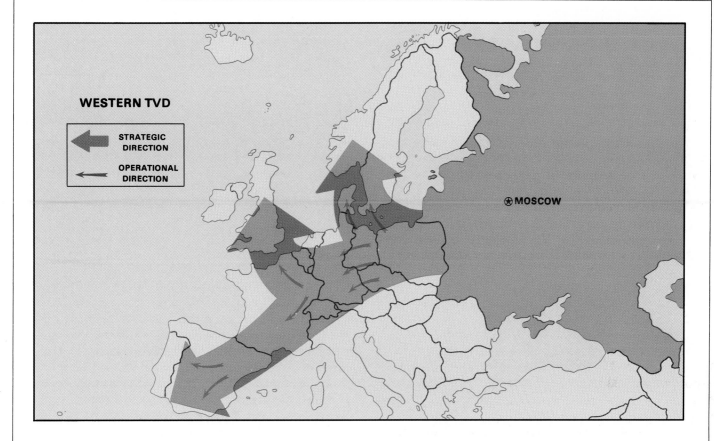

WESTERN TVD

STRATEGIC DIRECTION

OPERATIONAL DIRECTION

MOSCOW

Soviet strategic attack assets and to support naval operations in the Arctic and Atlantic Ocean TVDs. The objective of land operations in the Northwestern TVD would be to seize vital air and naval facilities in northern Norway, using the most favorable avenues of approach. Soviet control of northern Norway is important to the protection of Northern Fleet bases and assets, particularly ballistic missile submarines, and to the movement of Soviet naval and air forces into the Norwegian Sea and the North Atlantic Ocean. Soviet plans also call for a land offensive operation through Finland and possibly Swedish territory.

The Northern Fleet would conduct combat operations in the Arctic and Atlantic Ocean TVDs and on the seaward flanks of the Northwestern TVD. The vast majority of the Northern Fleet's assets would be dedicated to the Arctic Theater, which encompasses the Arctic Ocean and the Norwegian, Barents, and Greenland Seas—the main operating areas for strategic ballistic missile submarines. In addition to providing the ballistic missile submarine assets for strategic operations during conflict, the other tasks of the Northern Fleet in the Arctic Ocean TVD would be:

- to protect the USSR from sea-based at-

tacks by establishing naval superiority in the Arctic, Barents, Greenland, and Norwegian Seas; and
- to conduct ASW operations against NATO ballistic missile and general purpose submarines within this geographic area.

Combat operations in the Atlantic Ocean TVD would be considered less crucial by the Soviet military leadership than those in the Arctic. In the Atlantic TVD, the Northern Fleet would be tasked to conduct operations against NATO ballistic missile submarines and to interdict NATO sea lanes carrying reinforcements and supplies from North America to Europe. Soviet attack submarines would conduct most of these operations, which would probably entail minelaying and patrols off key North American, United Kingdom, and West European ports and bases. Some Naval Aviation and Air Force bombers probably would participate in these interdiction operations.

The Soviets plan operations in the Southwestern TVD to support their advance in the Western Theater and to establish dominance in NATO's Southern Region. In wartime, Soviet plans for offensive operations in the region include an attack through neutral Austria

61

into southern Germany and northern Italy. Soviet plans also include operations to seize the Bosporus and Dardanelles. Efforts to seize the Turkish straits would be accomplished by coordinated ground, airborne, and amphibious operations. Warsaw Pact naval forces in the theater organized into a combined Black Sea Fleet and the Soviet Mediterranean Squadron would attempt to clear the Black Sea of NATO naval forces and would attempt to prevent Allied forces from using the eastern Mediterranean to reinforce their defenses.

Soviet interest in the Southern TVD has been increased by the collapse of the pro-Western regime of the Shah in Iran as well as

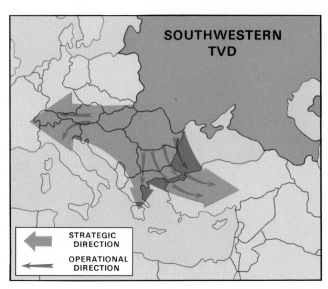

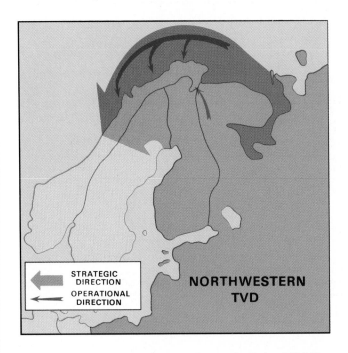

by other developments in the turbulent Middle East. The Soviets wish to establish dominance in this region and to deny the West access to its vital oil resources in wartime. Soviet forces are now engaged in combat in Afghanistan to ensure the success of the Communist regime installed by Moscow and to reduce that nation to a client state. In wartime, the Soviets would probably plan to conduct offensive operations from the USSR and Afghanistan through Iran to the Persian Gulf in order to obtain a stranglehold on the West's oil supplies. Also, the Soviets could use Afghanistan as a base from which to launch an attack on Pakistan.

The Far Eastern TVD is the largest continental TVD. Since the 1970s and into this decade, the Soviets have increased their forces in this

area. In this theater, priority for the assignment of new equipment is second only to the vital Western TVD. The Far Eastern TVD also contains the bases of the USSR's Pacific Fleet. In a war with NATO, the Soviets would hope to deter Chinese entrance into the conflict. If deterrence failed, the Soviets probably would engage in rapid offensive operations to seize relatively limited objectives in China in order to force a quick termination of the war on the eastern front. In this way the Soviets would hope to avoid a two-front war as well as becoming enmeshed in a prolonged conventional ground war in China.

The Pacific Ocean Fleet is tasked with conducting operations in the Far Eastern, the Pa-

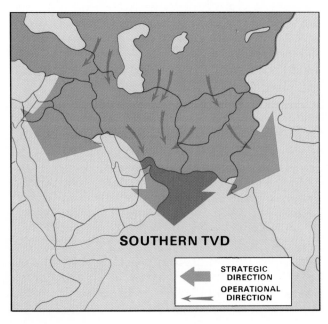

cific Ocean, and Indian Ocean TVDs. The Pacific Ocean Fleet is the largest of the four Soviet fleets. Its size can be attributed to its wartime missions, the increasing importance of the Pacific Basin in trade and commerce, and its geographic isolation from the western fleets and the major shipbuilding centers in the USSR. This remoteness would make reinforcement exceedingly difficult during wartime. The Pacific Ocean Fleet's wartime operations would be concentrated mainly in the northwest Pacific. In addition to protecting ballistic missile submarine assets, the Pacific Fleet's tasks would include:

- protecting the USSR from sea-based attacks by establishing naval superiority in the Sea of Japan, Sea of Okhotsk, along the Kuril Islands, and off the Kamchatka Peninsula;
- conducting operations against enemy sea-based strategic platforms; and
- interdicting enemy sea lines of communication.

The Pacific Fleet's sea-control effort would entail extensive surface ship, submarine, and naval aircraft ASW and antiship operations along the Soviet Far East periphery. Control of these seas would also be crucial to defending Soviet territory against possible US carrier-based airstrikes or amphibious assaults.

To complement its sea-control mission, the fleet would deploy attack and cruise missile submarines and strike aircraft into the northwest Pacific to engage US forces. In essence, the fleet would attempt to establish an echeloned defense of the Soviet Far East. Submarines and strike aircraft would spearhead the outer defense in the northwest Pacific; and surface combatants in combination with submarines and strike aircraft would form an inner defense along the Soviet coast.

Soviet attack submarines probably would deploy for ASW and possibly minelaying operations off the US ballistic missile submarine base at Bangor, Washington. Additionally, a few submarines might attempt to deploy near ports and bases off the US west coast and the Hawaiian Islands.

Operating primarily out of Cam Ranh Bay, Soviet naval forces would conduct antiship strikes against transiting enemy forces, interdict sea lines of communication in the South China Sea, and possibly attack US facilities in the region.

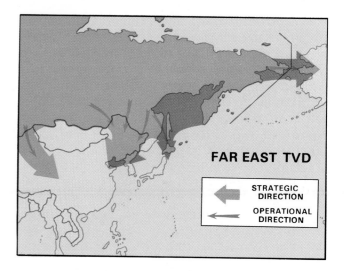

FAR EAST TVD

STRATEGIC DIRECTION
OPERATIONAL DIRECTION

In the Far East TVD, the Soviets have strengthened ground forces oriented against US allies. They have deployed a coastal defense division to the Japanese Northern Territories (south of the Kuril Islands) to the northeast of the Japanese island of Hokkaido. Four Soviet divisions are now deployed on the Pacific approaches to the USSR—the Northern Territories, Kurils, Sakhalin Island, and Kamchatka Peninsula. These divisions thus constitute the ground component of the Soviets' maritime strategy in the Pacific. In addition, those forces on the Northern Territories, Kurils and Sakhalin Island could threaten Japan.

To support their operations in the various TVDs, the Soviets have amassed large amounts of ground, air, naval, and air defense equipment and forces. These vast quantities in part reflect Soviet military planning to employ overwhelming power to achieve their objectives. They also reflect the offensive nature of Soviet military doctrine and strategy in that attacking forces are believed to require at least a 5:1 force ratio in anticipation of high losses inherent in offensive operations.

Wartime Air Force Employment

Since the mid-1960s, the Soviets have moved toward a doctrine and force capability to fight decisively at all levels of conflict, with or without nuclear weapons. A non-nuclear option, however, still requires a force posture capable of negating, or at least reducing, an enemy's air and nuclear resources. To achieve this, the Soviets have again looked to their historical experiences and developed a modernized version of the air operations of World War II.

The Soviets would, under non-nuclear conditions, substitute the mass employment of aviation forces for an initial mass nuclear strike. Such an operation would be performed simultaneously within the sectors of several fronts in an attempt to achieve air superiority and destroy or weaken an enemy's air and nuclear resources. The air operation has been developed into a crucial component of the theater strategic operation. The success of this operation is critical to the outcome of the theater campaign.

The principal targets of an air operation would be the enemy's aviation, nuclear resources, air defense, and command, control, and communications (C^3) facilities. Airstrikes would be directed to destroy tactical nuclear capabilities, disrupt any coordinated defense, and assure air superiority by neutralizing the main force of enemy aviation at the outset of hostilities.

The Soviet Union envisions an air operation lasting three or more days that would involve from three to seven mass strikes over the period. Two or three mass strikes would occur on the first day, with one or two additional mass strikes on subsequent days. Wartime employment of fixed-wing, tactical ground-attack airpower after completion of the air operation would probably fall into small and large strike packages. The small attacks would be two to four aircraft flying close support for troops, defense suppression, or perhaps armed reconnaissance missions. Large strike packages, on the order of 50 to 100 aircraft, would conduct major strike missions against nuclear storage depots, airfields, C^3 facilities, ports, and rear

area logistics and support bases. All Soviet air operations would occur as part of a planned and coordinated combined arms operation intended to achieve Soviet war aims. Pre- and post-strike reconnaissance, electronic countermeasures (ECM) escort support, and air defense support would be closely integrated with strike aircraft in major combat operations.

Soviet Military Transport Aviation's (*Voyenno-transportnaya aviatsiya,* abbreviated VTA) wartime functions would remain primarily paradrop and the landing of combat units as well as the provision of logistics support to all Soviet Armed Forces as needed. This could include rapid reinforcement and aerial resupply, nuclear weapons resupply, and medical evacuation. VTA, along with the mobilized Soviet Civil Aviation (Aeroflot) and the air transports of the other Soviet military elements, would probably provide sufficient numbers of air transport assets to perform their missions, especially since all Eurasian continental TVDs are accessible by rail and highway transportation networks.

Ground Forces

The USSR has traditionally maintained large, well-equipped ground forces as a primary component of military power. The ground forces are the largest of the USSR's five branches of the armed forces. An ambitious force development program is underway involving expansion, equipment modernization, training improvements, innovative tactics and operational concepts, and enhancement of command and control capabilities.

In peacetime, Soviet ground force personnel

USSR Selected Artillery

	2S3	2S1	M-1975	M-1975	2S5	M-1976
TOWED/ SELF-PROPELLED	Self-Propelled	Self-Propelled	Self-Propelled	Self-Propelled	Self-Propelled	Towed
CALIBER/TYPE	152-mm Howitzer	122-mm Howitzer	203-mm Gun	240-mm Mortar	152-mm Gun	152-mm Gun
MAXIMUM RANGE (M)	17,200	15,300	30,000	12,000	27,000	27,000
NUCLEAR-CAPABLE	Probably	No	Yes	Yes	Yes	Yes

number approximately 1.9 million. Their combat power resides in 213 maneuver divisions, including 12 mobilization base divisions (unmanned equipment that will be activated as divisions upon mobilization), with two additional divisions expanded to corps-type structures.

In peacetime, the ground forces within the USSR are subordinate to the 16 military districts, except for the 7 airborne divisions which are directly subordinate to Airborne Forces Headquarters in Moscow. Forces deployed in Eastern Europe are organized into four Soviet Groups of Forces, one each in East Germany, Poland, Czechoslovakia, and Hungary. Soviet forces in Mongolia and Afghanistan are each organized into an army subordinate to the adjacent military district. Assets of the Groups of Forces and military districts would be converted to fronts in wartime.

Tank, motorized rifle, and airborne divisions comprise the basic maneuver elements of Soviet ground forces. Tank and motorized rifle divisions are highly mobile armored forces. The Soviet tank division, which has 11,000 men, is comprised of three tank regiments and one motorized rifle regiment, while the motorized rifle division (13,000 men) is based on three motorized rifle regiments and one tank regiment. Both tank and motorized rifle divisions have a full complement of support elements, including aviation, artillery, air defense, signal, engineer, chemical, reconnaissance, maintenance, motor transport, and medical units.

The Soviet Union maintains the world's largest airborne force, currently seven divisions. Elements of an eighth division are operating in Afghanistan. Soviet airborne divisions do not have the same degree of land mobility as tank or motorized rifle divisions but are significantly more mobile than a US airborne division. They consist of three parachute regiments with airborne amphibious combat vehicles (BMDs) plus combat support and service units. In addition to the regular airborne divisions, the Soviets have formed air assault brigades at front level and air assault battalions at army level.

Current developments in Soviet ground forces are highlighted below:

- Tank and motorized rifle divisions are being expanded and reorganized. The resultant divisions are larger, more capable, and are configured for high-speed, combined arms operations on a conventional or nuclear battlefield.
- Two corps-type structures have been formed. These units are divisions expanded to almost twice the size of a tank division. The new formations contain over 450 tanks, 600 infantry fighting vehicles and armored personnel carriers (APCs), and 300 artillery pieces and multiple rocket launchers. They are ideally

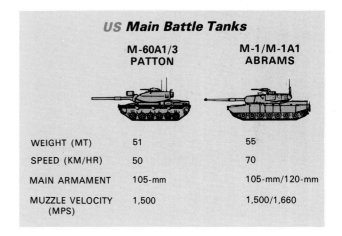

US Main Battle Tanks

	M-60A1/3 PATTON	M-1/M-1A1 ABRAMS
WEIGHT (MT)	51	55
SPEED (KM/HR)	50	70
MAIN ARMAMENT	105-mm	105-mm/120-mm
MUZZLE VELOCITY (MPS)	1,500	1,500/1,660

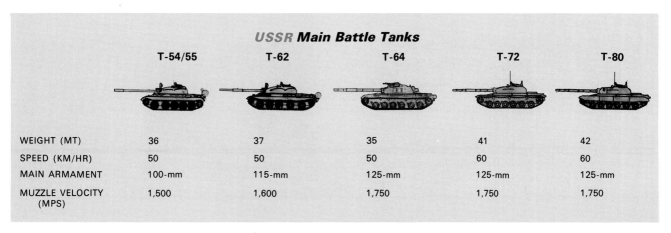

USSR Main Battle Tanks

	T-54/55	T-62	T-64	T-72	T-80
WEIGHT (MT)	36	37	35	41	42
SPEED (KM/HR)	50	50	50	60	60
MAIN ARMAMENT	100-mm	115-mm	125-mm	125-mm	125-mm
MUZZLE VELOCITY (MPS)	1,500	1,600	1,750	1,750	1,750

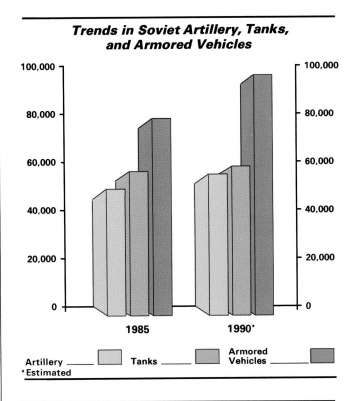

Trends in Soviet Artillery, Tanks, and Armored Vehicles

1985

1990*

Artillery _____ Tanks _____ Armored Vehicles _____
*Estimated

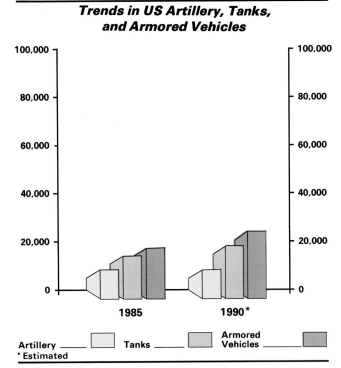

Trends in US Artillery, Tanks, and Armored Vehicles

1985

1990*

Artillery _____ Tanks _____ Armored Vehicles _____
* Estimated

suited to act as an Operational Maneuver Group (OMG), conducting high-speed operations deep in an enemy's rear area. Additional units of this type are expected to be formed once testing and evaluation are completed.

● Nondivisional artillery support for maneuver forces is also being expanded. Some army-level regiments are being expanded to brigade size with the addition of a fourth battalion. Battalions are concurrently expanding from 18 to 24 guns each. These changes have resulted in a 40-percent increase in artillery pieces in the brigades and are occurring primarily in units opposite NATO. New artillery units are also being formed; for example, two new artillery divisions have been formed since 1984.

Helicopters. To support ground operations, the Soviets continue to emphasize their helicopter forces, which are being expanded and modernized. At division level, helicopter detachments continue to expand to squadrons, and in some squadrons the number of HIND attack helicopters has been increased. At army level about 20 attack regiments have been formed, with up to 60 HIP and HIND attack helicopters in each. Over half of these are deployed opposite NATO forces. Most attack helicopters are the heavily armed Mi-24/HIND D/E and Mi-8/HIP E. Soviet emphasis on a heavy-lift helicopter transport capability is reflected in the development and recent appearance of the Mi-26/HALO. It is the world's largest production helicopter and is capable of carrying internally two airborne infantry combat vehicles or about 85 combat-ready troops. Much of the technology and hardware used in its production was obtained from the West.

The Soviets are now equipping their helicopters with infrared (IR) jammers and suppressors, IR decoy dispensers, and additional armor, thereby increasing their survivability—

The Mi-28/HAVOC, the USSR's newest attack helicopter, will be deployed in the near future.

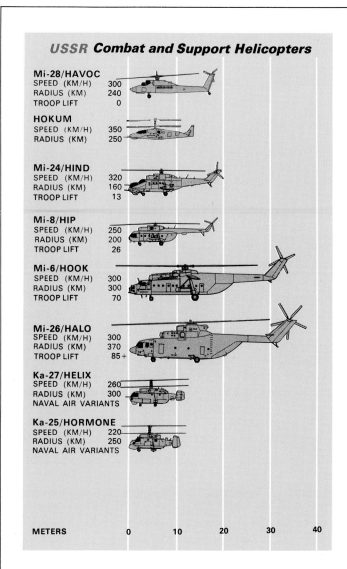

USSR Combat and Support Helicopters

Mi-28/HAVOC
SPEED (KM/H) 300
RADIUS (KM) 240
TROOP LIFT 0

HOKUM
SPEED (KM/H) 350
RADIUS (KM) 250

Mi-24/HIND
SPEED (KM/H) 320
RADIUS (KM) 160
TROOP LIFT 13

Mi-8/HIP
SPEED (KM/H) 250
RADIUS (KM) 200
TROOP LIFT 26

Mi-6/HOOK
SPEED (KM/H) 300
RADIUS (KM) 300
TROOP LIFT 70

Mi-26/HALO
SPEED (KM/H) 300
RADIUS (KM) 370
TROOP LIFT 85+

Ka-27/HELIX
SPEED (KM/H) 260
RADIUS (KM) 300
NAVAL AIR VARIANTS

Ka-25/HORMONE
SPEED (KM/H) 220
RADIUS (KM) 250
NAVAL AIR VARIANTS

METERS 0 10 20 30 40

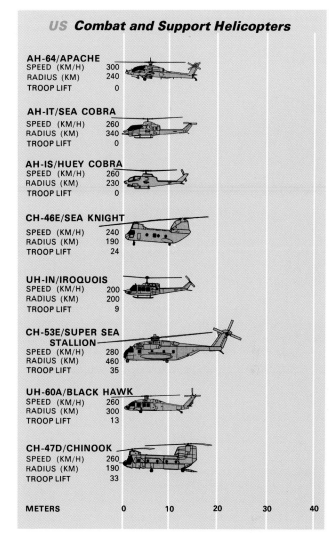

US Combat and Support Helicopters

AH-64/APACHE
SPEED (KM/H) 300
RADIUS (KM) 240
TROOP LIFT 0

AH-IT/SEA COBRA
SPEED (KM/H) 260
RADIUS (KM) 340
TROOP LIFT 0

AH-IS/HUEY COBRA
SPEED (KM/H) 260
RADIUS (KM) 230
TROOP LIFT 0

CH-46E/SEA KNIGHT
SPEED (KM/H) 240
RADIUS (KM) 190
TROOP LIFT 24

UH-IN/IROQUOIS
SPEED (KM/H) 200
RADIUS (KM) 200
TROOP LIFT 9

CH-53E/SUPER SEA STALLION
SPEED (KM/H) 280
RADIUS (KM) 460
TROOP LIFT 35

UH-60A/BLACK HAWK
SPEED (KM/H) 260
RADIUS (KM) 300
TROOP LIFT 13

CH-47D/CHINOOK
SPEED (KM/H) 260
RADIUS (KM) 190
TROOP LIFT 33

METERS 0 10 20 30 40

probably as a result of lessons learned in Afghanistan. A new attack helicopter, the Mi-28/HAVOC, similar to the US Army Apache, is expected to be deployed soon. The new HOKUM helicopter, which has no current Western counterpart, may give the Soviets a significant rotary-wing air-superiority capability. The Soviets are also employing helicopters as airborne command posts and electronic jamming platforms, as well as attack and transport platforms.

Soviet Ground Force Equipment

Armor

Soviet ground forces have some 52,600 main battle tanks in their active inventory, of which more than a third are the latest models, the T-64/72/80 series. These new tanks feature increased firepower, with a 125-mm main gun and

improved fire control systems, including a laser range finder on some versions. Both the T-80 and a variant of the T-64 can fire an antitank guided missile through the main gun. Survivability has been increased through the use of improved armor incorporating laminates and composites. Several thousand tanks currently not in the active inventory are also available if necessary.

The USSR's ground forces have about 59,000 armored personnel carriers and infantry fighting vehicles (IFVs) in their active inventory, with about 20,000 armored vehicles in reserve. Most of the inventory consists of the BTR-60 wheeled APC and the tracked BMP IFV. The BTR-80, which is a follow-on to the BTR-70 and BTR-60, is being fielded in limited numbers. It has an improved engine and drive train and better off-road performance. The improved BMP-2 is augmenting and replacing the BMP. It has

SCALEBOARD Coverage from the USSR and Eastern Europe

Potential SS-23 and SCALEBOARD Missile Coverage in an Advance Across Europe

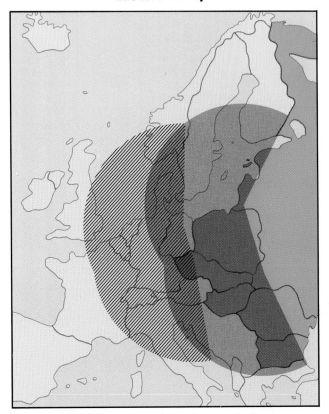

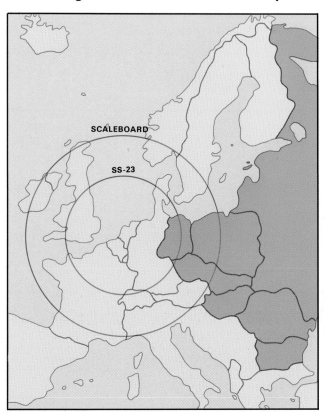

The Soviets' new main battle tank, the T-80, on field maneuvers.

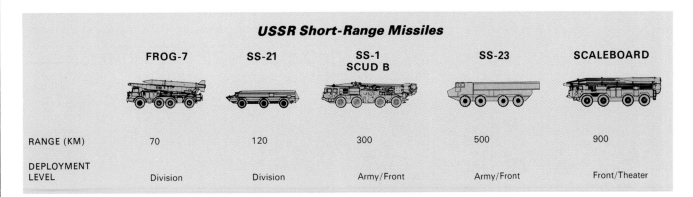

USSR Short-Range Missiles

	FROG-7	SS-21	SS-1 SCUD B	SS-23	SCALEBOARD
RANGE (KM)	70	120	300	500	900
DEPLOYMENT LEVEL	Division	Division	Army/Front	Army/Front	Front/Theater

Soviet SS-21 short-range missile on transporter-erector-launcher.

New 120-mm airborne amphibious combat vehicle.

a 30-mm rapid-fire gun in place of the 73-mm gun on the original BMP and carries the AT-5 antitank guided missile (ATGM). In addition to the BTR-BMPs, the Soviets have fielded the BMD with airborne and air assault units and a number of light-ground-pressure vehicles such as the GT-T/MTLB series for use in areas of poor trafficability.

Shorter Range Missiles

The Soviets have about 1,600 tactical and shorter range intermediate-range nuclear force (SRINF) ballistic missile launchers in their inventory. In 1985, the Soviets began to deploy their newest SRINF missile system, the SS-23. This missile, which has a longer range and improved accuracy over the SCUD, is expected to replace the latter at army and front levels. The front commander may also have a brigade of 12 to 18 SCALEBOARD missiles available. A more accurate version of the SCALEBOARD has been deployed. In 1984, the Soviets deployed the SCALEBOARD to East Germany and Czechoslovakia, marking

the first time this missile has been stationed outside the USSR. Much of Western Europe is now within range of these 900-kilometer missiles. The new generation of short-range missiles can be employed effectively with conventional warheads because of increased accuracy. Deployment will give the Soviets a formidable conventional deep-strike system.

In the area of short-range nuclear forces (SNF), Soviet armies and fronts have missile brigades equipped with from 12 to 18 SS-1C SCUD missile launchers. At division level, the predominant SNF weapon is the unguided free rocket over ground (FROG) found in a battalion of four launchers. The Soviets have begun to replace the FROG with the more accurate, longer range SS-21 missile in some divisions opposite European NATO.

Fire Support

The Soviets have traditionally placed great emphasis on fire support and currently have over 39,000 artillery pieces and multiple rocket launchers (MRLs) greater than 100mm in cal-

iber in their active inventory, with about 10,000 held in reserve. The ground forces are now fielding large numbers of self-propelled artillery at all levels.

Developing Operational Concepts

Soviet improvements in equipment and weapons developments reflect concepts to accomplish longstanding operational goals. The rapid penetration of forward enemy defenses on selected axes is designed to ensure that the focus of decisive action is shifted to an adversary's rear area. The rapid advance of Soviet forces is intended to bring about the collapse of the enemy's defense and the destruction of his forces while the attainment of deep strategic objectives is sustained by the continuous commitment of follow-on forces.

The Soviets are aware of the planned or programed enhancements of NATO theater forces. They believe the development of capabilities and strategies involving deep attack, such as the US Army Air-Land Battle and the NATO Follow-on Forces Attack concepts, could challenge their ability to execute a planned strategy. As a result, Soviet operational concepts and force planning are taking these enhancements into account. Recent Soviet force developments are designed to provide greater mobility, firepower, sustainability, and command and control capabilities to counter NATO force enhancements.

Innovations in traditional Soviet operational concepts feature increased emphasis on deep operations into an opponent's rear area early in a conflict. Adapting their experience with mobile forces in World War II, the Soviets have developed Operational Maneuver Groups (OMGs) to conduct mobile warfare in the enemy's rear area following a breakthrough of his forward defenses. The insertion of OMGs, consisting of tank-heavy formations supported by infantry fighting vehicles, mobile fire support, air defense, air assault units, and avia-

The Soviet 16-tube, 220-mm BM-27 multiple rocket launcher is capable of firing high-explosive conventional rounds, scattering mines, and delivering chemical warheads as far as 40 kilometers. The BM-27 is used extensively in Afghanistan, where it provides intensive long-range fire support against Afghan Freedom Fighters.

tion, is designed to isolate front-line defending forces, disrupt rear area logistics and reserves, threaten key command and control facilities and economic and population centers, and neutralize nuclear attack systems. The successful use of OMGs would facilitate the commitment of second-echelon forces and accelerate the overall rate of advance.

Special Operations Forces (SPETSNAZ)

The USSR maintains a complement of special operations forces, the most prominent of which are known as SPETSNAZ. These are managed by the Main Intelligence Directorate (GRU) of the Soviet General Staff and are trained to conduct a variety of sensitive missions, including covert actions abroad. Large numbers of SPETSNAZ troops have been assigned to Soviet forces in Afghanistan, where they have become known for their ruthless aggressiveness.

During peacetime, the GRU carefully coordinates reconnaissance programs that are geared to meet the intelligence requirements for Soviet forces in war. In wartime, SPETSNAZ forces would operate far behind enemy lines for extended periods of time where they would conduct reconnaissance and sabotage on a wide variety of military and political targets.

The KGB is assessed to have overall responsibility, under Central Committee guidance, for operational planning, coordination, and political control of special purpose forces that operate abroad in peacetime. This was the case in the Soviet invasion of Czechoslovakia in 1968 and of Afghanistan in 1979. The KGB maintains its own special operations capabilities in the form of clandestine assets dedicated to assassination and wartime sabotage.

Though organized into brigades, these forces would infiltrate and fight as small teams. In a war, each brigade can be expected to field about 100 SPETSNAZ teams. A typical team would be led by an officer, with a warrant officer or sergeant as second in command. At least one team member would be fully versed in the language and customs of the target country. Other members of the team are trained as radio operators and weapons and demolition experts. In addition to normal military training, all receive instruction in:

- reconnaissance and target location;
- infiltration tactics;
- sabotage methods using explosives, in-

cendiaries, and chemical and biological agents;
- clandestine communications;
- hand-to-hand combat and silent killing techniques;
- psychological operations;
- language skills; and
- survival behind enemy lines.

In wartime, naval SPETSNAZ teams would be transported to a target area by aircraft, submarine, or surface ship and would be inserted immediately prior to hostilities.

Once deployed, the teams would conduct reconnaissance and tactical operations against a wide variety of targets, such as ship and submarine bases, airfields, command and intelligence centers, communication facilities, ports and harbors, radar sites, and—of prime importance—nuclear weapons facilities. Though a small force, SPETSNAZ has the potential to achieve results disproportionate to its size against such a critical, yet often vulnerable, target list.

Theater Nuclear Capability

The Soviets believe nuclear weapons are decisive in theater operations. Even if a war is fought at the non-nuclear level, the Soviets recognize the constant danger of rapid escalation. If a theater operation is fought at or escalates to the nuclear level, the Soviets would employ nuclear weapons in a coordinated, massed theater strike which would allow the rapid attainment of deep theater objectives. The Soviets' capability to fight and win a theater war at the nuclear level would be predicated on three main factors:

- a formidable nuclear weapons delivery capability;
- the ability to destroy or degrade an adversary's nuclear systems and command and control capability while protecting Soviet assets during conventional operations prior to escalation; and
- a significant reconstitution capability in the post-strike period to ensure that critical Soviet forces would survive NATO nuclear strikes and regenerate their own offensive force structure.

Chemical Warfare

The USSR has the most extensive chemical warfare capability in the world. At the end of World War II, the Soviets captured from the Germans large stockpiles of chemical agents as well as the technology and equipment to make the nerve agents tabun and sarin and the German plans for production of soman. Two German nerve agent production plants were dismantled and removed to the Soviet Union where they were reassembled. The Soviets have continued to develop production capabilities based on this early design and have built agent manufacturing facilities in various locations around the Soviet Union. Since the late 1960s, the Soviets have continued to test, produce, and stockpile chemical weapons.

The Shikhany Chemical Warfare Proving Ground is one of the Soviets' primary chemical weapons test areas. It was established in the mid-1920s, and a number of chemical weapons tests were conducted in the late 1920s and 1930s. World War II reconnaissance photographs confirmed that Shikhany was an active chemical weapons test facility. Since that time it has grown in size and sophistication and continues to be a highly active testing facility.

Chemical agents are stored in a network of highly secure military depots located across the Soviet Union. These depots contain agents in bulk containers and agent-filled munitions as well as gas masks, protective suits, decontamination solutions, and decontamination vehicles. Many depots have rail lines allowing the rapid movement of chemical warfare materials. Since the late 1960s, the amount of agents, weapons, and material in storage at these deposits has increased significantly and this buildup continues. These depots support operational forces and report to the Headquarters of the Soviet Chemical Troops in the Ministry of Defense.

The Soviets have developed the doctrine for the use of chemical weapons, and Soviet tacticians have standardized the required procedures. If a commander determines that a particular battle situation is suited for the employment of chemical weapons and once approval has been granted by the highest Soviet authority, chemical strikes can be conducted against an array of targets including:

- nuclear delivery means;
- airfields;
- naval bases and seaports;
- command and control facilities;
- storage depots;
- supply routes;
- troop concentrations;
- artillery and armor; and
- amphibious/heliborne landing forces.

The Soviets have persistent and nonpersistent chemical agents as well as a variety of delivery systems. If Soviet forces have to cross contaminated areas, specially trained troops would be available for advice, reconnaissance, and decontamination.

The Soviet concept of maintaining the momentum of attack presupposes the capability to decontaminate armored fighting vehicles, equipment, and personnel rapidly and return them to combat. This begins at the unit level with a variety of decontamination devices allowing rapid, partial cleansing of contaminated equipment. Specialized decontamination units exist at regimental level and above. These units use a truck-mounted decontamination apparatus to cleanse equipment and personnel rapidly and thoroughly. One such item, the TMS-65, is an aircraft turbojet engine mounted

The Targets for Soviet Chemical Weapons

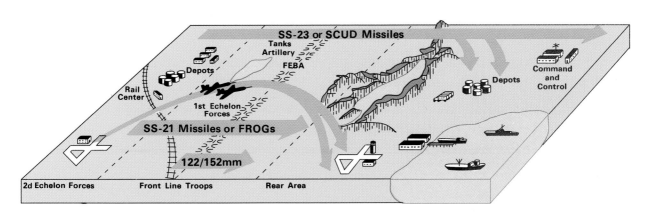

Chapter IV Soviet Forces for Theater Operations

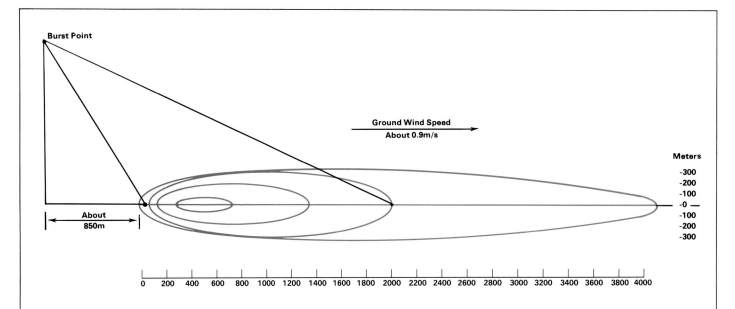

Burst Point

Ground Wind Speed
About 0.9m/s

Meters
-300
-200
-100
-0 —
-100
-200
-300

About
850m

0 200 400 600 800 1000 1200 1400 1600 1800 2000 2200 2400 2600 2800 3000 3200 3400 3600 3800 4000

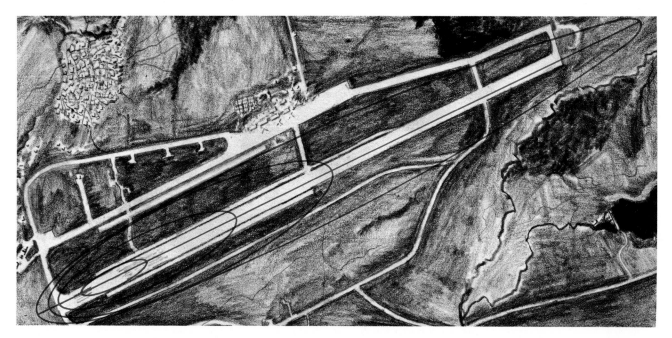

The SCUD-B ground contamination pattern superimposed on a military airbase runway. Operational flights from contaminated runways are extremely hazardous and difficult. In a Soviet chemical attack against a NATO airbase, many SCUD missiles would be used to ensure coverage.

on a URAL-375 truck chassis which sprays a decontamination solution on contaminated vehicles.

Several chemical agents, toxins, and combinations have been used by the Soviets in Afghanistan and by their client forces, the Vietnamese, in Laos and Cambodia.

Chemical agents known to have been developed by the Soviets include:

- nerve agents (sarin, soman, and a V-series agent);
- blister agents (mustard, lewisite, and a mixture of the two);
- a blood agent (hydrogen cyanide);
- a choking agent (phosgene); and
- one other agent not specifically identified but which causes unconsciousness for an hour or more and which has been widely reported as being used in Afghanistan.

The Soviets stock both persistent and nonpersistent agents. Persistent agents stay on the target from hours to days, depending on weather conditions, unless removed by decontamination, while nonpersistent agents will clear the target relatively quickly. The Soviets are also investigating binary weapons systems. This type of system, in addition to its inherent safe handling and storage characteristics, expands the possibilities for newer agent combinations. Complete protection from all the types of agents in the Soviet inventory requires special clothing and masks as well as rapid treatment for any exposed personnel.

Almost all Soviet conventional weapons systems from mortars to long-range tactical missiles have compatible chemical ammunition or warheads that are available to land, air, and naval forces. The Soviets have also developed the firing data required for employing chemical weapons in battlefield situations. This includes the types and numbers of weapons required to attack different targets under a variety of weather and combat conditions. They continue to test systems with improved dissemination, larger payloads, increased range, and better accuracy which afford them greater target flexibility and deeper strike capability. Two types of chemical warheads have been developed for tactical missiles—bulk agents and small bomblets—which can be dispersed over the target.

The Soviets' continuing chemical weapons activities are carried out by a large and well-trained chemical warfare organization directed by the Headquarters Chemical Troops in the Ministry of Defense. This organization is headed by a three-star general and numbers more than 45,000 personnel in the ground forces alone. Its size is expected to double during wartime. The primary responsibilities of Soviet chemical specialists include:

- providing technical advice to front commanders;
- conducting research and development programs;
- producing and storing chemical weapons and testing and evaluating protective materials;
- training Soviet forces in chemical weapons employment and survival on a contaminated battlefield;
- decontamination and reconnaissance; and
- operating the chemical academies.

This corps of specialists also has about 30,000

Soviet Chemical Weapons Depots, Production Centers, and Storage Areas.

Chapter IV Soviet Forces for Theater Operations

vehicles for decontamination and reconnaissance and has more than 200 locations for teaching and training Soviet forces in chemical protection and decontamination. Training includes the actual use of live chemical agents. Also, the Soviets have installed protective filtration systems in many combat and combat support vehicles and ships, allowing their forces to operate in a contaminated environment without wearing full protective clothing.

Biological Warfare

The Soviet Union continues to maintain and broaden its offensive biological warfare capabilities. Institutes and other facilities are rapidly acquiring state-of-the-art developments in biotechnology. This technology is being carefully screened for its potential to improve or alter well-known disease-producing agents for biological warfare purposes.

Agents the Soviets have developed for biological warfare purposes include anthrax, tularemia, and various toxins including the mycotoxins. Research and development on a variety of toxins continues. The use of mycotoxins in Southeast Asia and Afghanistan and the Sverdlovsk biological agent accident of 1979 that resulted in the release of anthrax from a bacteriological warfare institute show that the Soviets have violated the Biological Weapons Convention of 1972.

Air Forces

The Soviet Air Forces (SAF) are a crucial component of the USSR's theater force structure. The Soviets have organized their air forces to provide dedicated aviation support to combined arms commanders from maneuver divisions to the Supreme High Command and to allow commanders to mass high-value aviation assets at the most decisive place and time.

The Soviet Air Forces have three major combat components: Strategic Air Armies, Air Forces of Military Districts and Groups of Forces, and Soviet Military Transport Aviation (VTA). The USSR dedicates high priority to upgrading each component. New generations of strategic, tactical, and transport aircraft are in the development, test, production, and deployment stages.

The five Strategic Air Armies include one designed for intercontinental and maritime strike missions and four designed to operate in continental TVDs. Approximately 180 BEAR and BISON heavy bombers are assigned to the air army organized for intercontinental strikes. The four theater-oriented air armies are equipped with medium bombers, fighter-bombers, and fighters which constitute the principal deep-strike component of theater forces. The air armies are directly subordinate to the Soviet Supreme High Command (VGK) and are assigned to operate in TVDs in accordance with the dictates of the VGK. Eighty percent of the more than 500 medium bombers are based west of the Urals and would, most likely, be employed in operations in the Western, Southwestern, Northwestern, and Southern TVDs. The remainder would operate in the Far Eastern TVD.

There are 17 air forces in the Groups of Forces, peripheral military districts of the Soviet Union, Mongolia, and Afghanistan. These air forces are operationally subordinate to the military district, Group, or army commander (as in Afghanistan) and are comprised of combat fighters, reconnaissance aircraft, fighter-bombers, and helicopters. The latter are known as Army Aviation, although the mix is not standard. Fighter and fighter-bomber regiments can be organized into divisions or remain independent, reporting directly to the military districts and Groups of Forces. Reconnaissance regiments and squadrons are independent units, while helicopter units either report to the military districts and Groups of Forces or to armies or divisions. To ensure dedicated aviation support to ground forces, tank and combined arms armies are being assigned their own aviation components consisting primarily of helicopters. In wartime, the air forces of the military districts and Groups of Forces will become the air forces of the front.

Soviet Military Transport Aviation is the third operational element of the Soviet Air Forces. Its primary responsibility is to provide airlift for the Soviet airborne forces and air assault units. It also provides air logistics support for deployed Soviet and allied armed forces and supports Soviet political and economic interests, especially in the Third World.

The Soviet Air Forces have over 700 bomber aircraft, some 6,300 fighter and fighter-bombers, and about 600 VTA transports. Of the total, the air forces of the military districts and the Groups of Forces have about 5,440 fighter-interceptors, fighter-bombers, and reconnaissance and electronic countermeasures (ECM) aircraft deployed in nearly 140 regiments and squadrons. An additional 750 fighter and fighter-bomber aircraft are assigned to the Strategic Air Armies, and some 110 are in Afghanistan.

The air forces of the USSR's Warsaw Pact allies provide important adjuncts to the Soviets' air and air defense capabilities in the Western and Southwestern TVDs. Altogether the non-Soviet Warsaw Pact countries have approximately 2,350 fixed-wing combat aircraft.

Over the past decade, the Soviets have significantly enhanced the performance characteristics of their tactical combat aircraft. Older weapons systems had limited range and payload capabilities, short-range air intercept radars or range-only radars, little or no capability to employ precision-guided munitions, and were restricted primarily to clear-weather operations. Newer fighters and interceptors,

however, can conduct air intercepts at beyond-visual ranges. Moreover, they can operate at greater distances from their airfields, carry up to eight air-to-air missiles, and perform in all weather conditions. The newest generation of fighter-interceptors—FOXHOUNDs, FULCRUMs, and FLANKERs—has a true look-down/shoot-down capability that enables them to engage low-flying aircraft or cruise missiles.

The MiG-23/FLOGGER is by far the most numerous fighter-interceptor, with about 1,700 aircraft. Other fighter-interceptors include the FOXBAT, FLAGON, FIREBAR, FIDDLER, and the new MiG-31/FOXHOUND. The FLOGGER is likely to remain in the force in substantial numbers for the next five years. Almost 600 late-model MiG-21/FISHBEDs are still operational, although they are being replaced in a few regiments by the MiG-29/FULCRUM.

Deployment of the new Mach-2 MiG-29/FULCRUM air-superiority fighter proceeded

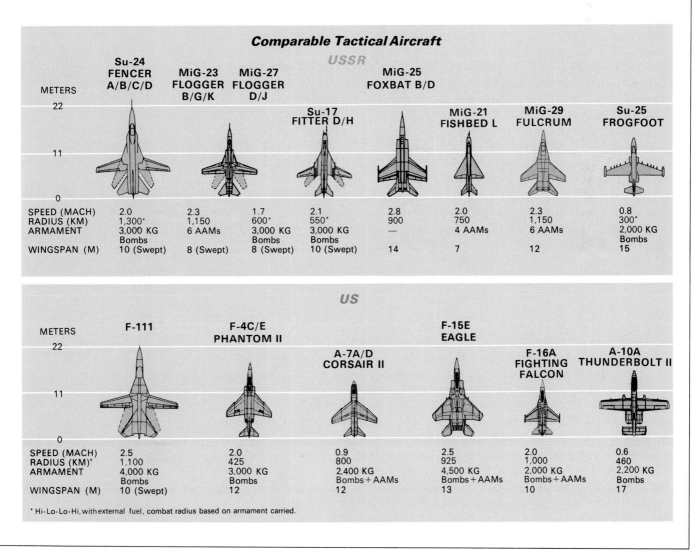

Comparable Tactical Aircraft

*Hi-Lo-Lo-Hi, with external fuel, combat radius based on armament carried.

77   **Chapter IV Soviet Forces for Theater Operations**

The new Su-27/FLANKER, equipped with the look-down/shoot-down radar and weapon system, has the capability to engage low-flying aircraft and cruise missiles.

throughout 1985 and into early 1986 at a steady, though still limited, rate. By the end of January 1986, Soviet forces in East Germany and the far eastern USSR had begun to receive this aircraft. Additional regiments inside the Soviet Union west of the Urals now possess FULCRUMs, and an increasing pace of deliveries is expected over the next several years.

The new Su-27/FLANKER also entered operational service by early 1986, with initial aircraft arriving in air defense regiments.

The FULCRUM and FLANKER, with true look-down/shoot-down radar, carry both the beyond-visual-range AA-10 and the short-range AA-11 air-to-air missiles. These aircraft, together with the FOXHOUND homeland defense interceptor, mark the Soviet Air Forces' transition to a new generation of far more capable combat aircraft. Although not fully matching the avionics capabilities of corresponding current US fighter aircraft, they pose a significant wartime air-superiority threat.

The Su-17/FITTER is the most common ground-attack aircraft. There are almost 800 in Soviet Air Force regiments, in military districts, or Groups of Forces. The next most numerous is the MiG-27/FLOGGER with over 700 aircraft. However, almost 700 Soviet Air Forces Su-24/FENCERs are the best deep-interdiction aircraft in the Soviet inventory. Other regiments are comprised of MiG-23/FLOGGERs, the new Su-25/FROGFOOT, and

older MiG-21/FISHBEDs and Su-7/FITTER As. A new improved FENCER variant, the D model, is currently being deployed primarily with Strategic Aviation FENCER regiments. Reconnaissance assets include MiG-21/FISHBEDs, Su-17/FITTERs, MiG-25/FOXBATs, and Yak-28/BREWERs. Newer aircraft are beginning to replace the BREWER, significantly increasing Soviet reconnaissance range capabilities.

Over 200 Tu-16/BADGER bombers still com-

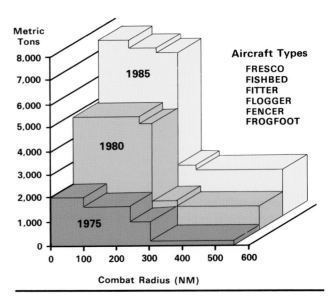

Bombing Capabilities of Soviet Tactical Ground-Attack Aircraft

The Su-24/FENCER nuclear-capable fighter-bomber, introduced in 1974, with new variants being produced, is the USSR's best deep-interdiction tactical aircraft.

prise nearly half of the Soviet medium bomber force. Approximately 150 BACKFIREs are currently operational and available to support theater mission requirements. The remainder of the Soviet Air Forces' medium bomber force consists of 135 Tu-22/BLINDERs.

The VTA aircraft force consists of almost 600 medium- and long-range cargo transports. Il-76/CANDID long-range jet transports have been replacing the older An-12/CUB medium-range turboprop transports in VTA units at a rate of about 30 per year. The CANDID offers obvious advantages over the CUB since it can carry twice the maximum payload over three times as far. The CANDID now predominates over the CUB in numbers as well as payload. The VTA holds over 290 CANDIDs and only 230 CUBs in its inventory. VTA also has about 55 An-22/COCK long-range turboprop transports, the only Soviet transports able to carry out-sized cargo such as main battle tanks or large missiles. Production and deployment of the new CONDOR transport will dramatically upgrade VTA's heavy-lift capability. The CONDOR should begin arriving in VTA units in 1987 or 1988.

The Warsaw Pact air forces hold a significant advantage over those of NATO in the degree of hardening completed at their tactical airbases. They have built several thousand concrete aircraft shelters, many of which are earth-covered for added protection and cam-

ouflage. In contrast, NATO has only about half as many aircraft shelters. A significant number of US reinforcement aircraft still lack European deployment bases until early combat attrition would free space. The Soviets have established secondary operating strips for a number of their forward-based units, although they still have some space limitations for potential later reinforcements as well.

The Su-25/FROGFOOT ground-attack aircraft has seen extensive action in Afghanistan. It is being deployed with Soviet forces in both the western and eastern USSR and is exported to Czechoslovakia and Iraq.

Air Defense Forces

The basic mission of air defense is to counter air threats to the Soviet homeland as well as to deployed forces. Soviet air defense forces include both strategic and tactical surface-to-air missile systems that have capabilities to engage aircraft, cruise missiles, and some types of ballistic missiles. Along most Soviet borders,

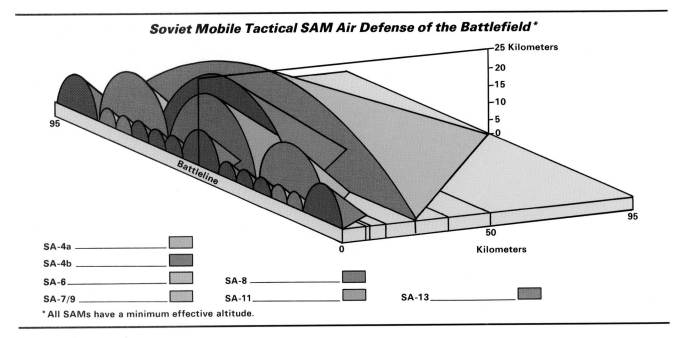

Soviet Mobile Tactical SAM Air Defense of the Battlefield*

SA-4a
SA-4b
SA-6
SA-7/9
SA-8
SA-11
SA-13

* All SAMs have a minimum effective altitude.

these assets are currently organized under a single command at the military district level.

Soviet strategic SAMs that are deployed for barrier, area, and point defense of key installations in the Soviet Union also are used to provide cover for frontal forces in garrison and at staging areas. After the deployment of the front, these SAMs would provide defense of the rear echelon and vital supply lines. Systems that are transportable (for example, the SA-2) or truly mobile (the SA-10 now in the process of being deployed) could also move forward with the front to establish air cover for newly occupied territory.

Tactical or troop air defense SAMs, AAA, and radars are designed to counter low-altitude threats and are inherently mobile. As noted in Chapter III, tactical air defense systems could be used to augment strategic systems for homeland air defense. However, these systems are principally intended to move with the front as organic elements of combined arms formations. Over 4,600 tactical SAM launchers and 12,000 AAA pieces are deployed with Air Defense Forces units at regimental through front level. In addition, as many as 25,000 shoulder-fired SAM launchers are at battalion and company level and with nondivisional units.

The antiair operation is a vital component of a theater strategic operation. Its primary objective is to disrupt or blunt enemy offensive air operations. An additional objective is to prevent hostile aircraft that are carrying out a deep-interdiction/deep-strike mission from attacking installations or troop concentrations. The operation is accomplished by using both air and ground assets to attack enemy aircraft either at their bases or in flight. This combined arms operation would be directed by the High Command of Forces in the TVD.

Naval Forces

The Soviet Navy is organized into four fleets —the Northern, Baltic, Black Sea, and Pacific Ocean Fleets—and the Caspian Sea Flotilla. The navy also maintains deployed forces in the Mediterranean Sea, the Indian Ocean, and off the coast of West Africa. The Soviets also continue to develop a naval and airbase at Cam Ranh Bay, Vietnam, where they now station submarines with supporting surface combatants and a composite air group of BADGER strike and combat support aircraft and an air defense force of MiG-23/FLOGGERS. In addition, combatant task groups often deploy to the Caribbean Sea, with stopovers at Cuban bases and ports.

Since the mid-1970s, the Soviet Navy has evolved toward a balanced ocean-going fleet capable of fighting at great distances from the USSR at nuclear and conventional levels. As recently as the mid-1970s, Soviet naval capabilities were configured for a short, intense war. Sustained combat was seriously restricted by the small weapon loads as well as the limited capabilities and endurance of most surface

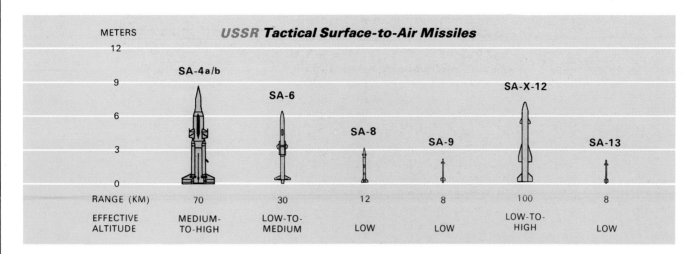

USSR Tactical Surface-to-Air Missiles

METERS						
	SA-4a/b	SA-6	SA-8	SA-9	SA-X-12	SA-13
RANGE (KM)	70	30	12	8	100	8
EFFECTIVE ALTITUDE	MEDIUM-TO-HIGH	LOW-TO-MEDIUM	LOW	LOW	LOW-TO-HIGH	LOW

combatants, some submarines, and naval aircraft. During this time, however, new classes of larger ships with more sophisticated weapons systems, sensors, electronics and communications, as well as improved endurance capabilities, began to enter the fleet. In combination with marked improvements in naval aircraft and submarines, Soviet capabilities to conduct sustained antiship, antisubmarine, and antiair warfare in distant waters were increased. However, the Soviets still do not have sufficient seaborne aircraft capabilities to conduct carrier combat operations outside the range of land-based aircraft.

Naval Force Growth

The USSR is constructing several new and improved classes of general purpose submarines and is transitioning to new designs such as the AKULA and SIERRA. This process decreased output of general purpose submarines in 1985, with only one new nuclear-powered attack submarine—a VICTOR-III-Class launched. The construction of KILO-Class diesel-powered attack submarines continued. Series production of the AKULA, SIERRA, and possibly other classes is expected to begin in earnest with additional launches in 1986. New Soviet general purpose nuclear-powered submarines, characterized by significant quieting, new weapons, and new sensors, pose a formidable challenge to Western naval forces.

The Soviets are also producing increasingly capable surface ships with greater displacement, firepower, and endurance, along with improved sensors and electronics—all of which result in ships with significantly increased self-sustainability. At present, ten new classes of surface warships are being produced.

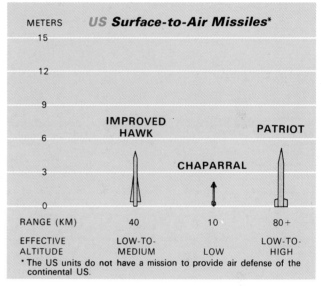

US Surface-to-Air Missiles*

METERS			
	IMPROVED HAWK	CHAPARRAL	PATRIOT
RANGE (KM)	40	10	80+
EFFECTIVE ALTITUDE	LOW-TO-MEDIUM	LOW	LOW-TO-HIGH

* The US units do not have a mission to provide air defense of the continental US.

The most noteworthy new platform under construction is an entirely new class of aircraft carrier. Launched from Nikolayev shipyard in December 1985 and now in a two- to three-year fitting-out period prior to its initial sea trials toward the end of the decade, the new carrier is approximately 300 meters long and will displace 65,000 tons

The new ship is an evolutionary step in the Soviet Navy's aircraft carrier program. It has a larger angled flight deck than the 37,100-ton KIEV-Class carriers, has deck-edge aircraft elevators fore and aft of the starboard island superstructure, and has a broad, upturned bow similar in configuration to a ski jump ramp used for short-take-off-and-vertical-landing aircraft. It is still too early to determine whether the new carrier will conduct over-the-bow flight operations or whether the forward area of the flight deck will be fitted, at least initially, with surface-to-surface mis-

sile mounts similar to those aboard the KIEV-Class carrier.

The aircraft for the new carrier's air wing are still under development. The test and evaluation program for candidate aircraft continues at the Saki naval airfield near the Black Sea. The Soviets are developing catapult and arresting gear systems that would be required by a carrier for launching and recovering high-performance fixed-wing aircraft. Installation of catapults and arresting gear on the new carrier cannot be confirmed, however, and the Soviets could choose to deploy this first unit with about 40 to 50 vertical take-off and landing aircraft.

The 14,000-ton OSCAR-Class submarine carries 24 nuclear-capable, 550-kilometer-range SS-N-19 antiship cruise missiles. Three OSCAR units are now operational.

The new carrier is expected to begin sea trials in 1989.

The Soviet Navy now has about 675 surface combatant ships. This total includes 280 principal surface combatants and 3 KIEV-Class aircraft carriers. It also includes 185 patrol combatants, 77 amphibious ships, and some

130 mine warfare ships. There are 300 underway replenishment and material and fleet support ships and 296 general purpose submarines. About 500 of these surface ships are ocean-going ships of greater than 1,000 tons displacement, with the remainder serving primarily in coastal defense and flank-support roles. Together, the navies of the Soviet Union and its Warsaw Pact allies have about 540 surface ships greater than 1,000 tons displacement, compared to more than 850 ships of this size in the navies of the United States and its NATO allies. The 37,100-ton KIEV-Class carrier is the largest operational ship in the navy's inventory and is the first modern Soviet-built ship to carry fixed-wing aircraft. Four have been constructed, and the last KIEV is fitting out. Its weapons and sensors differ from previous units, and it is expected to begin sea trials soon in the Black Sea.

The KIROV-Class guided-missile cruiser is the Soviet Navy's first nuclear-powered surface warship. Two, the *KIROV* and the *FRUNZE,* are now in service. Although their weapons systems differ somewhat, both have broad capabilities in all naval warfare areas—antisurface, antisubmarine, and antiair. A third KIROV-Class cruiser is likely to be launched in 1986, and construction of a fourth unit is expected to begin soon. The lead ship of the newest class of Soviet cruisers, the *SLAVA,* is active in the Black Sea and the Mediterranean. With its 16 SS-N-12 launchers, the SLAVA is mainly designed for antisurface warfare. It also has a modern air defense system with eight SA-N-6 launchers and two twin-armed SA-N-4 launchers. The second and third units are expected to begin sea trials in late 1985 and 1986, respectively, and a fourth unit is under construction at a Black Sea shipyard.

Two guided-missile destroyer construction programs continued during 1985. The fifth SOVREMENNYY-Class guided-missile destroyer began sea trials last August, and five additional units are in varying stages of construction. The SOVREMENNYY, which has eight launchers for antiship cruise missiles—twice as many as any other Soviet destroyer—

USSR Attack Submarines

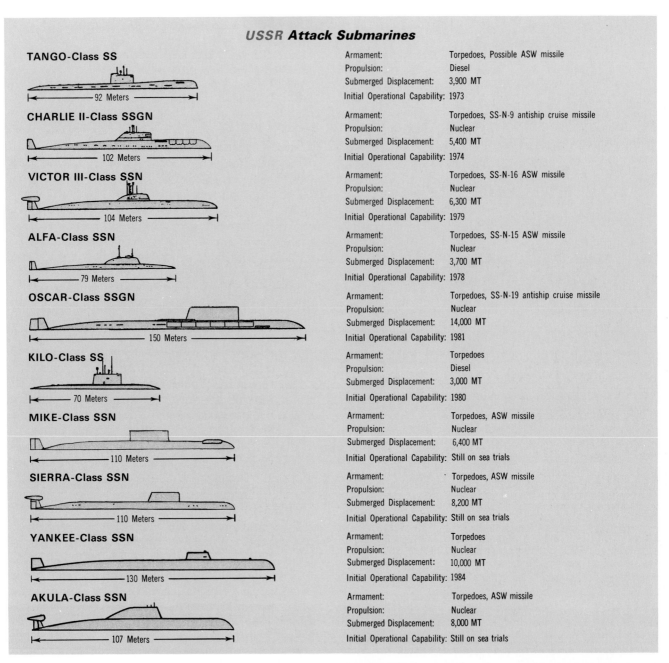

TANGO-Class SS
92 Meters

Armament: Torpedoes, Possible ASW missile
Propulsion: Diesel
Submerged Displacement: 3,900 MT
Initial Operational Capability: 1973

CHARLIE II-Class SSGN
102 Meters

Armament: Torpedoes, SS-N-9 antiship cruise missile
Propulsion: Nuclear
Submerged Displacement: 5,400 MT
Initial Operational Capability: 1974

VICTOR III-Class SSN
104 Meters

Armament: Torpedoes, SS-N-16 ASW missile
Propulsion: Nuclear
Submerged Displacement: 6,300 MT
Initial Operational Capability: 1979

ALFA-Class SSN
79 Meters

Armament: Torpedoes, SS-N-15 ASW missile
Propulsion: Nuclear
Submerged Displacement: 3,700 MT
Initial Operational Capability: 1978

OSCAR-Class SSGN
150 Meters

Armament: Torpedoes, SS-N-19 antiship cruise missile
Propulsion: Nuclear
Submerged Displacement: 14,000 MT
Initial Operational Capability: 1981

KILO-Class SS
70 Meters

Armament: Torpedoes
Propulsion: Diesel
Submerged Displacement: 3,000 MT
Initial Operational Capability: 1980

MIKE-Class SSN
110 Meters

Armament: Torpedoes, ASW missile
Propulsion: Nuclear
Submerged Displacement: 6,400 MT
Initial Operational Capability: Still on sea trials

SIERRA-Class SSN
110 Meters

Armament: Torpedoes, ASW missile
Propulsion: Nuclear
Submerged Displacement: 8,200 MT
Initial Operational Capability: Still on sea trials

YANKEE-Class SSN
130 Meters

Armament: Torpedoes
Propulsion: Nuclear
Submerged Displacement: 10,000 MT
Initial Operational Capability: 1984

AKULA-Class SSN
107 Meters

Armament: Torpedoes, ASW missile
Propulsion: Nuclear
Submerged Displacement: 8,000 MT
Initial Operational Capability: Still on sea trials

US Attack Submarines

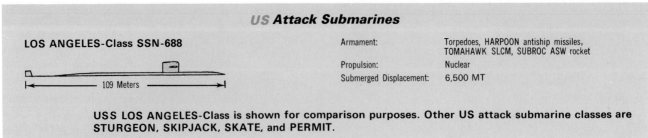

LOS ANGELES-Class SSN-688
109 Meters

Armament: Torpedoes, HARPOON antiship missiles, TOMAHAWK SLCM, SUBROC ASW rocket
Propulsion: Nuclear
Submerged Displacement: 6,500 MT

USS LOS ANGELES-Class is shown for comparison purposes. Other US attack submarine classes are STURGEON, SKIPJACK, SKATE, and PERMIT.

is designed for antisurface warfare. It complements the ASW-configured UDALOY-Class guided-missile destroyers, which carry eight long-range cruise missile-delivered ASW weapons. Two UDALOYs entered the inventory during 1985, bringing the total of active units to seven. Four additional units are under construction.

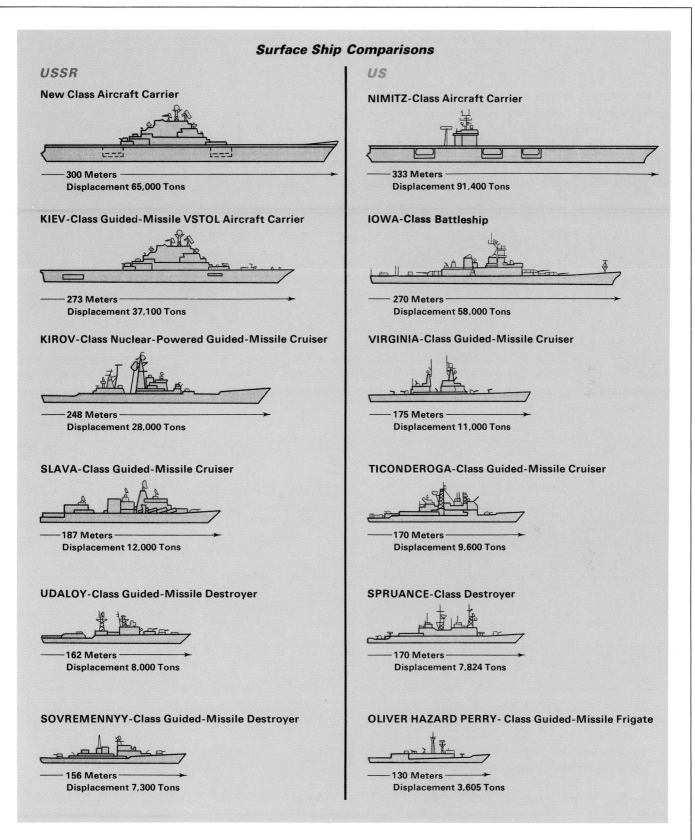

Surface Ship Comparisons

USSR

New Class Aircraft Carrier
—— 300 Meters ——
Displacement 65,000 Tons

KIEV-Class Guided-Missile VSTOL Aircraft Carrier
—— 273 Meters ——
Displacement 37,100 Tons

KIROV-Class Nuclear-Powered Guided-Missile Cruiser
—— 248 Meters ——
Displacement 28,000 Tons

SLAVA-Class Guided-Missile Cruiser
—— 187 Meters ——
Displacement 12,000 Tons

UDALOY-Class Guided-Missile Destroyer
—— 162 Meters ——
Displacement 8,000 Tons

SOVREMENNYY-Class Guided-Missile Destroyer
—— 156 Meters ——
Displacement 7,300 Tons

US

NIMITZ-Class Aircraft Carrier
—— 333 Meters ——
Displacement 91,400 Tons

IOWA-Class Battleship
—— 270 Meters ——
Displacement 58,000 Tons

VIRGINIA-Class Guided-Missile Cruiser
—— 175 Meters ——
Displacement 11,000 Tons

TICONDEROGA-Class Guided-Missile Cruiser
—— 170 Meters ——
Displacement 9,600 Tons

SPRUANCE-Class Destroyer
—— 170 Meters ——
Displacement 7,824 Tons

OLIVER HAZARD PERRY- Class Guided-Missile Frigate
—— 130 Meters ——
Displacement 3,605 Tons

The backbone of the navy's ASW corvette force is the GRISHA. Although first introduced into the inventory in 1968, construction of this class continues and some 40 are operational.

Even with the first deployments of the Soviets' new aircraft carrier in the 1990s, Soviet Naval Aviation (SNA) will continue to be primarily a land-based force. Within the bomber

Chapter IV Soviet Forces for Theater Operations

force, production of the BACKFIRE continues, and the C variants with improved performance have begun to enter the fleet. The BACK-FIRE, with its AS-4 air-to-surface missiles, is replacing the BADGER as the navy's primary antiship strike aircraft. The BACKFIRE substantially extends the range at which SNA bombers could attack US and allied surface forces, such as aircraft carrier battle groups or amphibious task groups. With respect to ASW force developments, production of a variant of the BEAR F long-range ASW aircraft has resumed. This aircraft's improved sensor system and 5,000-kilometer radius considerably enhances Soviet capabilities to conduct ASW operations at greater distances from the USSR.

Soviet amphibious forces generally receive lower priority than submarine and surface war-

© Mistsuo Shibata

The Soviets' ability to project power into the Pacific Ocean region has increased with the deployment of the KIROV-Class nuclear-powered guided-missile cruiser FRUNZE to the Pacific Fleet.

produce air cushion vehicles (ACVs) mainly for an amphibious warfare role. The USSR now maintains the world's largest force of ACVs. Those classes currently in the inventory include the AIST, LEBED, TSAPLYA, UTENOK, and GUS. The first unit of the new PELIKAN-Class joined the Baltic Fleet in 1985, as did the first unit of the POMORNIK-Class. The latter craft is 56 meters long, making it the world's largest naval ACV. An additional class is also under construction. The ACV's high speed enables it to move troops and equipment more efficiently over short distances than conventional landing craft.

The Soviet Naval Infantry (SNI) is a small, elite force with the primary missions of conducting assault landings on the maritime flanks of the USSR in support of ground theater operations and of securing strategic straits in conjunction with other forces.

Since 1979, the SNI has undergone extensive reorganization and equipment modernization. All three former SNI regiments in the western fleets have been expanded to brigades, and combat support elements have been added to the single Pacific Ocean Fleet division. Further, SNI manning has increased from 14,000 to 16,000 troops. The introduction of artillery and antitank battalions as well as new equipment such as T-72 tank and 82-mm automatic mortars has increased SNI's organic firepower and operational capabilities.

Naval Operational Concepts

The USSR's concept of wartime operations appears to be influenced as much by geography as by potential enemies. Soviet military planners face four separate maritime frontiers—Arctic/North Atlantic, Baltic, Black Sea, and Pacific—which have necessitated the development of four different and nearly self-contained fleets. To facilitate command and control and wartime operations of the widely separated fleets and to meet the navy's varied and expanding wartime roles, a theater of military operations (TVD) structure encompassing the world's oceans has been established.

Within these oceanic TVDs, the missions of

ship programs. Although no new, large amphibious ships have been produced since completion of the second IVAN ROGOV amphibious assault transport dock (LPD) in 1982, construction of amphibious vehicle landing ships (LSTs) for the Soviet Navy has continued in Poland, and a new, large LST class is believed to be in the planning stages.

The Soviet Navy continues to develop and

Chapter IV Soviet Forces for Theater Operations

The Yak-36/FORGER vertical/short takeoff and landing (VSTOL) fighter is the main strike aircraft carried aboard the KIEV-Class aircraft carrier.

the Soviet Navy are to contribute to Soviet deterrence and strategic strike capability and to defend the USSR from enemy sea-based strike forces. The wartime tasks associated with these missions include:

- protecting Soviet strategic ballistic missile submarines;
- countering enemy sea-based strategic forces;
- securing the sea approaches to the USSR and Warsaw Pact countries;
- conducting operations in selected areas to deny Western forces freedom of action;
- supporting Soviet and Warsaw Pact ground operations in continental TVDs;
- protecting Soviet sea lines of communication; and
- interdicting enemy sea lines of communication.

Although the traditional fleet mission of

strategic submarine protection and homeland defense remain dominate themes in Soviet planned wartime operations, coordinated combined arms/joint force operations within continental TVDs, especially in the Baltic and Black Sea Fleets, are receiving increased emphasis. For the most part, these continental TVD-oriented exercises appear designed to prepare fleet units to protect the seaward flanks of the Warsaw Pact, to seize key straits and islands, and to conduct amphibious assaults in support of Soviet land operations.

Recent naval exercises in both the oceanic and continental TVDs have been conducted under realistic conditions approximating a wartime environment. In the Northern and Pacific Ocean Fleets, they have focused on command and control of multiple task groups and formations, the deployment of large numbers of warships and aircraft, and the establishment of echeloned combat zones stretching into the North Atlantic and Northwest Pacific Oceans. These exercises also reveal that Soviet naval operations are being conducted with larger and more powerful forces at increasingly greater distances from the USSR.

NATO and the Warsaw Pact

In 1984, the North Atlantic Treaty Organization published the second edition of the NATO and the Warsaw Pact Force Comparisons study. Charts from the 1984 NATO study were published in *Soviet Military Power 1985*.

The following charts and tables present a US estimate of updated data for 1985. Not included in the data are forces of France and Spain. Although both nations are members of the North Atlantic Alliance, they do not participate in its integrated military structure. In an invasion of Western Europe by the Warsaw Pact, France and Spain would defend their national sovereignty with the following forces: approximately 20 divisions, 2,000 tanks, 3,000 artillery/mortars, 1,000 antitank launchers, 8,000 combat vehicles, 450 helicopters, 900 aircraft, and 100 naval warships.

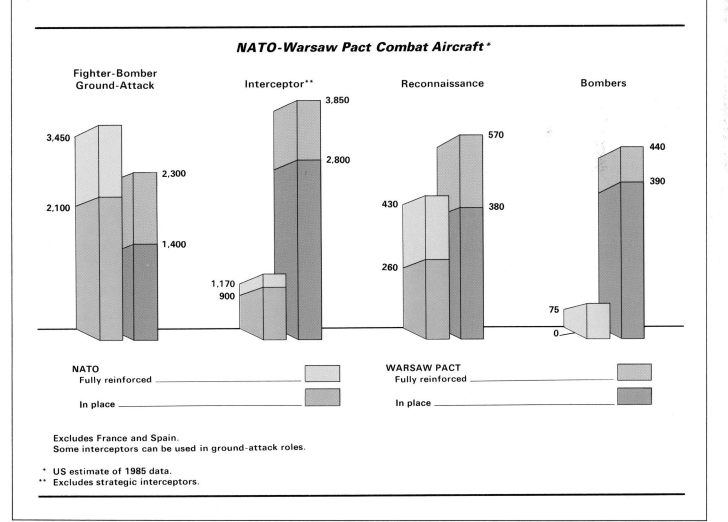

NATO-Warsaw Pact Combat Aircraft*

Fighter-Bomber Ground-Attack

Interceptor**

Reconnaissance

Bombers

NATO
Fully reinforced

In place

WARSAW PACT
Fully reinforced

In place

Excludes France and Spain.
Some interceptors can be used in ground-attack roles.

*   US estimate of 1985 data.
** Excludes strategic interceptors.

NATO and Warsaw Pact Maritime Forces in the North Atlantic and Seas Bordering Europe, 1985*

Category	NATO	Warsaw Pact
Aircraft Carriers VSTOL Carriers	10	—
KIEV-Class Ships	—	1
Helicopter Carriers	6	2
Cruisers	16	21
Destroyers, Frigates, Corvettes	303	199
Coastal Escorts and Fast Patrol Boats	269	520
Amphibious Ships - Ocean-going	50	21
- Other Ships/ Coastal Craft	69	181
Mine Warfare Ships/Craft	264	360
Total Submarines (All Types)	209	265
- Ballistic Missile Submarines	35	47
- Long-Range Attack Submarines	70	150
- Other Types	104	68
- % Submarines Nuclear Powered	50%	50%
Sea-based Tactical ASW and Support Aircraft Including Helicopters	831	145
Land-Based Tactical and Support Aircraft Including Helicopters	379	575
Land-Based Anti-Submarine Warfare Fixed-Wing Aircraft and Helicopters	462	220

Excludes France and Spain

* US estimate of 1985 data

Land-Based INF Aircraft Deployed at End of 1985*

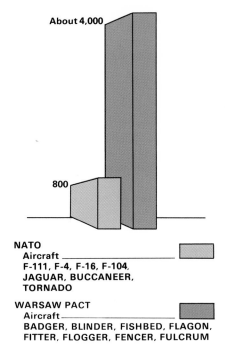

About 4,000

800

NATO
Aircraft
F-111, F-4, F-16, F-104,
JAGUAR, BUCCANEER,
TORNADO

WARSAW PACT
Aircraft
BADGER, BLINDER, FISHBED, FLAGON,
FITTER, FLOGGER, FENCER, FULCRUM

* US estimate of 1985 data
Numbers reflect NATO systems deployed in NATO Europe and Warsaw Pact systems opposite NATO

Short-Range Nuclear Forces (SNF) Deployed at End of 1985*

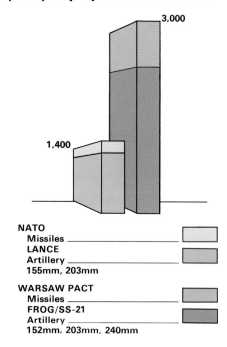

3,000

1,400

NATO
Missiles
LANCE
Artillery
155mm, 203mm

WARSAW PACT
Missiles
FROG/SS-21
Artillery
152mm, 203mm, 240mm

* US estimate of 1985 data
Numbers reflect NATO systems deployed in NATO Europe and Warsaw Pact systems opposite NATO

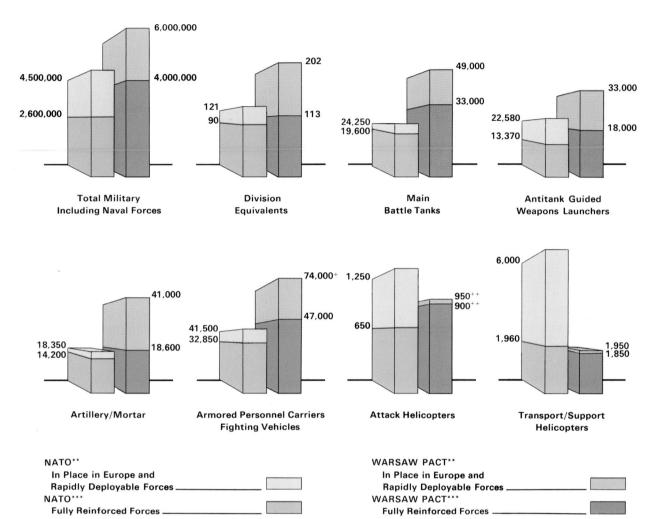

Total Military
Including Naval Forces

Division
Equivalents

Main
Battle Tanks

Antitank Guided
Weapons Launchers

Artillery/Mortar

Armored Personnel Carriers
Fighting Vehicles

Attack Helicopters

Transport/Support
Helicopters

NATO**
  In Place in Europe and
  Rapidly Deployable Forces _____
NATO***
  Fully Reinforced Forces _____

WARSAW PACT**
  In Place in Europe and
  Rapidly Deployable Forces _____
WARSAW PACT***
  Fully Reinforced Forces _____

Excludes France and Spain

Warsaw Pact divisions normally consist of fewer personnel than many NATO divisions but contain more tanks and artillery, thereby obtaining similar combat power.

* US estimate of 1985 data.

** Rapidly deployable forces—Include those US forces whose equipment is stored in Europe and high-readiness Soviet forces located in the Baltic, Belorussian, Carpathian, Odessa, Kiev, and North Caucasus Military Districts.

*** Fully reinforced forces—Include North American reinforcements and all Warsaw Pact forces located west of the Ural Mountains.

+ Excludes armored command vehicles and other carriers.
++ Excludes transport helicopters that can be configured for attack roles.

Chapter V

Readiness, Mobility, and Sustainability

The USSR's comprehensive commitment to support of its armed forces, in addition to the buildup and modernization of its weapons systems and forces, is reflected in programs that exercise and maintain a high degree of combat readiness. The development of extensive logistics bases and the expansion of strategic and theater mobility capabilities are designed to ensure that Soviet forces can make a rapid transition to war and can be moved and supported in combat.

A massive mobilization and combat support system underlies Soviet military power. It is designed to focus all the resources of the nation on waging war. Soviet doctrine stresses that its armed forces must be prepared to engage in any type of conflict ranging from short local wars to protracted global conflicts. Therefore, the Soviets are prepared to mobilize and sustain their forces in a variety of wartime contingencies. Moreover, support systems and resources paralleling the growth of strategic and theater combat forces have been developed. These include a trained military manpower base for expanding the active forces and replacing losses; a logistics system incorporating all classes of consumable supplies; war reserve equipment; and transport, repair, construction, and medical units.

Soviet R&D efforts to improve theater mobility include the development of wing-in-ground-effect craft. The ORLAN-Class, seen here, takes advantage of the increased aerodynamic lift that occurs when a wing operating near the surface experiences a reduction in induced drag. This greatly increases the craft's ability to carry heavy loads over long distances, especially over water, making it well-suited for amphibious warfare.

Mobility

Historically, the Soviet Union has possessed formidable forces suited for fighting in Europe, the Far East, and other areas contiguous to the USSR. During the past two decades, however, the Soviets have enhanced their posture by steadily increasing their military forces in size, capability, range, and scope of operations beyond the periphery of the USSR. Through continuous technological advancements in air, sea, and command and control systems, they are increasingly able to maintain lines of communication and sustain their expanding military reach. An enhanced capability to deploy light, well-armed, mobile forces in support of strategic goals and national objectives increases the potential for Soviet power projection into areas of vital interest to the Western Alliance.

Existing Soviet mobility capabilities encompass these developments:

- the formation of strategically mobile forces and compatible military transport assets;
- the design, modernization, and expansion of civilian transport systems that are easily adapted to military transport requirements; and

transportnaya aviatsia, abbreviated VTA) forces are the most visible of all the Soviet military mobility assets. In wartime, VTA forces would support airborne operations and provide logistic airlift to the armed forces. During peacetime, VTA aircraft make arms and equipment deliveries to client states in the Third World. VTA's worldwide presence is continually growing in numbers and scope—from famine relief operations in Ethiopia to combat support operations in Afghanistan. This force, comprised of about 600 aircraft, continues to modernize and improve in range, speed, and cargo capacity.

VTA holdings consist of the four-engine, propellor-driven An-12/CUB and its replacement, the long-range jet transport Il-76/CANDID, which now constitutes over half of the VTA inventory. The USSR's heavy-lift capability currently consists of 55 An-22/COCK aircraft. However, the Soviets are preparing to deploy the new An-124/CONDOR heavy-lift transport in 1987 or 1988. This aircraft, which is comparable to the US C-5B GALAXY, will be able to carry a payload of 150 metric tons, almost twice the capacity of the An-22. This increase in heavy-lift capacity, in conjunction with the continued improvements expected from additional Il-76/CANDID deployments, will significantly enhance the Soviets' ability to support their commitments abroad. The CONDOR, in particular, will be able to

The visor-nosed An-124/CONDOR, with its large payload capacity for outsized cargo and its drive-through feature, will add significantly to Soviet military airlift and power projection capabilities.

- the establishment of national-level planning and management bodies capable of mobilizing and assembling strategic assets from the civilian sector to meet military transport requirements.

Soviet mobility is based in part on amphibious assault ships and increasingly capable military air and air transport forces supplemented by civilian transport assets and associated personnel. The Soviet leadership has established procedures for mobilizing civilian transport resources for military employment and routinely uses these assets in various military exercises.

Military Transport Aviation *(Voyenno-*

carry larger quantities of outsized weapons such as the SS-20 transporter-erector-launcher, tanks, helicopters, missiles, and other critical equipment than could any of its predecessors. In peacetime, the Soviets will be able to supply client states with greater quantities of materiel in crisis situations. In wartime, the large lift capacity of the CONDOR, in conjunction with the CANDID, will facilitate the rapid movement of critical reserve stocks to forward areas or between theaters of war as well as increase the flexibility of Soviet airborne forces.

The Soviets' total aircraft capacity would be significantly increased by the mobilization of the state-owned airline, Aeroflot. These long- and medium-range transport aircraft, which number some 1,600, provide the Soviets with an immediate source of strategic air transport.

The close relationship between Soviet military and civil sectors is very apparent in the Ministry of Civil Aviation. For example, Minister of Civil Aviation Boris P. Bugayev is an active duty general officer who holds the rank of Chief Marshal of Aviation. Additionally, several key ministry members are active duty officers, and most Aeroflot aircrews hold reserve military commissions.

Sealift

The USSR's military sealift capability is based on the Navy's 77 amphibious warfare ships. For strategic sealift, the Soviets, however, depend on their large merchant fleet. This military-adaptable fleet has grown steadily during the past two decades. The foundations of strategic sealift consist of more than 1,700 ships

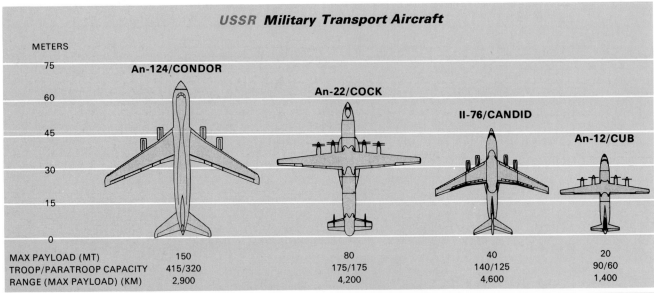

USSR *Military Transport Aircraft*

	An-124/CONDOR	An-22/COCK	Il-76/CANDID	An-12/CUB
MAX PAYLOAD (MT)	150	80	40	20
TROOP/PARATROOP CAPACITY	415/320	175/175	140/125	90/60
RANGE (MAX PAYLOAD) (KM)	2,900	4,200	4,600	1,400

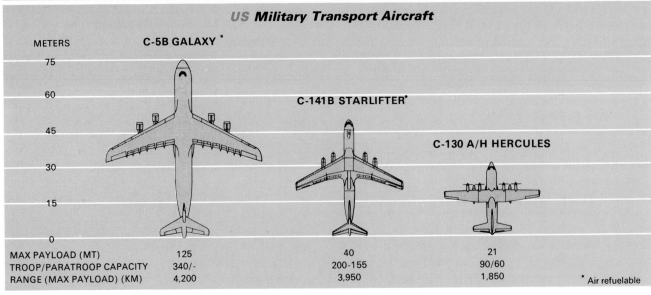

US *Military Transport Aircraft*

	C-5B GALAXY *	C-141B STARLIFTER*	C-130 A/H HERCULES
MAX PAYLOAD (MT)	125	40	21
TROOP/PARATROOP CAPACITY	340/-	200-155	90/60
RANGE (MAX PAYLOAD) (KM)	4,200	3,950	1,850

* Air refuelable

whose combined deadweight tonnage exceeds 21 million. This figure represents an increase of more than 500 percent over the past 20 years. Nearly half the cargo ships are self-sustaining and have cranes capable of lifting heavy military vehicles. Soviet ships have commercial as well as a military utility.

The Soviet merchant fleet is regularly used to support naval logistics operations. It consists of more than 60 roll-on/roll-off (RO/RO) and rail transport vessels. An element of the RO/RO technology, specifically the loading ramp, was acquired from the West. In wartime, the merchant fleet would allow the Soviets to move forces to the most remote areas of the globe. In peacetime, it is used to transport arms and the forces of client states in support of Soviet foreign policy objectives.

Soviet merchant ships produced over the last two decades have increasingly been constructed to military standards. Some key features they have incorporated include chemical-biological-radiological (CBR) protection; increased endurance and surface speeds; improved capability in handling gear and self-servicing features; advanced communication, navigation, and electronics systems, including identification-friend-or-foe (IFF) systems which are restricted to naval ships in the West.

The current Soviet merchant marine shipbuilding program emphasizes designs having direct military applications. These include roll-on/roll-off, roll-on/float-off (RO/FLO), lighter aboard ship (LASH), and container ships.

The operations of the merchant marine are closely coordinated with naval requirements from Moscow down to the smallest port facility. A significant amount of logistic support required by the Soviet Navy in peacetime, especially in distant areas, is routinely provided by Soviet merchantmen. This flexibility allows Soviet merchant ships to obtain supplies for naval use in ports where warship visits might be denied.

In a crisis, the highly organized, centrally controlled merchant fleet can provide military support quickly and effectively, particularly for amphibious operations, troop movements, and arms shipments. For example, in support of a military operation against Japan, the Soviet Far East merchant fleet has the estimated capacity to transport up to seven motorized rifle or tank divisions in a single lift operation, if given appropriate sea conditions and air superiority. To ensure readiness to perform

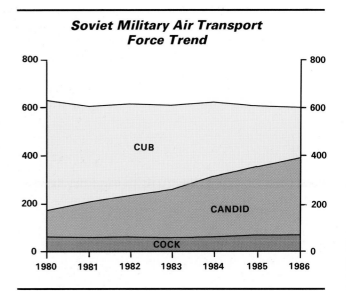

Soviet Military Air Transport Force Trend

such missions, Soviet merchant ships are commanded mostly by naval reserve officers who routinely participate in major naval exercises.

Augmenting the ocean-going merchant fleet is a river-sea fleet consisting of some 700 tankers and dry cargo carriers, with a deadweight tonnage of 2.5 million. These ships, which operate in coastal sea areas and in the Soviet and European inland waterway system, represent an added wartime capacity to transport supplies and materiel to continental military theaters of operation.

Realizing the vulnerability of their rail transport system, the Soviets have over the past two decades expanded their inventory of heavy-lift transporters, especially the MAZ-537 tractor, with a trailer capable of carrying armored vehicles weighing 50 metric tons. The Soviets have more than 3,500 heavy-lift transporters available for moving military vehicles. The use of these heavy-lift transporters facilitates the movement of combat forces from the Soviet interior to forward areas opposite NATO, Southwest Asia, China, Korea, and Japan. Heavy-lift vehicles provide the Soviets with a fast and flexible transport force for the movement of combat forces.

The Mi-26/HALO, the world's largest heavy-lift helicopter, is another example of Soviet enhancement of civil and military transport sectors through the acquisition of Western technology. With its obvious military applications, it has a payload and cargo hold capacity similar to that of the US C-130.

Intertheater movement of Soviet forces opposite NATO, Southwest Asia, and the Far East still is dependent on the rail system. The Soviet rail system is organized to facilitate its rapid conversion during wartime to a primary long-distance carrier. Upon mobilization, the rail system comes under military control and operation; thus, locomotives and rolling stock are made immediately available to support Soviet military needs. Construction of the Baikal-Amur-Magistral Railroad, which will be operational in 1990, will augment the vulnerable Trans-Siberian Railroad in support of Soviet forces in the Far East either for action against China or against US forces operating in the Pacific area.

The continued development and success of Soviet theater and strategic movement capabilities present a clear challenge to Western defense planners. Despite the impact that mobilization of the civilian transport sector would have on the economy—including severe disruptions of normal transportation of goods and services—the wartime employment of civilian assets is a major strength and key element in Soviet military power.

Readiness

Soviet military doctrine asserts that its armed forces must be maintained at a high state of combat readiness to ensure expeditious deployment under any conditions. Maintaining peacetime forces that are fully deployed at the strength required for war poses an economic burden to Soviet planners. Therefore, in peacetime many Soviet ground force units are manned at levels below their planned wartime strength. The Soviets are dependent on their well-organized and extensive mobilization system which allows a rapid fleshing out of their force structure for war.

Even with extensive preparations, the Warsaw Pact might experience some initial difficulties. Many Warsaw Pact tactical air force fighter regiments include some new pilots with limited experience. The inexperience of these pilots would limit the overall air combat potential of the Warsaw Pact. Further, Warsaw Pact aircrews usually fly at only about half the annual rate of US active duty aircrews. As a result, Warsaw Pact aircrews usually are limited to a single role and therefore lack the flexibility inherent in many US and some non-US NATO units. With the reorganization of Soviet Air Forces, the growth in the number of longer range intermediate-range nuclear force

(LRINF) missiles, and the high state of readiness of forward-deployed forces, the USSR is capable of executing the initial phase of an attack without the mobilization of additional forces. However, if the order is given to go to war, the Soviets would implement their national mobilization plan, drawing upon some nine million recently trained reservists. These reservists would be used to bring understrength units, cadre units, and mobilization bases to full manning in a matter of days. While mobilizing and moving over 200 divisions is an extremely large and difficult task, the Soviets can assimilate the reservists, train them for combat, and be ready to conduct offensive operations in less than 60 days.

The Soviets maintain their forces at what they term "ready" and "not-ready" levels. Ready units are manned with a high percentage of their planned wartime personnel, possess the most modern equipment, and train extensively in peacetime. They can begin combat operations after only a very short period of mobilization and preparation. These "ready" units constitute about 40 percent of Soviet forces and include all of the Groups of Forces stationed in Eastern Europe. The "not-ready" units are cadre and unmanned mobilization bases that require extensive mobilization and preparation and are generally equipped with older but still effective equipment such as T-55 or T-62 tanks. However, as increasing amounts of modern equipment are made available, many "not-ready" divisions are being equipped with the most advanced items in the Soviet inventory.

The survivability of Soviet weapons systems and personnel is enhanced by a very comprehensive dispersal system that would be executed during the transition to war. When alerted, Soviet and non-Soviet Warsaw Pact units would deploy to areas that would decrease their vulnerability to detection and targeting. Ground forces would disperse and camouflage themselves in field assembly areas while aircraft would proceed to alternate airfields. Surface ships and submarines would depart from their main operating bases.

Personnel, equipment, and spare missiles needed for refiring ICBMs would move to field locations. Alternate command posts have been constructed, and redundant, hardened, and mobile communication links have been established throughout the USSR. These preparations for dispersal at the outbreak of war reflect Mos-

Soviet underway replenishment ship, on left, refueling a SOVREMENNYY-Class guided-missile destroyer during summer naval exercises.

cow's perceived threat and expected deployment of forces.

Logistics

Soviet military planners continue to improve the logistic infrastructure and to enlarge the resource base available to support high-intensity combined arms operations. Substan-

tial quantities of supplies are stockpiled in forward areas for the initial stages of a conflict, and large strategic reserves exist to sustain operations. This comprehensive logistic support system is found in designated theaters of military operations in Eastern Europe, Mongolia, and throughout the USSR.

The Soviets have prestocked critical ammunition and fuel reserves in Eastern Europe and the military districts of the western USSR. Soviet ammunition stocks intended to support combat operations against NATO in central Europe are double 1975 levels. The growth of Soviet military fuel stocks opposite central Europe is also substantial. In addition, each non-Soviet Warsaw Pact country maintains large stockpiles of key military items. Moreover, the well-developed road and rail system within the Western Theater facilitates the forward movement of supplies in wartime. Overall, theater logistic stockpiles in Eastern Europe and the military districts along the border of the USSR are capable of supporting Warsaw Pact military operations against NATO for 60 to 90 days.

The Far East Theater encompasses the USSR's largest continental theater of military operations but historically has been of secondary importance as Soviet planners have placed greater emphasis on supporting Soviet forces opposite NATO. In the last decade, however, the Soviets have devoted considerably more attention to increasing the sustainability of their forces in the Far East because of the long lines of communication and the need to support large theater forces opposite China and Japan. Storage capacities for ammunition and POL, which account for about 80 percent of the Soviets' total war materials, have increased significantly at many depots. The prepositioning of such large quantities of war materials in the Far East reduces the dependence on logistic assets from the western industrial centers for resupply during the initial periods of actual warfare. Soviet ground and naval forces can now sustain defensive conventional wartime operations for more than 100 days.

The Trans-Siberian Railroad would be a critical supply line to the Far East in a war exceeding 100 days. This railroad is the only land transportation link to the Far East and is particularly vulnerable to interdiction where it closely parallels the Chinese border. The Baikal-Amur-Magistral Railroad, currently under construction, will parallel the eastern portion of the Trans-Siberian to the north. When completed, it will be less vulnerable to interdiction but will not significantly increase overall supply capacity.

The Pacific Ocean Fleet is the USSR's most far-reaching arm in the Far East and is especially dependent on the Trans-Siberian for supply of war materials. The fleet must defend more than 14,000 kilometers of coastline,

Major Soviet Military Storage Areas

Ammunition Depots
**12 million metric tons arms/ammunition
including storage in Eastern Europe**

Reserve Armor Storage Depots
**6,000 armored vehicles (tanks/APCs)
including storage in Eastern Europe**

**Petroleum, Oil and Lubricants
Storage Depot Concentrations**
**60 million metric tons
including storage in Eastern Europe**

Major Soviet Military Storage Areas

Reserve Artillery Storage Depots
18,000 artillery and AAA pieces
including storage in Eastern Europe

Bridge Equipment Storage Depots
27,000 meters of bridging materials
including storage in Eastern Europe

Nuclear Warhead Stockpile Concentrations
including storage in Eastern Europe

the largest maritime border of any Soviet fleet. In order to provide logistic support to the fleet and serve as a hedge against loss of the Trans-Siberian Railroad, the Soviets have developed large naval weapons and POL storage complexes throughout the region. The fleet's present logistic infrastructure is estimated to be capable of sustaining naval combat operations beyond 150 days.

Although Soviet planners believe that military objectives in some theaters can be achieved within weeks, additional logistic resources, termed strategic reserves, have been established for protracted operations. The strategic reserve depots concentrated in the interior military districts of the Soviet Union would be used to support theater operations. Some of these reserve depots store various types of military materiel, including spare parts, clothing, rations, and medical supplies.

Major weapons systems and other warfighting equipment have been placed in storage depots. These items include tanks, armored personnel carriers, field artillery, and air defense systems as well as maintenance, engineer, signal, and other types of support equipment. Many of these systems are older models but are capable of performing effectively in combat. They would be used to replace losses and create additional combat and support units. This equipment thus constitutes an important addition to Soviet military power.

The USSR has deployed a variety of well-equipped logistic units to move supplies, repair damaged equipment, build and maintain lines of communication, and treat personnel casualties. Motor transport units, many of which are kept loaded with ammunition and fuel during peacetime, possess large numbers of the most modern trucks, including the very capable KA-MAZ trucks, which were built with Western technology and assistance.

Tactical pipeline construction units add substantially to fuel transport capabilities. Soviet pipelaying units are capable of installing about 80 kilometers of pipe per day using the TUM automatic pipelayer or about 30 kilometers per day manually. The high pipelaying rate is consistent with Soviet offensive doctrine which holds that armies are to advance up to 100 kilometers a day. Some 15,000 kilometers of pipe are currently estimated to be available for operations against NATO's Central Region while about 12,000 kilometers of pipeline are with logistics units in the Soviet Far East.

Chapter V Readiness, Mobility, and Sustainability

©Mistsuo Shibata

The 12,000-ton IVAN ROGOV-Class amphibious assault transports enhance the USSR's capability to project military power beyond the Soviet Union.

Equipment repair units are highly mobile and designed to move forward with rapidly advancing combat formations. To facilitate the movement of combat and support forces, the USSR has bridge, rail, and road construction units that would maintain critical lines of communication at strategic and tactical levels. Medical units to treat and evacuate casualties

are also part of the USSR's combat logistic support system.

The Soviet Union is investing very heavily in mobilization and logistic support systems that are the underpinnings of its military capabilities. In the USSR's military planning process, every effort is made to ensure that the demands that would be placed upon these systems in war

Symbolic of the Soviet Navy's growing capability to project power is the KIEV-Class aircraft carrier.

are not left to chance. The Soviets' peacetime preparations indicate they have every intention of meeting the support requirements inherent in major conflicts, even those that are protracted.

Mobilization System

To support wartime goals, the USSR has developed a mobilization system backed by an extensive manpower and logistics base that integrates the military, government, economy, and general population. Although geared to the rapid buildup and wartime commitment of military units and other resources, the system is also designed to accommodate extended and selective mobilization of all types of military and civilian assets. Mobilization may be general, in which the entire nation is placed on a wartime footing, or limited, as that conducted in preparation for the Czechoslovakia and Afghanistan invasions.

Some 4,200 military organizations, called commissariats—which are subordinate to the Soviet General Staff—are crucial to the rapid mobilization of Soviet manpower and materiel. Dispersed throughout the USSR, these military commissariats have functions analogous to those of US draft boards and armed forces reserve centers in that their peacetime mission is conscription, reservist registration, and training.

In wartime, commissariats are responsible for mobilizing reserve manpower and equipment from the civilian economy to activate or create combat and combat support units. These would include motor transport, engineer, repair, signal, and medical units. During mobilization, reservists are notified, assembled, and dispatched to units with equipment drawn from the national economy and are then integrated into the armed forces. When executed, this system could activate several million reservists and tens of thousands of trucks and other equipment within a few days. Also, support systems such as the rail network, the civil airline Aeroflot, the merchant fleet, and elements of the national communications system can be militarized as part of the national mobilization effort.

Military Manpower Base

All eligible Soviet youths, by law, must serve two years or, in the case of naval personnel aboard ship, three years of active duty. Conscripts are subsequently discharged into the reserves. Thus, the Soviets have a military manpower base in which all able-bodied male citizens between 18 and 50 are either on active duty or are subject to reserve service.

The reserve manpower pool currently comprises more than 55 million men subject to callup, of which 9 million have been discharged from active duty within the past five years. Since only about 2.1 million reservists, or about 5 percent of the total reserve manpower pool, are needed to bring the Soviet Armed Forces to full wartime strength, a substantial base would remain available to create new units and provide replacements.

The process of fleshing out units involves mostly conscripts since Soviet force structure employs a cadre system comprised of a career officer corps of about one million personnel already in place. The career officer corps represents over 20 percent of the total Soviet Armed Forces strength of approximately 5.7 million.

Within the Soviet military establishment, women serve mainly in the enlisted ranks in auxiliary and specialist roles—notably, medical, administrative, communications, and other support areas. Military law in the Soviet Union also subjects women to conscription during wartime, thereby ensuring a large reservoir for expanding the forces and releasing men for combat duty.

Chapter VI

Research, Development, and Production

The Soviet Union's evolution as a global superpower has been based primarily on its military capabilities. Realizing that numerical superiority alone would not provide the leverage they sought in the world arena, Soviet leaders have endeavored to harness modern technology to make their weapons systems qualitatively equal to, or superior to, those of the Free World. This objective complements the Communists' dialectical perspective of history which predicts Soviet scientific ascendancy in the 21st century. In an attempt to fulfill this destiny, the Soviets have committed their best scientific personnel, their best research facilities and equipment, and the management skills of their elite to military research and development (R&D) and production efforts, often to the detriment of their civilian industry and the welfare of their populace. The Soviets have also invested large amounts of economic resources in their effort to gain military superiority.

Military Expenditures

Cumulative Soviet military expenditures from 1976 to 1985 greatly exceeded those of the United States. During this decade, the estimated dollar cost of the Soviet military program was one-third larger than the US defense outlay, using similar methods of

---

Su-27/FLANKER all-weather, air-superiority fighters, now being deployed, are equipped with a look-down/shoot-down weapon system and beyond-visual-range AA-10 missiles. The FLANKER, along with the Soviets' expanding inventory of new, high-performance, dual-capable MiG-29/FULCRUM supersonic fighters, is emerging from an expanding industrial base that gives highest priority to military production.

definition. Soviet expenditures for weapons systems during this period were 50 percent higher. Increased US defense spending has narrowed this differential, but in critical areas such as R&D, the Soviet effort still exceeds that of the US. Moreover, there has been an upturn in Soviet weapons procurement during the past two years.

Estimates of Soviet military spending in current rubles indicate a significant increase from the early 1970s to the early 1980s—at a rate significantly faster than their overall economic growth. The Soviet military effort now consumes an estimated 15 to 17 percent of their gross national product.

The costs of the Soviets' huge military R&D effort are very high. The USSR commits about 3 percent of its gross national product (GNP) to research and development—or about 20 percent of total Soviet defense outlays. The USSR has assembled the world's largest pool of scientists and engineers—over 900,000—working in R&D. This total plus the almost one million support personnel involved in R&D constitutes about one-fourth of the world's total. Over half of these Soviet scientists and engineers have defense-related specialties, and a large percentage are involved in military-related R&D on a full-time basis. By their own accounting and definitions, the Soviets employ over 12 million scientists and engineers throughout their economy.

Key Military Technologies

Technological gains in Soviet weapons systems rely not only on the contributions of the indigenous R&D base but also on the acquisition of Western technology and its timely incorporation into Soviet weaponry. While the United States continues to lead the USSR in most basic technologies, the gap in the military application of such technologies continues to narrow. The incorporation of critical Western technologies is permitting the USSR to avoid costly R&D efforts and to produce Soviet weapons comparable to or superior to fielded US weapons at a much earlier date than would otherwise be possible.

Materials. Driven by the increasingly demanding requirements of advanced weapons systems, the Soviets have devoted considerable effort in all the important materials disciplines. Their capability in metal alloys such as titanium for the fabrication of structural elements for aerospace and naval systems is the equal of

US and Soviet Procurement of Major Weapons Systems 1976-1985

	US	USSR
ICBMs and SLBMs	700	3,350
IRBMs and MRBMs	430	1,000
Surface-to-Air Missiles	1,600	112,000
Long- and Intermediate-range Bombers	2	345
Fighters	3,500	7,850
Helicopters	1,500	5,350
Submarines	40	96
Major Surface Combatants	90	83
Tanks	7,400	24,900
Artillery	2,400	32,225

any other nation and may lead in some areas. For example, their use of titanium for submarine pressure hulls and for aircraft structures is most impressive. Their ability to use steel, aluminum, and most other alloys as well as advanced processing techniques such as powder metallurgy and rapid solidification is as good as any in the world. They are emulating the US in applying advanced composite materials with excellent strength and stiffness ratios to aerospace structural components. The Soviets claim parity with the US in composite materials development and design know-how but admit their deficiency in fabrication techniques.

In ground weapons applications such as tank armor, the Soviets have made significant improvements, including the use of laminated materials and applique concepts to improve the ballistic protection of their newest tanks. They have conducted considerable research in ceramics, particularly for engine and armor applications. While the US still enjoys a lead in structural materials technology, the Soviets are making advances that are eroding that lead.

Manufacturing. The USSR has long recognized the need to develop the manufacturing and fabrication capabilities that permit the mass production of weapons systems. The Soviets have the world's largest forging and extrusion presses, allowing them to fabricate large, single-piece components with considerable savings in weight and cost. To support their vigorous program in joining technologies, they graduate nearly 3,000 welding engineers each year while the Free World has only a few schools that even offer this curriculum. The Soviets have demonstrated innovative welding techniques in such processes as electroslag, friction, electrogas, and pulsed arc welding. They are the world leader in this important industrial capability. However, the Soviets continue to trail the Free World in automated manufacturing technologies such as numerically controlled machine tools, flexible manufacturing systems, robotics, automated industrial control systems, and high-precision equipment. Although they are improving, further Soviet development depends on the acquisition of knowledge and equipment from non-Communist countries.

Propulsion. The Soviets continue to progress steadily in all aspects of propulsion technology. Their gas turbine aircraft engines are improving in performance and efficiency and are noted for their ruggedness and simplicity although constrained by short operating lifetimes. Until they sent an An-124/CONDOR wide-bodied transport aircraft with a Lotarev D18T engine to the 1985 Paris Air Show, they had not displayed a high-thrust, high-bypass engine similar to those used by the US since 1969. The Soviets also have a very extensive R&D effort in all aspects of rocket propulsion. There has been a noticeable trend from liquid- to solid-propellant engines on their new land-based strategic systems, with the technology only slightly behind that of US systems.

They remain the world's leader in liquid rocket propulsion though they still have not successfully applied a liquid-hydrogen, liquid-oxygen cryogenic engine to their space launch vehicles. The Soviets have consistently been at or near the forefront of world developments in applications of power engineering, particularly for space and marine propulsion systems. Their work in nuclear power, particularly for space and marine applications, has been very innovative and effective.

Directed Energy. The Soviets continue major R&D efforts on all types of directed-energy weapons technologies. Their commitment to high-energy lasers began in the mid-1960s and is now considerably larger than that of the US. They have built more than six laser development and test ranges which dwarf their counterparts in the US. During the last ten years, the floorspace dedicated to this work has quadrupled. Moreover, articles by Soviet sci-

entists publishing on laser research have doubled to approximately 12,000. The Soviets have developed several unique power sources that could support mobile or remote directed-energy weapons, including a rocket-driven magneto-hydrodynamic (MHD) device that produces 15 megawatts of pulsed power. Further, recent Soviet developments in radio frequency generation devices could enable them to build weapons to degrade or destroy electronics or cause disorientation of personnel. They have generated single pulses with peak power exceeding one gigawatt and repetitive pulses over 100 megawatts. Similarly, since the early 1960s the Soviets have been working on many of the technologies needed to develop particle beam weapons. In some of the needed disciplines such as powerful accelerators, their work is at the leading edge of the state-of-the-art. They are still encountering difficult engineering problems, and the technology needed to build a particle beam weapon capable of propagation for a meaningful distance requires additional research.

Chemical and Biological Warfare. The USSR has a well-established, longstanding, and very extensive research, development, and test base for chemical and biological agents. It includes facilities such as the biological agent research facility at Sverdlovsk, where an accidental release of a large amount of anthrax spores in 1979 resulted in many casualties. It also includes the facility at Shikhany which dates to shortly after World War I. Shikhany has been active and under almost continuous expansion since that time.

The Soviets have developed a wide range of chemical agents including nerve, blister, blood, and choking substances as well as incapacitants that cause unconsciousness for an hour or more. They are continuing research on toxins and binary agents as well as ground and air delivery systems. Of great importance is the willingness of the Soviets to use the various agents, both lethal and incapacitating. As demonstrated by their actions in Afghanistan, the Soviets and their surrogates have inflicted a large number of deaths and casualties on native populations. These attacks have served as an excellent testing ground for the Soviets to evaluate their various chemical agents.

Bioengineering. The Soviets are also fully aware of the potential of bioengineering for medical, agricultural, and industrial benefits.

Further, they realize the potential of bioengineering to develop a predictable, controllable, and effective biological warfare agent that would offer a tempting alternative to other weapons of mass destruction. Soviet bioengineering has progressed very rapidly over the past five years, and policy directives of the Council of Ministers suggest continued high-level support. Free World genetic engineering is also progressing rapidly, and it is unlikely that the Soviets can keep pace in all areas.

Electronics/Computers. At the end of World War II, the Soviets' electronics capability was either extremely outdated or mostly destroyed. Since then, they have invested a large amount of resources to reestablish their electronics R&D capability and acquire Free World know-how to meet military requirements. These investments have paid off with significant advances in militarily critical systems—including phased-array and over-the-horizon propagation radars, millimeter wave devices, and high-power radio frequency generators.

Computers and microelectronics are of great importance in any advanced weapon system. Soviet computer technology continues to be based on US and Western developments. Although the Soviets have a solid understanding of the basic technology, they continue to have problems in transferring this knowledge to the production of microelectronic devices and computer hardware. The low reliability and poor quality of these devices reflect continuing problems with manufacturing. Soviet efforts in the crucial area of software development also suffer from fundamental problems. The Soviets' centralized economy, which is directed at meeting military requirements first, puts new electronics, either developed indigenously or obtained from the Free World, in the hands of military designers more rapidly than ours.

Technology Transfer

To correct shortcomings, the Soviets have come to rely heavily on Free World sources for much of the technology employed in their military systems. This is not a random effort, but a massive, centrally controlled campaign to obtain needed products and technical knowledge selectively through legal and illegal means. Virtually all of the 5,000 ongoing Soviet research projects with military applications or implications have benefitted to some

extent from know-how acquired from the Free World.

The Soviet technology acquisition program has two distinct but complementary aspects:

- The Military-Industrial Commission (VPK), which coordinates the development and production of military systems, is also the prime coordinator for technology acquisition to support the defense industrial ministries. It seeks one-of-a-kind military and dual-use hardware, documentation, blueprints, product samples, and test gear to improve the technical levels and the capability of Soviet weapons and military equipment and associated industrial machinery. This is accomplished by copying or exploiting the advanced designs and engineering contained in the equipment and technical data acquired. The VPK coordinates the requirements of the defense industrial ministries and levies them for collection through espionage by the KGB and GRU. Collection is accomplished by Soviet scientists, engineers, and officials, by exploitation of scientific exchanges and journals, and through illegal trade diversions. The Soviets spend the equivalent of $1.4 billion per year to underwrite their acquisition effort.

- The Ministry of Foreign Trade and the intelligence services administer a trade diversion program to obtain significant numbers of manufacturing and supporting equipment for direct use on Soviet military-industrial production lines. Although this effort targets many export-controlled technologies, it concentrates on microelectronics and computers, communications gear, robotics, and advanced machinery. Its purpose is to improve Soviet capabilities to produce reliable modern weapons.

Soviet efforts to acquire foreign technology have been very successful. Under the VPK program, over 3,500 requirements were levied each year during the late 1970s and early 1980s, and about one-third were satisfied annually. About half of the 6,000 to 10,000 pieces of hardware and one-fifth of the 100,000 documents obtained each year are used by the Soviets in transferring Free World technology to military research projects. During the 10th Five-Year Plan (1976-80), two prime users of ac-

Rank Ordering of Soviet Industries by Military Industrial Commission (VPK) Requirements Fulfilled, by Hardware Received, and by Rubles Saved, 1976-80

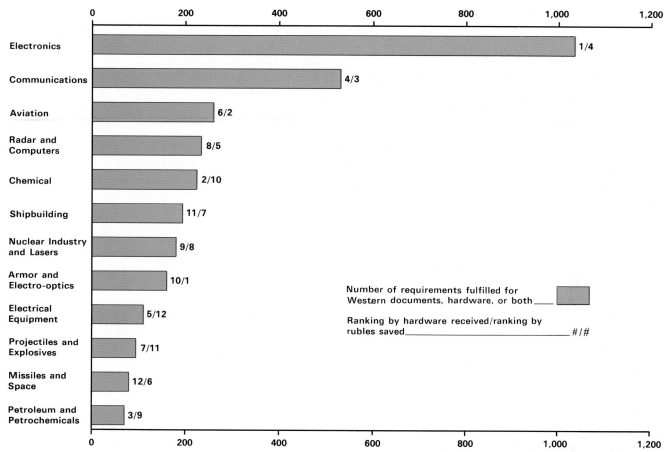

About 50 percent of the VPK requirements that were fulfilled during the 10th Five-Year Plan for Western hardware and documents were satisfied on behalf of two defense industries — electronics and communications. These are key areas where the Soviets' need for militarily significant technology and the West's need for better controls are greatest.

The four industries receiving the most Western military hardware and dual-use products were electronics (over 6,000 pieces of equipment, a large percentage involving microelectronics), chemical (almost 4,000 pieces), petroleum/petrochemicals, (over 1,500), and communications (over 1,500) ranked in that order.

The top four industries saving the most rubles in research project development costs in terms of manpower and other resources were the armor and electro-optics industry (almost 20 percent of the 1.4 billion rubles saved in research project costs) and the aviation, communications, and electonics industries. These four industries consistently appear to be the Soviet leaders in requesting, absorbing, and generally getting the most use out of Western hardware and documents. In some cases, such as in the armor area, the Soviets are using Western technology not to catch up, but to enhance a capability that already is equal to or better than that of the West.

quired technologies, the Ministries of Defense Industry (armor and electro-optics) and Aviation Industry, estimated that they saved almost one-half billion rubles in research project costs, translating to over 100,000 man-years of scientific research.

To cite one significant example, by using documentation on the US F-18 fighter, Soviet aviation and radar industries saved some five years of development time and 35 million rubles (the 1980 dollar cost of equivalent research activity would be $55 million) in project manpower and

other developmental costs. The manpower portion of these savings probably represented over a thousand man-years of scientific research effort and was one of the most successful individual exploitations ever of Western technology. The documentation on the F-18 fire control radar served as the technical basis for new look-down/shoot-down engagement radars for the latest generation of Soviet fighters, including the MiG-29/FULCRUM and the Su-27/FLANKER. US methods of component design, fast-Fourier-transform algorithms, terrain

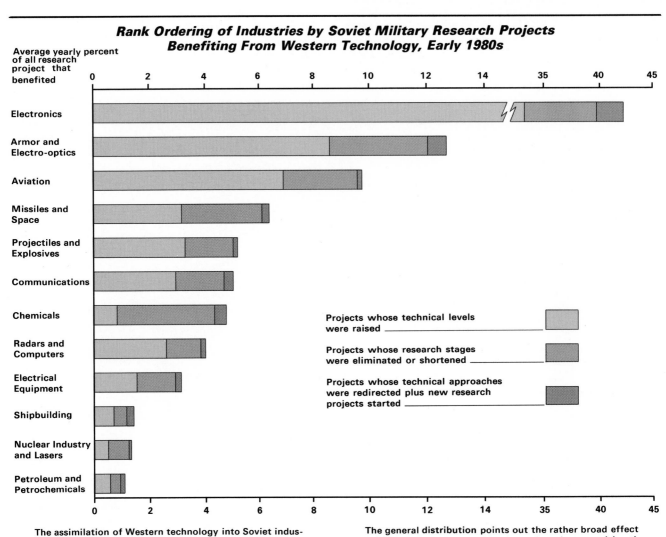

Rank Ordering of Industries by Soviet Military Research Projects Benefiting From Western Technology, Early 1980s

Average yearly percent of all research project that benefited

Electronics

Armor and Electro-optics

Aviation

Missiles and Space

Projectiles and Explosives

Communications

Chemicals

Radars and Computers

Electrical Equipment

Shipbuilding

Nuclear Industry and Lasers

Petroleum and Petrochemicals

Projects whose technical levels were raised

Projects whose research stages were eliminated or shortened

Projects whose technical approaches were redirected plus new research projects started

The assimilation of Western technology into Soviet industries conducting military research is considerable. The greatest beneficiaries were the electronics and armor and electro-optics industries, which accounted for over 50 percent (equaling thousands) of all military research projects benefiting from Western technology in the early 1980s.

The general distribution points out the rather broad effect that Western documents and hardware have just on raising the technical levels of Soviet military research. This is particularly true for the top three industries, where advanced technology and innovative design concepts play a significant role in weapons developments.

mapping functions, and real-time resolution-enhancement techniques were cited as key elements incorporated into the Soviet counterpart.

Moreover, F-18 and F-14 documentation served as the impetus for two long-term research projects to design from scratch a new radar-guided air-to-air missile system. The documentation also was instrumental in formulating concrete specifications to develop new Soviet airborne radar countermeasures equipment against the F-18 and F-14.

Hundreds of Soviet military systems and weapons of the 1980s and 1990s have benefited or will benefit from technologies obtained from the Free World. In the early 1970s, the technical levels of some 66 percent of their military research projects were raised and 27 percent of the completion dates were accelerated principally because the Soviets have copied concepts embodied in Western technical documents, military hardware, or dual-use products. US and allied efforts to counter this are covered in Chapter VIII.

The Soviets are not exclusively dependent on Free World technology to advance the quality of their military systems. Innovation, new concepts, new directions, higher technical levels of research, accelerated development of more advanced weapons, and the avoidance of major pitfalls are among the benefits the Soviet military derives from US military R&D projects. Free World technology gives the Soviet designer another option, often better than his own research establishment can produce, from which to choose. The Soviet practice of incorporating technology in small bits from many systems, however, permits the efficient, rapid assimilation of equipment or knowledge obtained from the West.

The Soviet R&D Base

Capital investment in research laboratories, design bureaus, key military technologies, and test facilities has kept pace with the drive for military technological supremacy. The USSR's military R&D capability, which is concentrated within nine defense industrial ministries, has grown about 28 percent during the last ten years. Some sectors involved in high-priority, high-technology projects such as directed-energy weapons and electro-optics have shown an even more dramatic growth rate. The Soviets have concurrently developed a full range of well-equipped, comprehensive test facilities permitting them to evaluate military systems under realistic conditions. This capability extends from subsystems to full-scale systems and includes all types of aerospace, ground, and naval components.

This focus on military R&D has not always been evenly applied. Various sectors have received special emphasis because of leadership perspectives of foreign military threats, mission requirements, and/or high-level patronage. Consequently, certain weapons systems have received concentrated developmental support. However, as high-level support has shifted, the Soviets typically did not transfer resources but rather added incremental resources so that previously emphasized sectors continued to receive strong support. The cumulative effect of this trend has been to provide the Soviets with a huge, broad-based R&D capability which can and does provide weapons for all segments of the Soviet arsenal.

To manage their massive R&D effort, the Soviets have evolved a complex, effective, if not always efficient, organizational structure. This structure operates within the framework of two interlocking bureaucracies, the Communist Party and the government. Military R&D programs are marked by top-level involvement and strong centralized management. The De-

fense Council, which is chaired by General Secretary Gorbachev, is comprised of top leaders of the Party, government, and military who make the important decisions on major weapons programs and R&D policies.

Approval of resource commitments for research programs is influenced by the technical bent of many senior Soviet leaders. Defense Minister Marshal Sokolov, while lacking the long, detailed experience in military-industrial programs of his predecessor Marshal Ustinov, is quite knowledgeable regarding the management of these complex projects. Additionally, the personnel changes General Secretary Gorbachev has implemented have brought more technocrats into positions of power. More than three-fourths of the Politburo and the Council of Ministers have technical backgrounds which create an environment conducive to understanding resource and managerial requirements.

The Military Industrial Commission (VPK) is a powerful supraministerial agency which coordinates all the efforts of the defense industrial ministries and centrally supervises all weapons programs. Operating across ministerial lines, the VPK is charged with implementing the joint resolutions of the Politburo and Council of Ministers which approve weapons programs. These resolutions provide one-time, multiyear approval for the entire duration of the program, including, in some cases, follow-on modifications. Under such a resolution, any state asset—that is, any individual or resource regardless of affiliation—can be coopted to support a particular weapons program. This includes the Soviets' 127,000 senior scientists and the resources of the academies of sciences and the Ministry of Higher and Secondary Education (MinVUZ).

The academies of sciences are charged with conducting basic research to support the national economy. The MinVUZ supports the national R&D effort by conducting exploratory research and educating the scientists and engineers who will fill its ranks. Both the academies and MinVUZ are becoming increasingly involved in military R&D in cases where development is dependent on advanced technology or where their specific expertise is needed.

The Ministry of Defense, as the prime consumer of the defense industries' products, also enjoys the unique privilege of direct quality control. Its representatives participate in every aspect of the process, including requirements generation, design, testing, production monitoring, and deployment. The powerful State Planning Commission integrates the military's R&D resource requirements into national plans.

The system integrator in the Soviet military R&D structure is the design bureau within the defense industrial ministry assigned to build the system. Each design bureau usually takes the name of the chief designer and has a specialty on which it concentrates. It works closely with the ministerial research institutes to translate their discoveries into practical applications. The design bureau staff then conducts the needed engineering, documentation, prototype construction, and testing to develop the new or improved system. The staff also coordinates with the production plants to facilitate series production. Design teams are formed in response to a requirement for a specific system and remain with the program from inception to completion and often through follow-on systems.

Soviet weapons designers have historically adhered to strict state industrial standards, used off-the-shelf components, and employed proven design methods detailed in official handbooks to ensure producibility, maintainability, and ease of operation. They build large numbers of weapons that are technologically adequate and well-engineered to meet mission requirements. Technological advances are usually assimilated in small steps, with the underlying assumption that new or improved components or subsystems will be incorporated in follow-on modifications or new systems.

As a result, the Soviets produce many more new and significantly modified weapons systems than the US. Their weapons often reflect functional, single-mission designs that can be manufactured in labor-intensive factories. They take a somewhat different approach to maintenance than the US by planning and designing for limited field maintenance by relatively unskilled personnel while emphasizing frequent depot maintenance by specialists.

Despite their tendency toward design conservatism, the Soviets have been quite successful in raising the relative technological stature of their weapons systems. The weapons they are

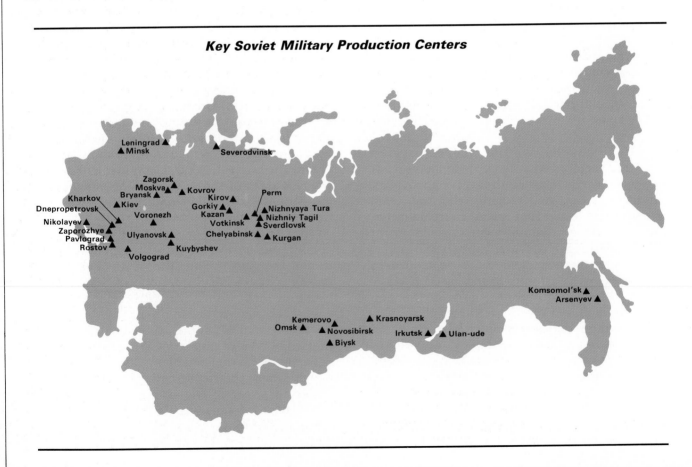

Key Soviet Military Production Centers

currently deploying which incorporate technology they developed or acquired from the Free World in the mid-1970s have narrowed, and in some cases, eliminated the Free World's qualitative lead. Particularly ominous is the fact that the Soviets have not yet fully realized the advantages of the last ten years' economic investments because of the timelag between resources committed and actual production. As resources and knowledge obtained from Free World sources further enhance Soviet capabilities, the West's qualitative edge could further erode and, in some critical military capabilities, result in Soviet superiority.

Military Industrial Production

General Secretary Gorbachev's industrial modernization program for the 12th Five-Year Plan seeks to raise the technological level of the machinery and equipment manufacturing sector, which provides the basis for Soviet economic and military might. Key areas within this sector that are likely to receive priority investments and undergo rapid growth include electronics, computers, robotics, machine tools, and instruments. Soviet military authorities widely agree that military requirements have moved into the·arena of high-technology and that without a strong, technologically advanced industrial base, the Soviet economy will have difficulty producing the complex weaponry required in the 1990s and beyond. The ultimate beneficiary of Gorbachev's modernization program will be the So-

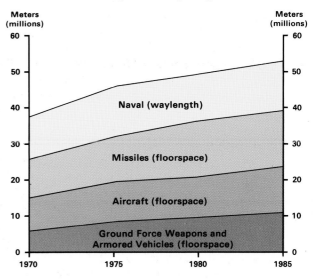

Soviet Military Industrial Expansion Floorspace/Waylength

viet military-industrial complex. Wide-spread modernization of the Soviet industrial base will ensure future military production capabilities.

Critical Industries

Metals. The dramatic increases in Soviet metals production underscore the USSR's emphasis on crucial materials to build their industrial base. Historically, the Soviets have exploited their impressive national resource base of strategic minerals, thereby assuring independence from foreign manipulation. The

Production of Ground Forces Materiel USSR/NSWP and NATO[1]

Equipment Type	USSR	NSWP	USSR	NSWP	USSR	NSWP	NATO		
	1983		1984		1985		1983	1984	1985
Tanks	3,000	550	3,200	450	3,000	700	1,600	1,600	1,800
Other Armored Fighting Vehicles	5,000	1,300	3,800	1,200	3,500	1,200	1,700	2,500	2,700
Towed Field Artillery	1,800	300	1,900	250	2,000	200	650	450	550
Self-Propelled Field Artillery	950	200	1,000	300	1,000	350	600	250	300
Multiple Rocket Launchers	900	100	900	100	700	100	50	75	75
Self-Propelled AA Artillery	100	0	50	0	100	10	0	50	25
Towed AA Artillery	0	150	0	225	0	225	25	25	0

[1] Revised to reflect current total production information. Includes United States; excludes France and Spain.

Soviet shipyards continue to produce new generations of major surface combatants with greater firepower including, from top to bottom, UDALOY- and SOVREMENNYY-Class destroyers, and KIROV-, and SLAVA-Class cruisers.

recent introduction of modern processing and fabricating techniques has further strengthened the Soviets' industrial autonomy.

To overcome their tendency for emphasizing only quantity in industrial production, the Soviets have designated sectors within each basic industry to develop the best state-of-the-art materials for advanced weapons systems. As would be expected, they are controlled and operated by the military ministries. Producers of strategic metals such as aluminum and titanium are totally merged with industries producing weapons for the Soviet arsenal. For example, the Ministry of Aviation Industry runs the metal fabrication plants of the aluminum industry. These plants produce components for aerospace industries and are located near the final assembly plants. This system streamlines production and delivery to assembly plants and ensures continuity of supplies for critical aerospace programs. Similarly, the titanium industry has been heavily influenced by military requirements, particularly for the production of titanium-hulled submarines.

Energy. The USSR is the only major industrial nation that is energy-independent. It is also the world's foremost producer and exporter of petroleum, with the largest proven oil reserves outside the Persian Gulf. Soviet natural gas reserves are even more impressive. Comprising over 37 trillion cubic meters and equivalent to about 200 billion barrels of oil, these reserves represent about 40 percent of the world's total, enabling the Soviets to continue as the largest producer and exporter of natural gas. The substitution of natural gas for petroleum for industrial and consumer use is well underway in the USSR, assuring the availability of large quantities of oil for exports to both Eastern and Western Europe.

The Soviet fuel and electric power base continues to expand and to provide surplus quantities of these most valuable commodities. Though dedicated primarily to supporting the military and related industries, the fuels and energy base provides over 50 percent of Soviet export earnings and fills the bulk of requirements of Soviet client states for imported energy as well. Growing fuels and energy exports to Western Europe could potentially provide the Soviet Union with economic leverage over some nations. If this condition were to evolve, it could have significant implications for the unity and viability of NATO.

Military Production

The USSR has consistently allocated a larger share of its national resources, both natural and industrial, to the peacetime production of military systems than any other country in modern history. Despite recent increases in output by the US, the Soviet Union still turns out roughly half of all weapons systems produced in the world and up to three-quarters of some types of military-related materiel. This phenomenal output has been achieved through the investment of huge amounts of money, raw materials, and manpower. The Soviets are implementing a three-pronged approach for military production. First, there is a thrust to use the huge R&D base they have assembled to upgrade the quality of their weapons and to produce more capable equipment. Second, the Soviet Union is expanding existing factories, building new ones, and providing on a priority basis new and modern manufacturing technologies to those industries that support military-related production. Finally, the Soviets are further integrating East European industries into their military-industrial complex.

The Soviet thrust toward increased weapons sophistication and modernization of the nation's military-industrial capacity has caused some decrease in the number of weapons systems being produced during the 1980s as well as an extension of their procurement cycles. Despite this current emphasis on intensive rather than extensive growth, the trend toward the production of more and more sophisticated weapons will not only continue but also probably increase in the 1990s. Huge numbers of each system will probably not be produced as in the past as Soviet military strategy assimilates the advanced capabilities of newer systems.

The vast number of industrial facilities committed to military requirements ensures that the Soviets will meet most production goals, even though some schedules may slip. At present there are over 150 major factories and shipyards producing weapons, armored vehicles, ships, aircraft, missiles, ammunition, and explosives. Additionally, 150 other plants provide combat support equipment such as radar, trucks, and communications gear. These major facilities, in turn, draw on literally thousands of parts and components factories. These facilities are continually being expanded and modernized; since 1970 they have increased in size by over 50 percent. This growth has been

From top to bottom, the OSCAR, SIERRA, AKULA, and KILO classes of attack and cruise missile submarines are currently in production.

Soviet production of large-bore self-propelled artillery includes, from top to bottom, 240-mm mortars, 203-mm guns, and 152-mm and 122-mm howitzers.

well-balanced across the entire spectrum of military equipment. For example, in recent years, the ammunition industry has been greatly expanded.

At the Severodvinsk Shipyard, the world's largest submarine production yard, shop space has increased by over 50 percent and covered building space by over 85 percent since 1965. Severodvinsk is only one of five Soviet shipyards producing submarines. Since 1970, the 24 naval construction yards that produce most Soviet naval ships have enjoyed a 16-percent increase in new building ways. The Soviet aircraft industry, while producing huge numbers of aircraft annually, continues to reflect growth and modernization. A notable example is the new plant at Ulyanovsk which will produce heavy-lift transports.

Industrial Modernization

The Soviet leadership has shown the same inclination to upgrade the country's industrial capacity, particularly the military sector, as it has for military systems by the introduction of new technologies. Since the 1960s, a concerted effort has been made to introduce computers and automation, and programs started in the 1970s have already resulted in the introduction of thousands of computer-aided design and automated production control systems. The current emphasis is on applying robotics and sophisticated machine tools as widely as possible. This objective is totally compatible with the production of technologically sophisticated weapons. If they succeed, the Soviets will realize increased efficiency in all phases of industrial production.

Ground Forces Equipment

The USSR continues to be the world's largest producer of ground forces equipment. Currently, emphasis is being placed on improving capabilities by incorporating new technologies into the equipment as well as into the means of production.

Tanks and Armored Vehicles. Overall tank production in 1985 included the T-72, T-64, and newer T-80 models. The time required for manufacturing modern tanks such as the T-80 exceeds that of their simpler predecessors. The tank plant in Nizhniy Tagil is supported by at least three other plants in Kharkov, Omsk, and Chelyabinsk. T-72s are also produced in Eastern Europe. Output of the T-80 tank is expected to increase. Production of other armored vehicles in 1985 included eight different types manufactured at seven Soviet plants as well as at two factories in Eastern Europe. The most important of these are the BMP infantry combat vehicle (ICV) series, the BMD airborne ICV, the BTR-70 and BTR-60 armored personnel carriers (APCs), and the BRDM-2 armored reconnaissance vehicle. Currently, the last two are produced only for export. Soviet BTR-70 and BMP production is supplemented by imports from other Warsaw Pact nations.

Artillery. Approximately 4,000 artillery pieces, mortars, and multiple rocket launchers were manufactured in 1985. Included were towed 85-mm and 100-mm antitank guns, 122-mm and 152-mm howitzers, and 130-mm and 152-mm field guns. Overall output of towed artillery increased. Self-propelled models included 122-mm and 152-mm howitzers and guns up to 203mm. Little change was noted in the output of three models of rocket launchers—two 122-mm models and a 220-mm piece are being built. Production of antiaircraft artillery increased as a new self-propelled model entered production. Most artillery production is accomplished at plants in Sverdlovsk and Perm.

Helicopters. The Soviets excel in design and production of these important weapons systems, producing over 800 per year since 1982. Five helicopters are now in production. The HIP, HIND, HALO, HAZE, HELIX, and at least two others are nearing production at five different airframe plants. The Mi-26/HALO is the world's largest helicopter. The HALO's lift capability is comparable to the US C-130 Hercules transport aircraft. The HIP is built at plants in Kazan and Ulan Ude. Thousands of these helicopters have been produced, including four new specialized military variants. Over 2,300 Mi-24 HIND helicopters designed to attack enemy tanks have been produced in Arsenyev and Rostov. A new attack helicopter, the HAVOC, which has a mission similar to the US AH-64 Apache, and the HOKUM, the world's first fighter helicopter, are in prototype testing and may enter production in 1986.

Naval Forces

Soviet naval production in 1985 continued at a high level. Unit completion numbers and tonnage produced in the principal surface combatant and small surface combatant categories

Besides manufacturing the new FLANKER and FULCRUM fighters, Soviet aircraft production includes, from top to bottom, the FROGFOOT and FOXBAT tactical aircraft as well as BEAR H and BACKFIRE bombers.

set this pattern. Quantitatively, submarine production was at about the 1984 level while auxiliary ships were built at the same rate observed since 1980.

Submarines. The Soviets continue to series-produce a variety of submarine classes. At present, they are building two classes of nuclear-powered ballistic missile submarines (SSBNs)—the TYPHOON and the DELTA IV. A third unit of the OSCAR-Class nuclear-powered cruise missile submarine (SSGN) class has joined the fleet, and further production is expected. Activity is also proceeding on four classes of nuclear-powered attack submarines (SSNs). Lead ships of three impressive new classes also continue to undergo trials and evaluation. These include the MIKE as well as the SIERRA and the AKULA. The latter two probably will replace the VICTOR III as standard fleet SSNs. Construction of the KILO-Class diesel-powered submarine (SS) now is underway at three different shipyards, indicating that it is intended to replace the FOXTROT as the standard fleet diesel-powered submarine. In addition, the Soviets are also producing experimental submarines and are converting SSBNs dismantled under the SALT accords.

Surface Ships. Soviet shipyards have ten classes of major surface combatants under series production. The third KIROV-Class nuclear-powered cruiser (CGN) is under construction. Construction proceeds on the second, third, and fourth units of the SLAVA-Class guided-missile cruiser (CG) and the out-

Naval Ship Construction USSR and NATO[1]

Ship Type	USSR			NATO		
	1983	1984	1985	1983	1984	1985
Submarines	10	9	8	8	12	8
Major Combatants	10	9	8	23	19	16
Minor Combatants	50	50	50	30	34	30
Auxiliaries	6	5	5	7	11	5

[1] Revised to reflect current total production information. Includes United States; excludes France and Spain.

A VICTOR III-Class nuclear-powered attack submarine, in foreground, and an OSCAR-Class nuclear-powered cruise missile submarine participated in the Soviets' major naval exercise in the North Atlantic in 1985.

Soviet BACKFIRE bombers, being produced at the rate of about 30 per year, are in service with Soviet Air Forces and Soviet Naval Aviation.

fitting of the fourth unit of the KIEV-Class guided-missile aircraft carrier (CVHG). Series construction continues on the SOVREMENNY, UDALOY, and Mod KASHIN classes of guided-missile destroyers (DDGs) at about one ship per class, per year. The Mod KASHIN, as well as the KONI-Class frigate (FF), are only for export. A variety of smaller combatant and auxiliary classes are also under construction.

The first of a new class carrier was launched at the Nikolayev shipyard. Use of this new ship to accommodate high-performance aircraft—possibly conventional take-off and landing (CTOL)—has been widely suggested. The ultimate flight deck configuration and the type of aircraft to be embarked are, however, still undetermined. It is possible that the Soviets intend to deploy the ship initially as a vertical/short take off and landing (V/STOL) carrier for Yak-36/FORGER aircraft as well as for helicopters, but could later perform modifications to accommodate modern, high-performance aircraft. The propulsion system is probably a combined conventional/nuclear plant similar to that of the KIROV-Class CGN. Sea trials of this unit are expected by early 1989.

East European nations have continued to contribute to Soviet naval power by providing additional ship construction. The non-Soviet Warsaw Pact countries have produced approximately 75 percent of Soviet amphibious landing ships and roughly 35 percent of Soviet naval auxiliaries.

Aircraft

The USSR is second only to the US in total aircraft production, but in the category of military aircraft is the world's number-one producer. This has allowed the Soviets to build and modernize the world's largest military air force. In addition, the continuous high output of all types of aircraft has enabled the Soviets

Aircraft Production USSR and NATO[1]

Aircraft Type	USSR			NATO		
	1983	1984	1985	1983	1984	1985
Bombers	35	50	50	0	0	2
Fighters/ Fighter- Bombers	950	800	650	650	550	550
Transports	250	250	250	290	250	300
ASW	5	5	5	15	10	5
Helicopters	550	600	600	725	720	525
Utility/ Trainers	10	10	0	425	305	300

[1] Revised to reflect current total production information. Includes United States; excludes France and Spain.

to amass the world's largest state-owned civil air fleet. The Soviet Union is also a major exporter of both civilian and military aircraft to the Third World.

Bombers. The USSR currently has three intercontinental-capable bombers in or nearing production: the BACKFIRE, the BEAR H, and the new BLACKJACK. The BACKFIRE is built at the huge plant at Kazan. The BEAR H, which carries the AS-15 long-range cruise missile, is being produced at Kuybyshev. Development of the latest advanced Soviet strategic bomber, the BLACKJACK, is progressing, and series production is expected at a massive new complex at the Kazan Airframe Plant.

Fighters. Overall Soviet fighter aircraft output has declined over the past several years, dropping from approximately 1,300 units in 1980 to about 650 in 1985. Output of newer fighters such as FULCRUM and FLANKER is not expected to offset production cutbacks in older, longstanding programs such as FLOGGER, FISHBED, and FITTER. Other active fighter production programs in 1985 included the FOXHOUND, FOXBAT, FROGFOOT, FENCER, and FORGER. The FOXHOUND interceptor, the FULCRUM counterair fighter, and the FROGFOOT ground-attack aircraft, produced at Gorkiy, Moscow, and Tbilisi, respectively, have achieved operational status during the last five years. In addition, four improved variants of older Soviet fighters, two each of FENCER and FITTER, have been in production since 1980. Deployment of the new MiG-29/FULCRUM is finally beginning to quicken, with Soviet units in Eastern Europe now receiving this aircraft.

The latest Soviet fighter, the Su-27/FLANK-

ER air-superiority fighter, built in Komsomolsk, achieved operational status early in 1986. The first Su-27s have begun arriving at operational bases in the USSR, after developmental difficulties delayed their introduction into the Soviet Air Force for a few years. Further, the Soviets probably have at least one new entirely different fighter design and several upgraded variants of existing models in different stages of development.

Transports. The Soviet Ministry of Aviation Industry ensures that all domestically produced high-performance transport aircraft meet military requirements. About 85 of the 250 transports produced in 1985 were for military use, primarily the Il-76/CANDID and the An-26/CURL, and, for foreign air forces, the An-32/CLINE. The CANDID is built at a huge facility in Tashkent. The Soviets produce two militarily important variants of this aircraft, an aerial refueling tanker and an airborne warning and control aircraft designated MAINSTAY. Other transports in production include CLASSIC, CRUSTY, CARELESS, CLOBBER, and CAMBER. Series production for the An-124/CONDOR heavy transport will probably start in 1987 or 1988. Six plants in the USSR manufacture transport aircraft as their main product. They, together with several other plants making multiple types of aerospace products, are expected to turn out an average of about 250 transports annually for the next several years.

Missiles

The Soviet missile industry has one of the highest priorities assigned to military programs and is engaged in continuous expansion and modernization. This results in not only

Missile Production USSR and NATO[1]

Missile Type	USSR			NATO		
	1983	1984	1985	1983	1984	1985
ICBMs	150	75	100	0	0	0
LRINF	125	125	125	110	80	175
SRBMs	500	500	450	50	25	50
SLCMs	650	700	700	1,300	1,100	800
SLBMs	100	50	100	75	70	75

[1] Revised to reflect current total production information. Includes United States; excludes France and Spain.

more advanced but also more classes of missiles being produced at more than 20 plants.

ICBMs. The Soviets continue to manufacture liquid-propellant ICBMs for troop training and to sustain the deployed force, producing approximately 100 during 1985. For the future, the Soviets are developing a new liquid-propellant ICBM to replace their SS-18 systems. A new solid-propellant ICBM (SS-25) now is in series production, and a second model (SS-X-24) is in prototype production.

SLBMs. Currently only the SS-N-20 for the TYPHOON SSBN is in series production, but developmental or prototype production on newer models is underway.

Cruise Missiles. The Soviets are serially producing six antiship naval cruise missiles—the SS-N-2, SS-N-3, SS-N-9, SS-N-12, SS-N-19, and SS-N-22—and three antisubmarine models—SS-N-14, SS-N-15, and SS-N-16—at an annual rate of about 700. This production program stretches from plants in the Far East maritime provinces to the Ukraine.

The AS-15, a long-range air-launched cruise missile designed to attack land-based targets as far as 3,000 kilometers from its BEAR H and BLACKJACK launch platforms, can be delivered against targets in the US and Eurasia.

Longer Range Intermediate-Range Nuclear Forces (LRINF). Production of LRINF has increased since 1980 and totaled approximately 125 missiles in 1985. The SS-20 is still in series production.

Short-Range Ballistic Missiles (SRBMs). The output of these systems has more than doubled since 1979. This increase is evidence of a major modernization effort to replace the thousands of FROG and SCUD missiles with new, more accurate SS-21s and SS-23s plus improved SCALEBOARDs.

SAMs. The USSR continues to turn out the world's largest variety of strategic and tactical surface-to-air missiles. The SA-10 and SA-11, which are now in series production, and the SA-X-12 are sophisticated, effective weapons. Soviet SAM production remains at more than 40,000 units of 12 systems from plants in Moscow, Leningrad, Sverdlovsk, Kirov, and Kovrov.

Radar and Military Support Items

Radar. The Soviets are currently developing approximately 20 new radars while those now in production include technological advances made or acquired during the 1970s. They continue to reflect Soviet doctrine to use more types of radars than Western forces. They embrace the full spectrum of systems, including mobile and transportable ground-based air defense radars, large fixed-site phased-array radars, as well as older ballistic missile radars. What probably is a new over-the-horizon radar under construction in the Far East could have an early warning capability against US SLBMs launched from the Pacific.

Trucks. Truck production in the USSR has increased over 20 percent during the past decade—from approximately 665,000 in 1974 to over 800,000 in 1985. The number of medium trucks procured by Soviet forces during this period decreased while the numbers of light and heavy trucks have been increasing. Of the more than 800,000 trucks produced by Soviet plants during 1985, some 25 to 30 percent were acquired by the military.

The Future

Despite extraordinary technological advances, the Soviet leadership is aware of the country's economic shortcomings. General Secretary Gorbachev has taken aggressive actions to accelerate technological changes and has pledged to enhance productivity and spur modernization and economic progress through intensive growth. Gorbachev has charged the scientific community, particularly its management, to bridge the longstanding gap between research and production. Concurrently, he has pledged to improve the quality and availability of consumer goods for the beleaguered Soviet populace, which even today has had to endure rationing and shortages. Satisfying the needs of both the civilian and military sectors of the economy, however, cannot be achieved simultaneously. Gorbachev, however, knows that military strength is the basis of the USSR's existence. He has explicitly expressed his continuing support for the Soviet military and is very unlikely to make shifts in resource allocations that would challenge the entrenched power of the Ministry of Defense or defense industries. It is very likely, therefore, that civilian programs will continue to suffer as the Soviet thrust for military technological supremacy focuses on qualitative improvements.

Chapter VII

Global Ambitions

Since the accession to power of General Secretary Gorbachev, the Soviets have characterized his foreign policy as more effective in dealing with the "dangerous situation" in the world and more responsive to international problems than that of the USSR's major adversaries. The new leader has been skillful in projecting a robust and decisive media image. Moreover, he has cultivated an impression of dynamism in foreign policy and has injected a more persuasive tone in the Kremlin's public diplomacy. While proclaiming domestic reform to be his top priority, he has also maintained a heavy schedule of meetings with foreign delegations and has repeatedly proposed arms control and peace initiatives.

The new General Secretary inherited powerful military forces as well as an effective and assertive foreign policy establishment. Parts of this establishment are the Central Committee departments, the Ministry for Foreign Affairs, and the Soviet intelligence and security services. All of these entities have proven their ability to advance and defend Soviet interests throughout the world. There is little chance that the General Secretary's moves to improve the Soviet economy portend a modification of Moscow's fundamental goals. The USSR still seeks to divide the West and destabilize much of the Third World through its foreign policy and military actions.

A large percentage of the weapons systems the USSR exports to client states, Third World proxies, and repressive regimes flows from the enormous military port at Nikolayev on the Black Sea. SA-5/GAMMON surface-to-air missiles for Libya and helicopter gunships and tanks for Angola and Nicaragua are among the hundreds of thousands of tons of weaponry being shipped each year from the port's steadily expanding facilities dedicated to military cargo.

Soviet Naval Reconnaissance Aircraft Operating Areas-1965

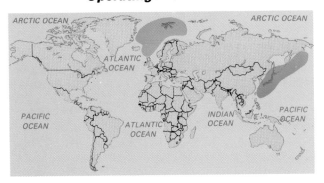

Soviet Naval Reconnaissance Aircraft Operating Areas-1986

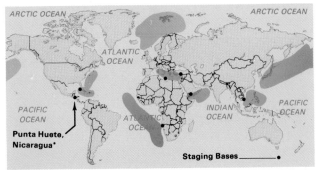

*Newly constructed airfield capable of handling Soviet long-range reconnaissance aircraft.

The Soviet Union has concentrated on castigating the United States and pushing highly publicized, skillfully timed, but one-sided arms control schemes. The Soviets are attempting to foment discord between the US and its NATO and Pacific allies, to strengthen their hold over Eastern Europe, and generally to pose as the champion of Third World interests. By resurrecting an array of one-sided arms reduction concepts, the Soviets have sought to portray the US as intransigent and bellicose and therefore a threat to European security and world peace. Moscow continues to pursue actively the normalization of ties with China and to woo some Western allies while maintaining a stream of press invectives against others such as Japan and West Germany. Third World affairs have occupied little of Gorbachev's public time, although these regions remain prime targets for continued exploitation. The Soviet leader has insisted that the Kremlin will not look at the world "solely through the prism" of US-Soviet relations. The Soviets will continue their efforts to undermine US support for the Freedom Fighters in Afghanistan and Nicaragua.

In East Asia, the Soviet-North Korean relationship has expanded significantly in recent months. The Philippine political situation and the Southwest Pacific continue to offer potential opportunities for exploitation. Attention has been paid to shoring up what Moscow calls its "special relationship" with India and expanding its support to Vietnam. Initial indications are that the war in Afghanistan will be prosecuted with greater vigor, and Moscow has increased pressure on Pakistan to reduce

its support for the Mujahideen. There are also signs of increased Soviet efforts to improve relations with Japan.

In the Middle East, the USSR has courted moderate states like Egypt, Jordan, and Kuwait while strengthening ties with Syria, establishing relations with Oman and the United Arab Emirates, and continuing to insist on a role in the peace process. In Sub-Saharan Africa, the scene of the USSR's greatest Third World gains in the 1970s, the Soviets continue to concentrate on Angola, Ethiopia, and Mozambique while attempting to exploit turmoil in South Africa. Meanwhile, Latin America continues to offer an opportunity for the Soviets to foment conflict. Nicaragua has already received additional assurances of direct Soviet support.

Overall, Soviet global ambitions are expected to be pursued through an active foreign policy. Attention will remain focused on the US-Soviet strategic relationship coupled with a renewed emphasis on Third World affairs.

Soviet Support to Terrorism

The Soviets have a long history of maintaining relations with groups that are linked to terrorism. Moscow's historical experience with the use of terror as an instrument of internal state control suggests its leadership is not averse to creating and exploiting opportunities for covert support to terrorists and insurgents.

Within the broader context of foreign policy objectives, the Soviets seek to achieve specific goals through support of violence, insurgencies, and wars of "national liberation." In the Third World, they seek the creation and exploitation of instability in pro-Western and anti-Soviet regimes. Consequently, the accession to power of a pro-Soviet regime anywhere in the Third World would lessen Western political and economic influence and thus make access to raw materials less secure. Another Soviet objective is to weaken NATO and foment discord in the Western democracies that would lead to disunity and increased security problems.

Publicly, the Soviets have disavowed any connection with international terrorist groups and individual acts of terrorism. However, the Soviets openly support wars of national liberation and leftist insurgent groups as an integral element of foreign policy. Moreover, the fact that acts of terrorism or revolutionary violence are appendages to insurgent activities does not hinder Soviet support and backing in light of Leninist doctrine.

Soviet subversive activities are orchestrated by the Communist Party Central Committee's International Department. Support to terrorism involves the intelligence and security services—specifically Department 8, Directorate S, of the KGB's First Chief Directorate and the GRU's "Special Branch" and "Special Center." Additional aid is provided by various state ministries as well as by Soviet diplomatic, military assistance, aid, trade, and cultural missions abroad. Terrorist training activities are carried out by the International Department in conjunction with the KGB and the GRU. Complementing this apparatus are similar organizations in East European states and Cuba. Other countries and groups with regional objectives that have mutual interests with the Soviets in destabilizing Western-oriented regimes also receive Soviet support. These nations, such as Libya and South Yemen, in turn harbor, train, and equip selected terrorist groups, sometimes in cooperation with the Soviets but often for their own purposes. They also fund and coordinate certain terrorist activities.

The best documented links between Soviet intelligence and security services (the KGB and GRU) to international terrorism are through the training, funds, and weapons provided by the Soviet Union and its East European and non-Bloc allies to Third World and Western "revolutionaries." The Soviets spend large sums of money training such personnel worldwide. Instruction in guerrilla warfare,

sabotage, assassination, terror, and espionage occurs at special Soviet training facilities and camps near Moscow and locations along the southern Soviet border. Some evidence exists that terrorist training is also conducted in Czechoslovakia, Bulgaria, and East Germany.

Thousands of Palestinians, other Arab recruits, and selected non-Arabs and members of the South West African Peoples' Organization (SWAPO) and the African National Congress (ANC) have received training in insurgency and terrorist techniques at facilities in the Soviet Union. Additionally, arms shipments from Eastern Europe as well as arms purchases on the open market by terrorist groups using funds derived from Soviet proxies and clients are significant indicators of Soviet support. Czechoslovakia and Bulgaria, through their state-controlled arms shipment agencies, have originated arms transfers that end up in terrorists' hands. The passage of terrorists through and their maintenance of temporary residence in Eastern Europe, including Czechoslovakia, East Germany, and Bulgaria, highlight Soviet Bloc security service collusion in sanctioning terrorist activities.

Soviet support for terrorist training camps in South Yemen, Libya, Iraq, and Lebanon has been the clearest evidence of substantial Soviet investment in terrorism in the Middle East. These training camps have been used

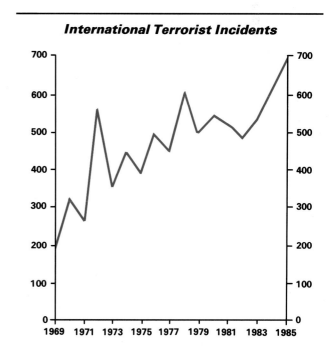

International Terrorist Incidents

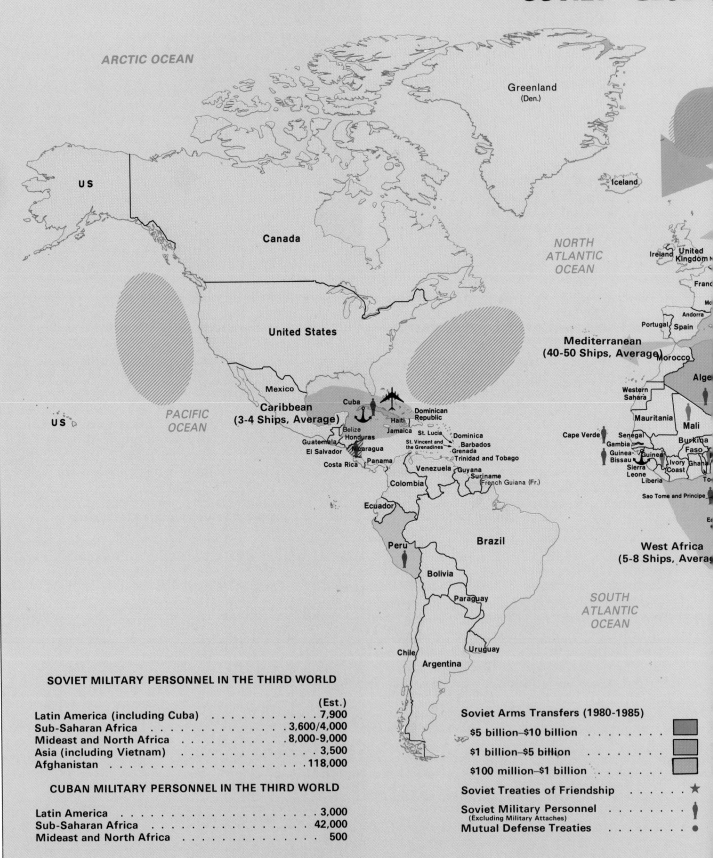

ARCTIC OCEAN

Greenland
(Den.)

US

Iceland

Canada

NORTH
ATLANTIC
OCEAN

Ireland United
Kingdom

Franc

United States

Andorra

Portugal Spain

Mediterranean
(40-50 Ships, Average)

Morocco

Alge

Mexico

Western
Sahara

Caribbean
(3-4 Ships, Average)

Cuba

PACIFIC
OCEAN

Dominican
Republic

Mauritania

Mali

US

Haiti

Belize
Honduras

Jamaica

St. Lucia

Cape Verde

Senegal
Gambia
Guinea-
Bissau

Burkina
Faso

Guatemala

Dominica

El Salvador

Nicaragua

St. Vincent and
the Grenadines

Barbados
Grenada

Guinea

Sierra
Leone

Ivory
Coast

Ghana

To

Costa Rica

Panama

Trinidad and Tobago

Liberia

Venezuela

Guyana

Sao Tome and Principe

Colombia

Suriname
French Guiana (Fr.)

Ec

Ecuador

Peru

Brazil

West Africa
(5-8 Ships, Averag

Bolivia

SOUTH
ATLANTIC
OCEAN

Paraguay

Chile

Uruguay

Argentina

SOVIET MILITARY PERSONNEL IN THE THIRD WORLD

	(Est.)
Latin America (including Cuba)	7,900
Sub-Saharan Africa	3,600/4,000
Mideast and North Africa	8,000-9,000
Asia (including Vietnam)	3,500
Afghanistan	118,000

CUBAN MILITARY PERSONNEL IN THE THIRD WORLD

Latin America	3,000
Sub-Saharan Africa	42,000
Mideast and North Africa	500

Soviet Arms Transfers (1980-1985)

$5 billion–$10 billion

$1 billion–$5 billion

$100 million–$1 billion

Soviet Treaties of Friendship

Soviet Military Personnel
(Excluding Military Attaches)

Mutual Defense Treaties

POWER PROJECTION

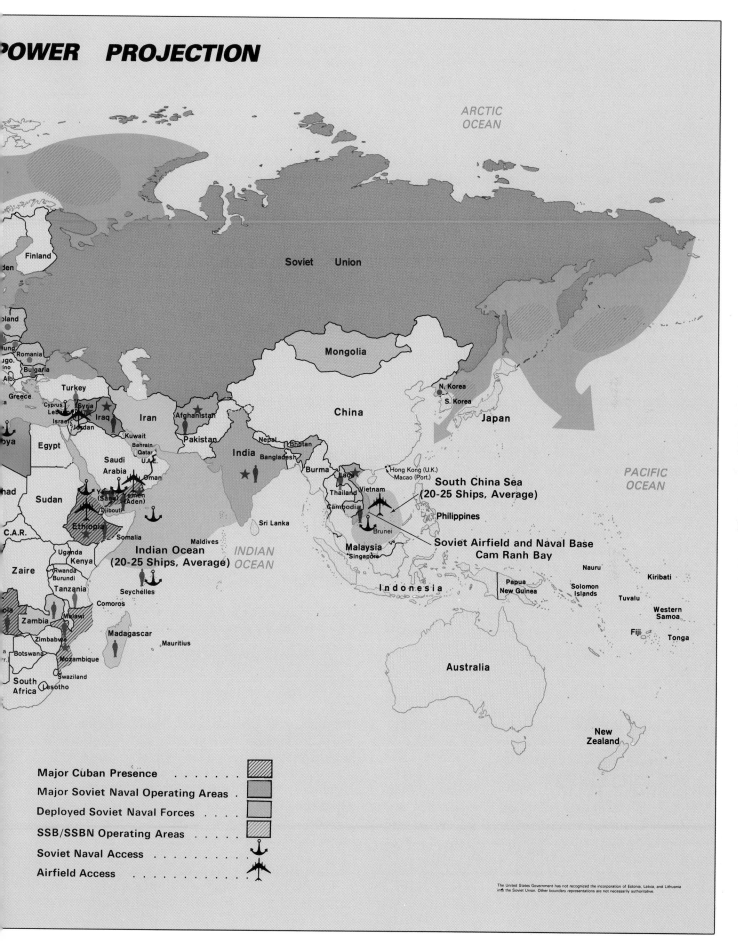

ARCTIC OCEAN

Finland

Soviet Union

Mongolia

N. Korea
S. Korea

Japan

PACIFIC OCEAN

Romania
Bulgaria
Greece

Turkey
Cyprus
Lebanon
Israel
Jordan
Iraq
Syria

Iran

Afghanistan

China

Egypt

Saudi Arabia

Kuwait
Bahrain
Qatar
U.A.E.
Oman

Pakistan

Nepal
Bhutan

India

Bangladesh

Burma

Laos

Hong Kong (U.K.)
Macao (Port.)

South China Sea
(20-25 Ships, Average)

Sudan

Yemen (Sana)
Yemen (Aden)
Djibouti

Thailand
Vietnam
Cambodia

Philippines

C.A.R.

Ethiopia

Somalia

Maldives

Sri Lanka

INDIAN OCEAN

Indian Ocean
(20-25 Ships, Average)

Brunei

Malaysia
Singapore

Soviet Airfield and Naval Base
Cam Ranh Bay

Zaire

Uganda
Kenya
Rwanda
Burundi
Tanzania

Seychelles

Comoros

Indonesia

Papua
New Guinea

Nauru

Solomon
Islands

Kiribati

Tuvalu

Zambia
Malawi
Zimbabwe

Madagascar

Mauritius

Western
Samoa

Fiji

Tonga

Botswana
Mozambique
Swaziland
Lesotho
South Africa

Australia

New Zealand

Major Cuban Presence . . . .

Major Soviet Naval Operating Areas .

Deployed Soviet Naval Forces . . . .

SSB/SSBN Operating Areas . . . . .

Soviet Naval Access . . . .

Airfield Access . . . .

127

extensively by radical elements of the Palestine Liberation Organization (PLO) as well as by guerrillas and terrorists from Latin America, Africa, Asia, and Europe. Libya, in particular, has emerged as a pivotal force in world terrorism.

On the opposite side of the globe, Cuban leader Fidel Castro has provided terrorist groups millions of dollars in arms and supplies to escalate and foment insurgency and revolutionary violence throughout Central and South America.

While the evidence indicates that the Soviets bear a substantial responsibility for fostering international terrorism, they appear to believe that direct Soviet control is not desirable or politically expedient in terrorist activities as long as terrorist aims and objectives parallel or complement Soviet goals. A substantial amount of the weapons and training support for terrorist groups originates with the Soviet Union and its clients or allies. Soviet support for revolutionary violence and international terrorism is expected to continue and perhaps escalate as a means of challenging the West.

Latin America

Central and South America remain important regions of the Third World in Moscow's pursuit of its global ambitions. Moscow seeks to build its own influence throughout Latin America while diminishing that of the US. By developing political and military relations and supporting subversion, the Soviets can challenge the US and gain access to military facilities. Also, securing economic ties in Latin America provides markets for Soviet goods and ensures supplies of grain and raw materials.

Cuba

The preeminent importance of Cuba to Moscow is evident in the vast amounts of Soviet military and economic support that have been provided to Castro's regime. Cuba has received nearly $6 billion worth of military aid from Moscow since 1960. Only Vietnam and East Germany among the Communist countries have received more. Economic assistance has reached almost $4 billion per year and is bolstered by the presence of possibly as many as 8,000 civilian advisors and technicians.

Throughout this decade, the Soviets have made an accelerated effort to upgrade Cuba's armed forces. Nearly 60 percent of all Soviet

military assistance to Cuba has been delivered since 1980. In 1985, this small island nation received 5 percent of all Soviet military assistance worldwide. Significant weapons systems noted in 1985 include the SA-13 and shoulder-fired SA-14 surface-to-air missile systems and STENKA-Class fast patrol craft. Soviet aid and the efforts of 2,800 military advisors have led to across-the-board improvements in Cuban military capabilities that pose a significant threat to maritime commerce routes in the Caribbean Sea and Gulf of Mexico.

Growth Trends in Cuban Forces

	1975	1980	1985
Air Force			
MiG 23s	0	12	45
MiG 21s	95	140	160
L-39 trainers	0	0	30
SAM launchers	105	165	215
An-26 transports	2	25	30
Il-76 transports	0	0	2
Navy			
FOXTROT submarines	0	2	3
KONI frigates	0	0	2
Missile patrol boats	22	18	20
TURYA hydrofoils	0	4	9
POLNOCNY landing ships	0	0	2
Army			
T-54/55 and T-62 tanks	300	720	1,000+
Other armored vehicles	120	1,000	1,200
Artillery	500*	1,400	1,500

*Estimated

In addition to military advisors, permanent Soviet military presence in Cuba is represented by a 2,800-man combat brigade and a major communications intercept site at Lourdes. This facility enables Moscow to monitor sensitive US maritime, military, and space communications as well as US domestic telephone calls. Furthermore, Cuban ports and airfields support Caribbean deployments by Soviet naval task forces and long-range naval aviation aircraft. The 25th naval task group to visit the Caribbean was active in Cuban waters and the Gulf of Mexico from late-September to mid-November 1985. There were seven deployments of Tu-95/BEAR D naval reconnaissance aircraft and six deployments of Tu-142/BEAR F antisubmarine warfare aircraft during 1985.

Castro provides cadre training, advisors, and material support to many regional subversive

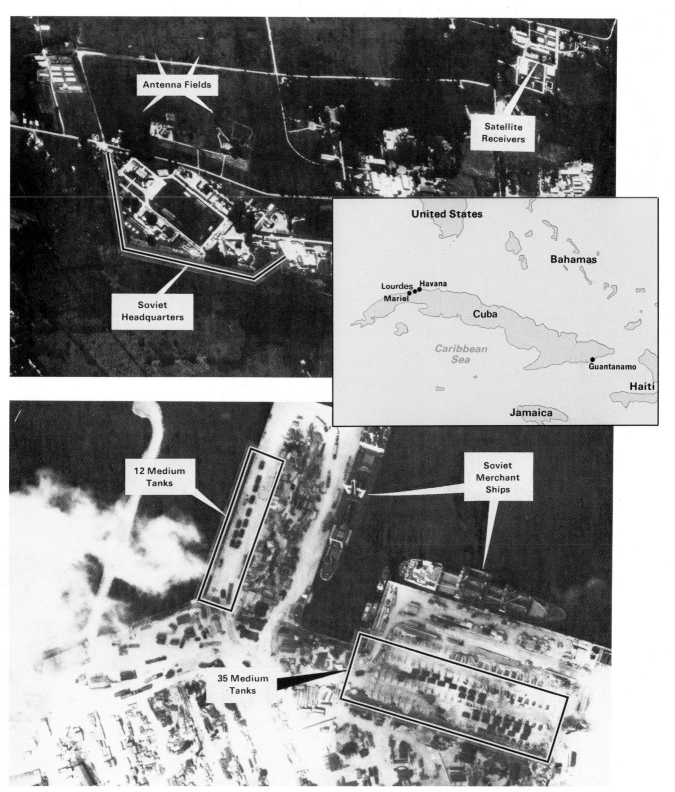

Soviet intelligence-collection facility at Lourdes, top, near Havana, Cuba. This listening post, the largest such facility outside the USSR, enables the Soviets to monitor sensitive US maritime, military, and space communications as well as telephone conversations in the United States. The Mariel port facility, bottom, serves as the primary Cuban port for the delivery of military hardware. In 1985, over 35,000 metric tons of Soviet/Soviet Bloc equipment were delivered to Cuba. Military hardware for Nicaragua is transshipped from this port facility.

129

groups and insurgencies, capitalizing on common Hispanic ethnic and regional associations to develop inroads that would otherwise be closed to the Soviets. For some time, Cuba has been seeking increased contacts with leftist parties and labor unions in the Caribbean, urging them to merge to oppose democratic governments in future elections. In Central America, Cuba remains heavily involved in supporting the Nicaraguan regime and provides about 3,000 military and 3,000-4,000 economic and technical advisors. Castro continues to undermine the legitimate government of El Salvador by providing logistical support as well as military and terrorist training to insurgents at bases in Nicaragua and Cuba.

In 1985, Castro achieved significant political and diplomatic successes in South America. He reestablished diplomatic relations with Uruguay, established the foundations for diplomatic relations with Brazil, and received a new Bolivian ambassador, marking the first official Bolivian presence in Cuba in several years. Peru, under President Alan Garcia Perez, plans to normalize relations with Cuba in 1986. Castro has loaned two deep-sea fishing vessels to Peru in an effort to increase commercial ties. Cuba hosted Ecuadorean President Febres Cordero while cultural, scientific, and technical cooperation between Argentina and Cuba grew.

Castro sought to capture Latin America's attention with his emphasis on the longstanding debt crisis. In July and August 1985, Cuba hosted a conference on the Latin American debt that was attended by several leftist leaders from the region. The conference blamed the US for the Latin American debt problem and called for a moratorium on payment of American loans.

In addition, Cuba maintains ties with several guerrilla groups, including Colombia's M-19, the Chilean Movement of the Revolutionary Left, and militant Ecuadorean groups. At the same time, however, Castro is trying to improve diplomatic relations and cultural ties with Colombia, Ecuador, Peru, Venezuela, Uruguay, Suriname, Guyana, and Bolivia.

Nicaragua

Moscow is gradually and cautiously consolidating its ties with Nicaragua. Of the $580 mil-

SHERSHEN-Class torpedo boats, left, and OSA-Class missile attack boats, below, being delivered aboard a Soviet RO/FLO. Units of both boats have been sold to eight different Third World nations.

lion in Communist military aid delivered since 1980, Moscow's share has been about $240 million. New military equipment, along with 50 to 70 Soviet and 2,500 to 3,500 Cuban military and security advisors, has helped to create the largest armed forces in Central America.

The regime in Nicaragua poses both a military and psychological threat to neighboring countries like Honduras and Costa Rica. The governments of El Salvador and, to a lesser degree, Guatemala, are threatened by Soviet- and Cuban-supported insurgents trained in Nicaragua.

The Kremlin is also making a substantial effort to bolster the Sandinistas economically. Moscow now provides, directly or indirectly, about 80 percent of Nicaragua's petroleum requirements. The Soviets also have provided significant amounts of grant food aid and disaster-relief assistance and have signed agreements to extend economic cooperation.

South America

Throughout South America, the Soviets patiently persist in their efforts to develop economic, political, and military relations while engaging in anti-US propaganda and covert measures. However, Moscow's relations are mostly limited to economic activity. Moscow's closest ties are with Peru, the only South American country to have purchased large amounts of Soviet military equipment. Since 1973, the value of Soviet military assistance to Peru has totaled about $1.5 billion. Peruvian

ports support nearly 200 Soviet fishing vessels in South American waters, resulting in $120 million in revenues. Peru also provides the Soviet state airline, Aeroflot, a point of entry into South America.

Sub-Saharan Africa/Indian Ocean

Soviet involvement in Sub-Saharan Africa over the past year has been significant in two important respects. Moscow has increased its support to the counterinsurgency efforts of its client states Angola, Ethiopia, and Mozambique. It has also continued its efforts to exploit discord and instability in South Africa.

Angola

Moscow is concerned about the survival of the Popular Movement for the Liberation of Angola (MPLA) regime. Luanda is one of the largest and best natural harbors on the west coast of Africa and is the main support base for the Soviet Navy's West Africa Patrol. Other assets there include a floating drydock, a communications station, and access for Tu-95/BEAR Ds, which patrol the South Atlantic sealanes. To assure the survival of MPLA control, Moscow has significantly increased the amount of military aid provided to the MPLA. In 1985, the Angolans received Mi-24/HIND and Mi-17/HIP H helicopters, additional Su-22/FITTERs, MiG-23/FLOGGERs, and SA-13 SAMs. Angola has deployed the MiG-23s and SA-13 SAMs to the south to help detect and defend against alleged South African

Major Soviet Equipment Delivered to the Third World 1980-1985*

	Near East and South Asia	Sub-Saharan Africa	Latin America	East Asia and Pacific	Total
Tanks/Self-propelled Guns	3,600	630	505	280	5,015
Light Armor	6,565	1,000	280	250	8,095
Artillery	3,810	2,050	895	390	7,145
Major Surface Combatants	26	4	4	5	39
Minor Surface Combatants	27	21	49	48	145
Submarines	7	0	2	0	9
Missile Attack Boats	16	9	6	6	37
Supersonic Aircraft	1,340	340	135	270	2,085
Subsonic Aircraft	120	5	0	5	130
Helicopters	695	190	80	75	1,040
Other Combat Aircraft	250	70	40	80	440
Surface-to-Air Missiles	10,400	1,890	1,300	430	14,020

* Revised to reflect current information.

Chapter VII Global Ambitions

aircraft supporting the National Union for the Total Independence of Angola (UNITA). Prior to 1985, the Angolans also received an early warning radar net that covers almost the entire southwestern part of the country and other equipment intended to improve intelligence-gathering capabilities against UNITA. Luanda was visited last September by a Soviet task group, including a KIROV-Class nuclear-powered guided-missile cruiser and two new guided-missile destroyers, an UDALOY and SOVREMENNYY, transiting to the Soviet Pacific Ocean Fleet. In addition, a squadron of Soviet An-12/CUB transports has been supporting Angolan government forces for several years.

Between August and October, Angolan forces launched an ambitious offensive against the guerrillas in the southeast. While this operation achieved mixed results, the tactics and weapons used indicate a more direct Soviet role in Angolan military operations.

Ethiopia

Ethiopia remains the USSR's most important East African client, a fact reinforced by Ethiopian leader Mengistu's favorable treatment in Moscow in November 1985 and by the provision of almost $4 billion in Soviet arms. The delivery of equipment to the port of Aseb for the 1985 campaign in Eritrea consisted of APCs, T-55 tanks, and additional MiG-23/FLOGGER fighters. The Ethiopian redeployment of 50,000 troops in less than three weeks in August at the height of the rainy season was facilitated by direct Soviet logistic and advisory assistance, resulting in the successful capture of an important Eritrean line of communication from Sudan and the key town of Barentu. Despite such aid, however, a second offensive made little headway against the insurgent stronghold of Nakfa.

Seychelles, Mozambique, and Madagascar

The Kremlin's push for access to Sub-Saharan Africa and the Indian Ocean is relentless, particularly in the Seychelles, Mozambique, and Madagascar. Permanent access would provide Moscow with significant advantages: a partial counterbalance to the US presence on Diego Garcia, greater staging capability for military airlift flights to southern Africa, and more intelligence-gathering opportunities against Western naval activity in the Indian Ocean.

The Soviets continue to seek regular military access to port and air facilities in the Seychelles. The USSR is the Seychelles' largest arms supplier, having delivered some $18 million in weapons and related equipment. Continuing Soviet ship visits indicate Moscow's resolve to maintain some influence in the Seychelles. Previously, during periods of instability or President Rene's absence, the Soviets have sent naval vessels to support the regime. Since February 1983, Soviet transport aircraft, many of which may be military, also have been making stopovers at the Seychelles' main airport on Mahe en route to southern Africa. However, the number of Soviet military advisors has decreased in the past year to only 10—down from 25—as the Seychelles attempts to balance its foreign policy to ensure Western economic assistance and improve tourism.

The USSR has continued to pay significant attention to the Samora Machel regime in Mozambique, largely because of Maputo's inability to quell the insurgency of the National Resistance of Mozambique (RENAMO). Moscow has provided about $1 billion in military aid. Among the significant 1985 deliveries were Mi-24/HIND helicopters, several PT-76 light tanks, BTR-60 APCs, artillery pieces, BM-24 multiple rocket launchers, SA-3 launchers, YEVGENYA-Class minesweepers, and SO-1 patrol boats. The approximately 850 Soviet advisors and technicians are heavily involved in planning and supporting Mozambican operations against RENAMO.

Since Mozambique is not near the normal operating areas of the Indian Ocean Squadron, Soviet combatants visit its ports infrequently; however, hydrographic research ships are often present in the Mozambique Channel. Arms carriers have unloaded their cargoes at Nacala several times in 1985, and a small contingent of An-12/CUBs has rotated to and from the USSR. Although the Soviets deployed two Il-38/MAYs to Mozambique in early 1985 and continue to make substantial improvements at Nacala airfield, they appear unable to gain more frequent access.

In 1983 and 1984, relations between the USSR and Madagascar suffered a setback as President Ratsiraka pursued a more balanced foreign policy. Madagascar provided a concrete demonstration of moving toward genuine nonalignment, and in 1985 a small US security assistance program was initiated. In an effort to shore up its ties to Madagascar, the Soviets in November 1984 provided $20 million in military equipment, including the first multiple rocket launchers in the Malagasy inventory. Soviet advisors number about 100. Although military access has not been granted, the Soviets probably continue to view the harbor of Diego Suarez (Antsiranana) and the airfield at Andrakaka, both on the northern tip of the island, as highly desirable locations.

South Africa

In addition to working for South Africa's diplomatic isolation, the USSR seeks to exploit internal discord in that country. Although domestic opposition to the South African Government is not united, Moscow attempts to influence events through:

- deliveries of weapons to and the military training of armed forces located in regional countries hostile to South Africa;
- ties with the South African Communist Party; and
- support of the African National Congress, a group that seeks to topple the present government.

By supplying military equipment to opposition groups, whether ideologically tied to communism or independently seeking equality and democratic reform, the Soviets hope to gain greater influence in the area.

Middle East/North Africa

Arms sales are the Soviets' principal means of gaining leverage in the Middle East and provide Moscow with its most effective entree into regional politics. The Soviets have provided some advanced models of weapons systems not yet deployed to their Warsaw Pact allies. Moscow has relied almost exclusively on its major arms clients, particularly Syria and Iraq, to further its regional influence. The USSR also provides large quantities of arms to Libya, although this does little to enhance its standing among the other Arab states. The Soviets have also stepped up efforts to improve relations with Arab moderates, notably Jordan, through arms sales. Recent military agreements with Jordan, worth some $300 million, include ZSU-23/4 antiaircraft guns and SA-8, -13 and -14 air defense missiles.

Moscow persists in its efforts to expand its presence in Egypt. Since the restoration of ambassadorial-level relations in September 1984, the Soviets have been unsuccessful in resolving debt and trade problems with Egypt and have thus been unable to exploit Cairo's economic problems and its need for military spare parts. At the same time, Moscow continues policies designed to undermine not only the Camp David peace agreement but also to sabotage the current Egyptian-supported Amman accords between Jordan and the PLO. Thus, while proclaiming its unswerving desire for peace, the Soviet Union continues its attempts to sabotage the peace process.

The Soviets continue their buildup of naval and airlift capabilities in the region, both to project power and to support their political objectives. The Soviet Mediterranean Squadron (SOVMEDRON), which averages 40-50 ships, is the Kremlin's most powerful naval force permanently operating outside its home waters. Soviet naval access, from port visits to permanent presence, occurs at some 12 locations in the Mediterranean. SOVMEDRON units have held combined exercises with both Syria and Libya, and Soviet Naval Aviation deployments to those countries have increased dramatically.

Syria

Syria is the largest Soviet arms client in the Third World, having contracted for about $19 billion in military hardware. There are more Soviet military advisors in Syria—4,000—than in any other Third World country. These advisors assist the Syrians in operating and maintaining equipment and provide training in military tactics and doctrine. Particular attention is directed to Syrian air defense systems, highlighted by advanced SA-5/GAMMON missile complexes at three locations.

The Soviets also have provided extensive economic assistance to Syria, although less than that given to Damascus by other Arab nations. This aid has focused on large-scale projects such as the Euphrates hydroelectric complex, the Tartus-Homs railway, and various land reclamation and oil development projects. New projects include the development of nuclear power and research facilities. Over 1,000 Soviet economic technicians work in Syria to support these programs. Moscow has extended over $1 billion in economic credits since 1983, indicating a significant expansion in Soviet-Syrian economic ties.

The foundation of the relationship, however, remains Soviet military support to Damascus. Recent deliveries include helicopters, SA-5 air defense missiles, patrol boats, STYX and SEPAL antiship missiles, additional

The large military production capability of the Soviet Union has made it one of the world's largest suppliers of all types of major arms for Third World clients.

T-72 tanks, and attack submarines. MiG-29/ FULCRUM aircraft are expected by 1987.

In return for military and economic assistance, the Syrians provide the Soviets access to the ports of Latakia and Tartus as well as to the airfield at Tiyas. Tartus has become the primary maintenance facility for Soviet submarines operating in the Mediterranean, with a submarine tender, oiler, and water tanker located there. Additionally, Moscow receives political support from Damascus on many international issues, particularly regarding Soviet actions in Afghanistan.

Libya

The basis for Soviet-Libyan relations is largely military. Since 1970, Libya has received over $10 billion in Soviet military equipment. About 2,000 Soviet military advisors are in Libya as well as approximately 1,200 East European advisors and technicians. The Soviet advisory mission assists with the assembly and maintenance of advanced Soviet equipment such as MiG-25/FOXBAT fighters and Mi-24/HIND helicopters. The Soviets also provide pilot instruction and assist in training Libyan military personnel. Despite its large surplus of arms, Libya continues to receive modern military equipment. Recent deliveries have included the long-range, medium-to-high-altitude surface-to-air missile, the SA-5. The Libyans are building at least two SA-5 sites, enabling them to attack aircraft operating close to or over the Gulf of Sidra. In return for supplying Libya with arms, the Soviet have received additional access to Libyan ports and airfields, thereby enhancing Soviet military capabilities in the region. The number of Soviet naval combatant port visits and Il-38/MAY antisubmarine warfare aircraft deployments to Libya has risen over the past few years. In January 1986, following the Rome and Vienna airport terrorist attacks, the Soviet cruiser, *SLAVA,* deployed into the Mediterranean to join the guided-missile cruiser, *GROZNYY,* in providing a Soviet presence during the tensions.

Algeria

Algeria's relationship with the Soviet Union

is tied to continued dependence on Soviet military equipment. Soviet-supplied equipment includes T-62 and T-72 tanks, MiG-21/FISHBED, MiG-23/FLOGGER, and MiG-25/FOXBAT fighters, as well as Soviet air defense missiles such as the SA-2/GUIDELINE, -3/GOA, -6/GAINFUL, -8/GECKO, and -9/GASKIN. By the end of 1985, Soviet equipment deliveries will have virtually fulfilled a $3.5 billion arms agreement signed in 1980.

For the near term, Algeria will remain dependent on Soviet arms and military assistance, especially for spare parts, but has indicated a willingness to diversify to Western sources. In keeping with its policy of nonalignment, Algeria has consistently refused Soviet requests for permanent base rights and combined military exercises. Further, the number of Soviet advisors has fallen from a high of 2,500 in early 1980 to approximately 800 in 1985.

Southwest Asia

The USSR is pursuing a cautious, calculated approach to cultivate its role as a major participant in the affairs of Southwest Asia. Moscow considers this region strategically important because it borders the Soviet Union and possesses large petroleum and gas reserves needed by the West. Throughout 1985, the Soviets used military assistance and diplomacy as their primary means of developing influence in the region. Overall, since 1954 the USSR has provided more than $19 billion in military hardware and supplies to various countries in Southwest Asia. In addition, the Soviets have an estimated 2,500 military advisors stationed in the region who perform maintenance on and provide training for Soviet-supplied military equipment.

Iran

Soviet-Iranian ties have been very strained for the past several years over the issues of Moscow's supplying arms to Iraq and its military activities in Afghanistan. In addition, Moscow has been at odds with Iran over its unwillingness to agree to a cease-fire and negotiations with Iraq. Nevertheless, the Soviets remain interested in expanding ties with Iran despite strong anti-Communist attitudes of the clerical regime in Tehran.

Early in 1985, political activity appeared to herald an improvement in relations between Moscow and Tehran. Rapprochement peaked in April, when Soviet Foreign Minister Gromyko received the Iranian Deputy Foreign Minister, the highest ranking Iranian visitor to the USSR in over three years. In the end, however, Moscow concluded that the Khomeini regime was seeking to curtail Soviet support to Iraq in its war with Iran without making significant concessions in return. Moscow has repeatedly made it clear that relations can improve only if Tehran ends its anti-Soviet propaganda, its support to the Afghan insurgents, and its repression of the Communist Tudeh Party— actions the present regime is unlikely to take. Moscow believes improved relations can occur only after Khomeini's death.

Iraq

The USSR has sought to maintain its influence in Iraq through large deliveries of military aid, including very modern equipment. In 1984, Iraq received $2.5 billion in military assistance and in 1985 took delivery of the Su-25/FROGFOOT ground-attack aircraft. Iraq is the first country to acquire this aircraft outside the Warsaw Pact. The Soviets also delivered SA-13/GOPHER SAM systems to Iraq. The Soviets intend to keep Baghdad supplied with highly sophisticated weapons at levels necessary to maintain its position in the war with Tehran. The USSR and Iraq signed a significant new arms accord in December during President Hussein's visit to Moscow. In addition, Moscow has tried to limit the shipment of arms by other nations to Iran.

South Yemen

Since 1977, South Yemen has been the primary focus of Soviet efforts to expand its influence in the Arabian Peninsula. Moscow has succeeded in creating an authentic patron-client relationship with Aden, based primarily on the provision of over $2 billion in military assistance. In return, the Yemeni Socialist Party has loyally responded to a variety of Soviet policies such as the export of revolution, support for terrorism, and subversion in North Yemen and Oman.

The Soviets' opportunism in South Yemen was highlighted by their role in the violent overthrow of the government in January 1986. Initially, the Soviets announced support for the established leadership, which had moderated its policies toward its neighbors in an effort to gain new sources of economic aid. Then, they attempted to mediate a cease-fire between the two factions, both of which were Marxist and pro-Soviet. Moscow eventually backed the hardline rebels when they began to consolidate power. If they are to maintain their military access, the Soviets will have to provide considerable assistance to South Yemen to repair the widespread damage done to the country during the fighting. Moreover, recent Soviet gains in the Persian Gulf region may be undermined if a new regime pursues radical policies toward its neighbors. The Soviet role in the fighting in South Yemen will also rekindle Arab suspicions of Soviet ambitions in the Third World.

North Yemen

The Soviets have relied on military assistance as their primary means of gaining influence in North Yemen. Moscow has delivered approximately $1.4 billion worth of arms since 1962, including a shipment of 16 T-62 tanks in mid-1985. The Soviets maintain a 500-man military advisory group that provides maintenance, repair, and training for North Yemen's Soviet-made military hardware. Over the past year, however, the North Yemenis have become increasingly displeased with the quality, and perhaps quantity, of the Soviet military aid program. This attitude, combined with North Yemen's recent oil discoveries and its intense suspicion about the Soviet role in the January coup in South Yemen, could weaken Moscow's standing in Sana.

Gulf Cooperation Council Members

For a long time, Kuwait was the only member of the Gulf Cooperation Council (GCC) with which the Soviets maintained relations. However, Moscow has readily responded to political openings that have recently come about within some GCC countries by undertaking cultural exchange programs. Last August, the Soviets sent a tourism official to Bahrain. Moscow also had contact with Qatar and Saudi Arabia when those countries sent delegations to participate in the opening ceremonies of the Youth Games held in the USSR during the same month. Moscow's increasing focus on the conservative Persian Gulf states has been rewarded. In September and again in November, it was announced that diplomatic relations would be established with Oman and the United Arab Emirates. The Soviets could use this entree to try to undermine Oman's security relationship with the US. Moscow is likely to try to continue to expand its influence among the other Arab principalities in the Gulf.

South Asia

India

Soviet influence in South Asia stems primarily from its close relationship with the region's largest power, India. Moscow employs several measures to sustain its influence in New Delhi but relies primarily on military assistance. In order to ensure continued Indian reliance on Soviet arms, the USSR has provided some of its most modern weapons systems at excellent prices with low interest rates and long-term repayment schedules. Moscow's determination to limit New Delhi's arms diversification efforts has led to Soviet acceptance of payment in Indian rupees rather than a hard currency and to agreements for Indian coproduction rights.

Since 1980, Soviet arms deliveries to New Delhi have totaled over $4 billion, enabling India's armed forces, the fourth largest in the world, to undergo a massive modernization program. Over 500 Soviet T-72 tanks have been delivered, providing New Delhi with a main battle tank superior to that of any other nation in South Asia. Recent aircraft deliveries include the MiG-27/FLOGGER. During 1985, the Soviet Union also provided the Indian Air Force with three Il-76/CANDID military transport aircraft while continuing its deliveries of the An-32/CLINE twin-turboprop transport.

Delivery of one of the Soviet Union's most advanced fighters—the high-performance, all-weather MiG-29/FULCRUM interceptor—is expected in 1986, as is delivery of the first KILO-Class attack submarine. Neither weapon system has previously been exported by the Soviet Union.

The new leaders of both countries have underscored the continuity of the Indo-Soviet relationship. Following the assassination of Indira Gandhi, Moscow reaffirmed Soviet-Indian ties, expressing support for Rajiv Gandhi and praising his election victory. Moscow scheduled a series of high-level visits between the two nations and successfully lobbied for Rajiv Gandhi to visit the Soviet Union before his scheduled June 1985 trip to the United States. Gandhi's visit to Moscow in May provided an opportunity to cultivate further ties with New Delhi.

Afghanistan

In December 1985, the Soviet occupation of Afghanistan entered its seventh year still opposed by widespread and popular resistance. Soviet control continues to be limited to urban areas, primarily the capital, Kabul. Nevertheless, Soviet forces, which now number 118,000, have become steadily more effective in attacking the Mujahideen, and a coherent Soviet counterinsurgency strategy designed to break the military stalemate appears to be emerging.

Last year Soviet forces in Afghanistan continued to focus on establishing control over major urban areas and on protecting vital lines of communication. The security of Soviet garrisons and airfield defense continued to receive priority attention. However, during 1985 Soviet forces also were employed with greater frequency in assault operations against resistance strongholds designed to crush insurgent initiative throughout Afghanistan.

During one such operation in the Konar Valley, Soviet forces advanced with unusual speed and effectiveness, temporarily lifting a nine-month siege of an Afghan Army border outpost. The Soviet Army demonstrated a considerably improved ability to concentrate and employ forces quickly against suspected insurgent positions. Resistance forces were also confronted by the Soviet ability to insert air assault forces into areas previously considered inaccessible to Soviet formations.

Soviet troops in combat vehicles patrol the streets of Kabul, maintaining security and enforcing Moscow's control of the capital.

This significant improvement in force projection has been enhanced by the introduction of several Special Purpose (SPETSNAZ) battalions into Afghanistan. Trained to operate in small teams behind enemy lines, SPETSNAZ units exemplify the continuing Soviet effort to tailor forces in Afghanistan to counterinsurgency operations.

Soviet attacks on Afghanistan's rural population have become commonplace. Moscow has employed "scorched earth" measures calculated to destroy the Freedom Fighters' support structure, such as the village above.

As part of its qualitative improvement, the Soviet Army in Afghanistan has introduced new weapons systems, focusing on those with greater mobility and increased lethality. Soviet airborne forces have been upgraded with the introduction of wheeled BTR-60/70 armored personnel carriers (APCs), more capable of negotiating Afghanistan's rugged terrain. The introduction of BM-21 multiple rocket launchers (MRLs) and M1981/82 120-mm self-propelled artillery has provided airborne forces with the ability to strike the insurgents more accurately and at greater range. Soviet motorized rifle divisions have also received new systems, including the BM-27 MRL and self-propelled artillery. The introduction of these systems has largely offset recent improvements in Mujahideen weaponry.

In addition to specialized troops and improved equipment, Moscow has continued to implement "scorched earth" measures directed at restricting Mujahideen access to civilian support. Throughout areas of eastern Afghanistan, Soviet forces appear to have implemented a free-fire zone policy. Villages in the region are frequently bombed or fired upon without warning in an apparent effort to depopulate areas thought to be pro-Mujahideen.

However, the 1985 Soviet campaign suffered several setbacks. Insurgent forces in the Panjsher Valley under Shah Akmad Masood overran an Afghan Army outpost, taking large numbers of prisoners. In the fall, a Soviet ammunition depot near Kabul was destroyed by

Chapter VII Global Ambitions

the insurgents. Endemic desertion and widespread collaboration with the resistance have continued to frustrate Soviet efforts to improve the size and effectiveness of the Afghan Army—essential to Moscow's long-term strategy in Afghanistan. In response, the Soviet command replaced the Afghan Minister of Defense.

Afghan Air Force officers have generally been perceived as more responsive to Soviet directives. However, in mid-1985 pro-resistance officers in the Afghan Air Force dealt a major blow to Soviet airpower in Afghanistan by destroying about 20 Soviet-built combat aircraft. In July 1985, the Afghan pilots of two Soviet-built Mi-24/HIND helicopters flew to Pakistan and requested asylum.

With the war now in its seventh year, the Kremlin is finding it increasingly difficult to maintain the fiction domestically that the Soviet presence in Afghanistan is merely a "limited contingent" of troops involved in peace corps-type missions and fighting "bandits." The Soviet media has increasingly acknowledged the difficulties of combat in Afghanistan, often making strained comparisons with the struggle against Nazi fascism. One Soviet spokesman even noted the training advantages afforded by actual combat. The Kremlin, nevertheless, is clearly preparing its populace for a long war.

Southeast Asia

Vietnam

Since the 1978 signing of the Soviet-Vietnamese Treaty of Friendship and Cooperation, the Soviet presence in Southeast Asia has expanded dramatically. This development is primarily the result of vastly increased Soviet support for Vietnam as well as for Laos and Cambodia. Vietnam has become almost totally dependent on Moscow and its East European allies for economic, military, and political assistance to support its economy, maintain its occupation of Cambodia, and counter Chinese military pressure along the Sino-Vietnamese border. From 1978 through 1985, the Soviets have provided over $5 billion in arms aid to Hanoi along with direct aid to Cambodia. Over 2,500 Soviet military advisors are in Vietnam to support this program, and a contingent of An-12/CUBs has operated in Vietnam, Laos, and Cambodia since 1979. In addition to more than $7 billion in Soviet economic assistance through 1984, Vietnamese membership in

the Council for Mutual Economic Assistance (CEMA) obligates the Soviet Union's East European allies to provide aid to Vietnam.

In return, Moscow has gained access to Vietnamese military facilities. Cam Ranh Bay has become the largest Soviet naval forward-deployment base outside the USSR. The installation includes a naval base, a composite air unit, and a growing communications, intelligence-collection, and logistics support infrastructure. The three or four attack and cruise missile submarines operating from Cam Ranh Bay conduct patrols in the South China Sea and are well situated to operate against sea lines of communication in the region. If necessary, Soviet forces at Cam Ranh Bay can augment the Indian Ocean Squadron. These facilities service the 20 to 25 Soviet ships routinely deployed to the South China Sea. In addition, since late 1984 a Soviet air unit comprised of 16 naval Tu-16/BADGER and 8 BEAR D/F aircraft, as well as a squadron of MiG-23/FLOGGER C/Gs, has been deployed at Cam Ranh Bay airfield. The BEAR and BADGER aircraft conduct reconnaissance, intelligence-collection, and ASW missions throughout the South China Sea. The BADGERs' strike range from Cam Ranh Bay includes not only regional states but also the Philippines, Guam, and Palau and Yap—the western portion of Micronesia. These military forces indicate the increasing reach of Moscow's military power and the potential political influence of the USSR on regional decisions.

ASEAN

Moscow has increased its efforts to improve relations with the states of the Association of South East Asian Nations (ASEAN) through expanded trade and cultural ties as well as by stressing issues of regional concern. Increased economic ties are attractive to these states, especially Indonesia and Malaysia, as they seek ways to increase non-oil exports to improve their trade positions. The Soviets have also continued their efforts to sell military equipment in the region but without positive results.

South Pacific

After almost a decade of relative inactivity, the Soviet Union has renewed its efforts to improve relations with the South Pacific island states and to increase its maritime access to that region. These efforts are designed to disrupt Western maritime mobility. To achieve

The AGI MARSHAL NEDELIN, lead ship of the newest class of Soviet space support ships, is equipped to support both missile tests and space launch activities. It currently operates in the Western Pacific.

The PRIMORYE-Class intelligence-collection ship is equipped with a versatile array of collection, electronic warfare, and communications equipment. The PRIMORYE is one of the Soviets' most sophisticated intelligence-collection ships and has conducted operations against US facilities on the Kwajalein atoll.

this strategic objective, the Soviets are relying on both commercial and scientific programs to gain influence and access. For example, Soviet interest in hydrographic research reflects their desire to improve their submarine operations and develop methods to counter US undersea military activities in the region. It could also assist them in acquiring strategic minerals from deep seabed mining areas.

Since September 1984, Moscow has offered to negotiate fishing access agreements, including substantial Soviet hard currency payments, with Fiji, Kiribati, Papua New Guinea, Tuvalu, and Vanuatu. Kiribati concluded an agreement in August for an annual Soviet licensing payment of about $1.7 million. This agreement not only allows the Soviets access to a wide area of the mid-Pacific adjacent to the US missile testing range at Kwajalein, it also could in-

fluence other island states to follow Kiribati's lead. Further, Soviet inroads could create a political environment that would give them the ability to intimidate and bring the smaller Pacific island states under their influence.

Moscow has also sought to exploit the antinuclear sentiment in the Pacific island states, Australia, and New Zealand through calls for nuclear-free zones that would have a much greater impact on US ships and aircraft than on those of the Soviets. This, coupled with their efforts to have states in this area deny access to the US, could prove to be damaging to Western strategic interests.

Northeast Asia

Over the last two decades, the Far East—and Northeast Asia in particular—has become second in importance only to Western Europe for Soviet political-military policy. The Soviets cite geography and the rapid economic development of the Soviet Far East as justification for their claim that the USSR is an Asian power and should therefore play a major role in the Pacific. The primary Soviet concern, however, is security. Moscow has focused on achieving superior military power in the region through the quantitative and qualitative improvement of Soviet forces in the Far East. These forces include over 50 divisions along the Sino-Soviet border and northeast Asia, some 1,700 tactical aircraft—excluding BACKFIRE bombers—and more than one-third of the Soviet mobile SS-20 missile force. The effective Soviet use of other overt instruments of foreign policy, such as diplomacy, aid, and trade, has been hindered by the Soviet military buildup which has led to a widespread regional perception of the Soviet Union as a threat to peace.

One characteristic of the Gorbachev approach to foreign policy has been the advocacy of an updated version of Brezhnev's Asian Collective Security proposal. Gorbachev first made this new proposal during Rajiv Gandhi's visit to Moscow in May 1985. The proposal calls for convening an All-Asian Security Forum modeled after the European security conference that led to the 1975 Helsinki Accords. This Asian conference would focus on peace and disarmament issues. Unlike the earlier Brezhnev proposal, Gorbachev's scheme is directed less against China than against the US security presence in Asia. Moscow has been persistent in its advocacy of this purposefully vague proposal with Asian governments.

China

China remains the major focus of Soviet activities in Asia. Although the overall relationship remains adversarial, Moscow has incentives to preserve and deepen the current Sino-Soviet dialogue, which began in October 1982. Even a slight improvement in bilateral relations is interpreted by Moscow as a loss for the US on the global balance sheet and an enhancement of Moscow's image.

Moscow undertook several initiatives during Chernenko's funeral to maintain the momentum of Sino-Soviet relations. Gorbachev announced Moscow's desire "to have a serious improvement in relations" with Beijing and that, given "reciprocity," such improvement was "possible." This statement is consistent with the longstanding Soviet position that Beijing must make the first substantive concessions. In addition, Gorbachev met with Vice Premier Li Peng, marking the first such high-level contact between Soviet and Chinese leaders since 1969. In response, China publicly acknowledged the Soviet Union as "socialist" for the first time since 1967.

Despite these overtures, Sino-Soviet relations reflect a pattern of a gradual expansion of economic and cultural ties with no movement on fundamental strategic issues. The long-anticipated visit to Moscow of Chinese Deputy Premier Yao Yilin took place in July 1985 and resulted in the signing of a five-year economic agreement intended to produce reciprocal trade totaling $3.5 billion by 1990. Normalization talks also occurred in April and October 1985, but with no new overtures by either side. Moscow is unlikely to accede to Beijing's demands that normalization of relations be preceded by the withdrawal of Soviet forces from Afghanistan, the withdrawal of Vietnamese troops from Cambodia, and the removal of Soviet military forces from the Chinese border and Mongolia.

North Korea

Soviet-North Korean relations have expanded markedly since President Kim Il-song visited Moscow in May 1984, resulting in the most dramatic change in Pyongyang's foreign policy since the early 1970s. To date, these changes have had a military focus, with increased Soviet military assistance in exchange for expanded cooperation in intelligence-collection activities.

The delivery of MiG-23/FLOGGER aircraft to North Korea has been the most significant trend in the improving bilateral relationship. There are presently 26 MiG-23s in North Korea. A total of some 35 to 45 such aircraft are expected to be delivered. A limited number of surface-to-air missiles, probably SA-3s/GOAs, have been delivered to North Korea. These arms transfers reflect Moscow's conclusion that Pyongyang is seriously prepared to improve bilateral relations. This is the first concrete evidence of an agreement by Moscow to renew deliveries of sophisticated new military equipment to North Korea.

In exchange, it appears that the Soviets have received permission to make military overflights of North Korea. Increased activity is expected for both intelligence collection and strike mission simulation. These flights have been made by Tu-16/BADGER reconnaissance aircraft, Tu-95/BEAR G strike aircraft, and Tu-95/BEAR D naval intelligence collectors.

One important result of Soviet support has been an improvement in overall military relations. To mark the end of World War II in Europe, Soviet and North Korean fighter units in early May conducted their first exchange visits. In late summer, to commemorate the 40th anniversary of the liberation of Korea from Japan, the Soviets sent a record number of delegates and three naval combatants—one KARA-Class guided-missile cruiser and two KRIVAK-Class guided-missile frigates. This visit was the first such port call to North Korea by major Soviet naval combatants.

Japan

Soviet military policies continue to dominate relations with Japan to the detriment of Moscow's political and economic ties with Tokyo. Soviet-Japanese relations are also clouded by the ongoing dispute over the Northern Territories (south of the Kuril Islands). Moscow denies and refuses to discuss the Japanese claim to these illegally occupied islands and continues its military buildup there with the deployment of MiG-23/FLOGGERs to Etorofu Island. While the Soviets seek to improve economic ties with Japan to obtain technology and capital to develop Siberia, Moscow's military buildup and antagonistic policies have only encouraged Tokyo to strengthen its ties with the United States and to continue upgrading its own military self-defense capabilities.

Throughout last year, bilateral meetings have occurred in response to changes in the

The second ship of the KIROV-Class of nuclear-powered guided-missile cruisers, the FRUNZE, on its way to join the expanding number of major combatants in the Pacific Fleet.

Soviet approach. Building on the meeting between Prime Minister Nakasone and Premier Tikhonov during the November 1984 funeral of Indira Gandhi—the first heads-of-state meeting between the two countries in 11 years— Tokyo has responded favorably to Moscow's overtures. Most notably, Prime Minister Nakasone met with General Secretary Gorbachev during the March 1985 funeral for Chernenko. In mid-January 1986, Soviet Foreign Minister Shevardnadze paid an official visit to Tokyo. This was the first Soviet foreign ministerial visit to Tokyo since 1973 and resulted in a joint communique that implicitly allows for future discussion of the Territories issue.

Concurrently, Moscow has intensified its propaganda campaign, criticizing Tokyo for its interest in the US Strategic Defense Initiative program and charging Prime Minister Nakasone with seeking to remilitarize Japan. This propaganda effort, coupled with the persistent obstacle of the Northern Territories, points to continuing tensions despite the recent improvement in relations.

Outlook

Moscow's use of all the instruments of foreign policy—military assistance, diplomacy, trade, aid, propaganda, and overt and covert activities—demonstrates a determined effort to extend Soviet power and influence and to promote the USSR as the dominant world force. Its quest for overseas bases, coupled with its improving capabilities in strategic mobility, reflects Moscow's desire to advance the ideological goal of a Communist world order.

Chapter VIII

US Policies and Programs

The preceding chapters have documented developments in Soviet military power by describing the continuing major military buildup that has been sustained over the past quarter-century. The increase in Soviet military power presents a serious challenge to the United States and our allies and friends, stemming in part from three major developments:

- the quantitative and qualitative Soviet military buildup, which has produced a major shift in the nuclear and conventional balance;
- the dramatic increase in Soviet military offensive capabilities; and
- improvements in the global reach of Soviet military forces, enhancing the Kremlin's ability to project influence and power.

The US response to the Soviet challenge has involved a spectrum of security policies aimed at deterrence and defense. The basis for these measures stems from a hard look at our strategic concept to preserve peace not only for today but also for future generations. Some of the measures undertaken to assure peace are: arms control initiatives; modernization of our nuclear and conventional forces; efforts toward strategic defense research; improvements in the readiness, mobility, and sustainability of our forces; protection of our technology; improvements in our industrial base; strengthening our alliances and capabilities for coalition warfare; and providing security assistance

By the end of the 1980s, the Soviet strategic nuclear threat will include regiments of BLACKJACK bombers armed with the 3,000-kilometer-range, nuclear-tipped AS-15 air-launched cruise missile. With new and more capable nuclear attack systems continuing to enter the USSR's Armed Forces, the Soviet Union's military challenge to the United States and the Free World continues unabated.

to our allies and friends. These are essential measures if world peace is to be maintained. Unlike the Soviet Union, we do not seek to win any political or territorial advantage by force of arms. At the same time, we must face the sobering fact that our vital interests cannot be protected if the Soviets enjoy an advantage in every category of military strength.

The following discussion summarizes the United States' policies and programs initiated to meet the Soviet challenge. A more comprehensive report on these developments is regularly made available to the public in such publications as the *Annual Report to the Congress* by the Secretary of Defense and the *Military Posture Statement* of the Chairman of the Joint Chiefs of Staff.

Deterrence and Arms Control

The primary security objective of the United States is to defend our right, and that of our allies, to live in freedom. Since World War II, we have sought to accomplish this objective by maintaining military forces capable of deterring Soviet military aggression and of frustrating their attempts to use military strength for political intimidation. And while we believe that, in the words of President Reagan, "a nuclear war cannot be won and must never be fought," effective deterrence requires that we must be perceived as able and prepared, if Soviet aggression does take place, to impose unacceptable damage on key elements of Soviet power.

At the same time, the United States is committed to an arms control process that, if it were to lead to equitable and verifiable agreements, could strengthen deterrence and enhance stability while radically reducing the numbers and destructive power of Soviet and American nuclear weapons. Our proposals made to the Soviets at the Nuclear and Space Talks (NST) in Geneva reflect that commitment. We are also working to lower the risk of conventional war through the Conference on Security and Confidence-Building Measures and Disarmament in Europe (CDE) and the Mutual and Balanced Force Reduction Talks (MBFR) in Vienna.

Deterrence and stability, however, are conditions that can result only from a balance between Soviet and American forces. Given the Soviets' massive buildup of both offensive and defensive capabilities—as documented in previous chapters—failure by the United States to modernize its own forces and to proceed with its Strategic Defense Initiative (SDI) research program would weaken deterrence and increase the risk of war.

Similarly, arms control agreements must be complied with and cannot be isolated from the underlying competition between the United States and the Soviet Union. Thus, an arms control agreement that preserved areas of Soviet advantage while placing unfair and unilateral restrictions on the United States would threaten Western security and wreck any hope for extensive, equitable, and verifiable arms reductions in the future. The situation will worsen if the Soviets continue their violations and probable violations of the letter and spirit of numerous existing arms control agreements. For these reasons, the United States has carefully constructed its defense modernization and arms control policies to be an integrated and mutually reinforcing approach to preserving Western security in the face of an evolving Soviet threat.

Arms Control Compliance

As part of our continuing efforts to put the arms control process on a firm and lasting basis, we have paid close attention to the question of compliance while the Soviets have not. The pattern of Soviet violations and probable violations raises serious questions concerning the integrity of the arms control process and its ability to guarantee a more stable and secure international environment. We have stated our readiness to "go the extra mile" in giving the Soviets an opportunity to correct their activities involving noncompliance. But we cannot accept a double standard that amounts to unilateral treaty compliance and restraint by the United States.

The list of Soviet violations and likely violations of both the letter and spirit of arms control agreements is long and getting longer. A few of the significant examples include:

- Construction of a large phased-array, ballistic missile detection and tracking radar at Krasnoyarsk in central Siberia in direct violation of the 1972 ABM Treaty requirement that such early warning radars be located on the periphery of the Soviet Union and be oriented outward.
- Deployment of the SS-25 single-warhead, road-mobile ICBM in direct violation of

the Soviets' political commitment to refrain from undercutting the 1979 SALT II agreement, which limits each side to just one new type of "light" ICBM. The Soviets previously said that their soon-to-be-deployed SS-X-24 multiple warhead ICBM was their one allowable new missile.

- Encryption of ballistic missile telemetry in direct violation of SALT II provisions prohibiting deliberate concealment measures that impede verification of compliance by national technical means.
- Maintenance of an offensive biological warfare program and capability in direct violation of the 1972 Biological and Toxic Weapons Convention and involvement in the production, transfer, and use of chemical and toxic substances for hostile purposes in Southeast Asia and Afghanistan in direct violation of the 1925 Geneva Protocol.
- Underground nuclear testing activities that constitute a probable violation of legal obligations under the Threshold Test Ban Treaty of 1974, which prohibits underground nuclear tests with yields exceeding 150 kilotons.

In December 1985, the President again reported to the Congress concerning Soviet non-compliance with arms control agreements. The report reaffirmed previous findings concerning Soviet violations and announced several additional findings. In relation to the SALT I and II Treaties, the additional findings were:

- Soviet violation of SALT I Interim Agreement by using facilities remaining at dismantled or destroyed SS-7 sites to store, support, or launch ICBMs;
- Soviet violation of the SALT II strategic nuclear delivery vehicles limit;
- Soviet violation of the SALT II prohibition on concealment of missile/launcher association;
- Soviet action inconsistent with BACKFIRE bomber commitment—Arctic staging; and
- evidence of BACKFIRE production at slightly more than the permitted 30 from 1979 to 1984 and production at slightly less than 30 from 1984 to 1985.

In the case of the ABM Treaty, it was determined that Soviet activities associated with rapid reload were ambiguous in relation to treaty compliance but were a serious concern.

Soviet activities relating to ABM-capable surface-to-air missiles (SAMs) were also held to be ambiguous.

The expanding pattern of Soviet violations is clear and has important political and military implications. Militarily, the Krasnoyarsk radar violation goes to the heart of the ABM Treaty. It appears even more menacing when considered in the context of other Soviet ABM-related activities. Together, they cause concern that the Soviet Union may be preparing an ABM territorial defense. Moreover, most worrisome is the technical argument by which the Soviets sought to justify the SS-25, for it might be applied to additional prohibited ICBMs in the future.

Soviet violation of the Geneva Protocol and the Biological Weapons Convention has given them a prohibited biological warfare capability which we do not have and against which we have no defense. Soviet violations of the SALT II verification provisions have impeded our ability to verify Soviet compliance with existing treaties, present special obstacles to maintaining existing arms control agreements, and are indicative of a Soviet attitude contrary to the fundamentals of sound arms control agreements.

The United States is seeking through diplomatic channels to obtain Soviet explanations, clarifications, and, where necessary, corrective actions. So far, the Soviets have refused to address seriously our compliance concerns. In addition, some Soviet violations—for example, the flight-testing and deployment of the SS-25— are, by their very nature, irreversible. For these reasons, in June 1985 President Reagan directed the Department of Defense to identify specific actions that could be taken in proportionate response to, and as a hedge against the military consequences of, those violations that the Soviets fail to correct.

Modernization Programs

Strategic Modernization
In 1981, President Reagan committed the United States to reversing the potentially dangerous erosion of the credibility of our strategic nuclear deterrent that resulted from the massive expansion and modernization of Soviet strategic forces during the 1970s.

The net result of the combination of Soviet modernization and deployment programs for their nuclear attack forces and US restraint in modernizing its offensive nuclear forces was to allow the Soviet Union a "sanctuary" for its ICBM force and for the other key assets that were protected by hardening. This, combined with the Soviets' ability to attack our Minuteman force, using only a portion of their ICBMs, significantly eased the problems of Soviet nuclear planners. They could begin to envision a potential nuclear confrontation in which they could threaten to destroy a very large part of our force in a first strike while retaining overwhelming nuclear forces to deter any retaliation we could carry out.

This ability to conduct a first strike also threatened to make less credible the deterrent linkage between our strategic nuclear force and our forward-deployed conventional and nuclear forces. In addition, the increasing Soviet emphasis on blunting the effects of US retaliation held open the prospect of undercutting deterrence further because the Soviet leadership could come to believe that their hardening programs would permit them to emerge from a major conflict with their forces, command and control system, and other support systems damaged but still functioning.

Since 1981, the Soviets have continued to press ahead with development and deployment of new generations of ICBMs, submarine-launched ballistic missiles (SLBMs), and aircraft capable of strategic missions. However, over the last five years, the United States has begun significant improvements in its strategic triad which—if carried to completion—will help restore high confidence among both friends and adversaries in the credibility of our deterrent forces. The purpose of our modernization programs is not to achieve strategic superiority over the Soviets but to frustrate their determined efforts to shift the strategic balance irrevocably in their favor.

Our strategic modernization programs consist of four key elements:
- In response to the threat posed by Soviet fourth-generation deployments and to the survivability and retaliatory capability of our land-based ICBMs, we will begin deploying a limited number of Peacekeeper missiles in selected Minuteman silos in 1986. Research and development will also continue on a new, single-warhead ICBM.
- To replace our aging Poseidon nuclear-powered ballistic missile submarine (SSBN) force, which will face block obsolescence in the 1990s, the United States is building Trident submarines at the rate of one per year. Deployment of the D-5 missile in the Trident in the late 1980s will strengthen our vital sea-based deterrent by giving it a hard-target capability not possessed by existing SLBMs.
- The usefulness of our B-52 bombers—the newest of which was built 23 years ago—has been extended for a few more years owing to the standoff capability of the air-launched cruise missile (ALCM) being deployed on selected B-52s. Introduction of the B-1B will ensure a continued penetration capability against Soviet defenses, at least until the deployment of a new advanced-technology bomber in the 1990s. At that time the B-1B will assume the role of ALCM carrier.
- In addition to fielding more survivable delivery vehicles, we are improving the survivability, endurance, and effectiveness of our command, control, and communications systems. This strengthens stability by making it less attractive to the Soviets to attempt a preemptive attack against our command system. Also, these improvements will further ensure our capability to manage our strategic forces effectively.

Our strategic modernization programs do much more than deter Soviet aggression against the United States. They also serve, as they have for the past four decades, to deny the Soviets the ability—either real or perceived—to use or threaten to use their strategic forces against our allies and friends.

Non-Strategic Modernization

The growth over the past decade of Soviet theater nuclear capabilities—in particular, their SS-20 deployments—has posed a unique challenge for the United States. Although these weapons do not threaten contiguous US territory, they do affect our vital national security interests because they significantly increase the threat to our friends and allies in Europe and Asia. It has been necessary, therefore, to respond to this threat by formulating and implementing a collective Western response.

Our NATO allies are meeting the challenge. In accordance with its 1979 dual-track decision,

NATO has completed deployment of the Pershing II, and deployment of ground-launched cruise missiles continues on schedule. At the same time, the United States, in close consultation with NATO allies, is seeking to negotiate an agreement with the Soviets at Geneva that would totally eliminate, or at least greatly reduce to equal global warhead limits, the entire class of longer range intermediate-range nuclear force (LRINF) missiles.

NATO is also following through on the 1983 Montebello decision to withdraw 1,400 nuclear weapons from the NATO stockpile within the next few years. Taken together with the 1,000 warheads already withdrawn, the number of nuclear warheads in the Alliance's stockpile will be reduced to the lowest point in 20 years. This is in stark contrast to the massive Soviet buildup of nuclear forces facing NATO.

Space Command

On 23 September 1985, the United States Space Command was activated in Colorado Springs, Colorado. This new unified command has operational control over the US Air Force Space Command, the US Naval Space Command, and the US Army Space Planning Group. The new command provides centralized planning and daily mission operations for space systems support of US military forces worldwide. Additionally, the mission of integrated warning of strategic attack against the continental United States has been assigned to this command. The formation of this command recognizes the importance of space systems in safeguarding the interests of the United States and its allies and is not directly related to the Strategic Defense Initiative research program.

Conventional Forces Modernization

Land Forces

To meet the Soviet threat, the United States is working to improve the antiarmor capabilities and tactical mobility of our ground forces as well as to provide better command, control, and communications (C^3) support. Over 400 modernized combat systems are being fielded, including the M1 Abrams tank, the M2/3 Bradley Fighting Vehicle (BFV) equipped with TOW antiarmor missiles, the Multiple Launch Rocket System, and the AH-64/Apache attack helicopter, which carries Hellfire antiarmor missiles. In addition, many support systems such as the Black Hawk helicopter and the high-mobility multipurpose wheeled vehicle have improved the effectiveness of our land forces. We have stepped up the pace of our ground force modernization programs, adding more M1s, BFVs, and AH-64s to the procurement levels planned by the previous administration.

The effective use of tactical mobility can help counter a numerically superior opposing force by permitting the rapid concentration of personnel and materiel at places where they can best exploit enemy vulnerabilities. A new generation of highly mobile helicopters and support vehicles will allow us to make better use of this tactic. For example, the UH-60/Black Hawk helicopter, which proved its worth in Grenada, is larger, more agile, and more reliable than the UH-1 it replaces.

Also supporting our ground forces are highly capable new weapons such as the Multiple-Launch Rocket System (MLRS). In less than a minute, a single launcher can fire 12 rockets beyond cannon range, covering an area the size of 6 football fields with approximately 7,700 grenade-like submunitions that are effective against both personnel and lightly armored targets. Additionally, the MLRS is an excellent example of US-NATO armaments cooperation.

Complementing these improvements in combat systems are upgrades to the command and control systems that would support our forces in battle. During the mid-to-late 1980s, our commanders will receive lightweight, jam-resistant C^3 equipment to assist them in managing their forces on a high-technology battlefield.

Maritime Forces

Strong maritime forces are needed to support our forward defense strategy, to fulfill the responsibilities associated with our network of overseas alliances, and to protect the vital sea lanes linking the US to Europe, Southwest Asia, and Northeast Asia. We rely heavily on maritime forces to respond to a wide variety of crises—a role for which their global reach, rapid responsiveness, and integrated combat power are particularly well suited.

The warfighting capability of our naval forces has improved markedly, with substantial increases in the quality and quantity of our ships, which numbered 540 in October 1985 and which are now well along toward our goal of a force of 600 ships. Modern aircraft carrier battle groups enable our naval forces to respond rapidly to crises throughout the world and to conduct sustained operations in areas where we do not have access to airfields or other major land bases.

With the delivery of 3 new nuclear-powered Nimitz-Class carriers over the next six years, we will expand to a force of 15 aircraft carriers. Four Iowa-Class battleships, now being refurbished and armed with long-range Tomahawk and Harpoon cruise missiles, are rejoining the fleet and will provide a potent supplement to our carrier force. At the same time, we are arming a variety of surface ships, attack submarines, and combat aircraft with Tomahawk and Harpoon weapons systems, giving them greater effectiveness against a wide array of targets.

To enhance our amphibious assault capabilities, we are building new high-speed air-cushion landing craft and two new classes of amphibious ships. By the middle of the next decade, our amphibious lift capability will have expanded by one-third. Ship-to-shore mobility will also be improved by the powerful CH-53E helicopter, now joining the force in large numbers, and by the new MV-22A Osprey tilt-rotor aircraft, currently under development. The combination of these assets will permit assaults to be launched from points over the horizon, thereby reducing vulnerability and increasing the likelihood of surprise. Once ashore, our Marines will be provided greater mobility and firepower by the addition of the Light Armored Vehicle (LAV).

We are working hard to improve our ability to locate and combat enemy submarines. One example is a new attack submarine scheduled for production near the end of this decade. A key design objective is to build a quieter boat with better sensors, enabling it to hunt down and engage enemy forces while remaining undetected. At the same time, we are continuing to construct improved versions of the Los Angeles-Class attack submarine as replacements for older boats that are approaching obsolescence; some 33 of the 52 Los Angeles-Class boats authorized to date are now operational. In addition, LAMPS helicopters, new towed-array sonar systems, and lightweight torpedoes are upgrading the antisubmarine capabilities of our naval surface and air forces.

Our defense against antiship missiles will be improved by the wide-area surveillance systems now under development and by strengthened area air defense systems. Central to these efforts is the development of tactical over-the-horizon radars that can detect enemy aircraft hundreds of miles away, thus enabling our land- and carrier-based interceptors to mount a more effective defense of our ships at sea. Likewise, the deployment of new CG-47 cruisers and DDG-51 destroyers, both of which incorporate the Aegis air defense system, will improve our ability to intercept high-speed cruise missiles and aircraft at extended ranges. Ultimately, we plan to build 27 CG-47 cruisers and 29 DDG-51 destroyers.

Tactical Air Forces

Well-trained and properly equipped tactical air forces can quickly destroy targets on land and at sea as well as provide an air defense umbrella in support of ground and naval forces worldwide. To retain our qualitative edge in this area, we must continue to improve our tactical aircraft. To that end, we are acquiring systems that will allow for rapid, multiple engagements beyond visual range while being highly maneuverable and lethal at close-in ranges. The overall capability of our tactical air forces to destroy enemy forces in the air and on the ground has improved substantially.

The Navy is modernizing its carrier-based force of combat aircraft. The F-14, our primary fleet air-defense fighter, and the long-range Phoenix missiles it carries are being upgraded. By the end of the decade, all the Navy's fighter and medium-attack squadrons will be equipped with F-14s and A-6Es, and the F/A-18 will have replaced almost 80 percent of the A-7E light-attack inventory.

The Air Force is continuing to modernize its tactical fighter forces with the new model F-15 and F-16 aircraft. Since 1980, it has more than doubled its inventory of F-15s and F-16s, bringing the combined total to nearly 1,400 aircraft. New, more durable, and easier-to-maintain engines, scheduled for installation on these aircraft in the early 1990s, will further enhance their combat effectiveness. These high-performance engines will enable the upgraded but heavier models of our fighters to keep pace with the new generation of Soviet-built fighters.

The Air Force also is upgrading its ground attack systems. Currently in development are a new airborne targeting system, the Low-Altitude Navigation and Targeting Infrared System for Night (LANTIRN), and new infrared air-to-surface missiles that will allow F-15s, F-16s, and A-10s to strike enemy targets whenever they present themselves. In addition, much-needed improvements in air-to-ground munitions have been initiated which will bring munitions effectiveness up to the high level of quality represented by these aircraft. Finally, some squadrons of B-52G aircraft have been assigned general purpose missions, such as minelaying, sea surveillance, antiship attack, and conventional bombing, supplementing their strategic duties.

Overall, our inventory of tactical aircraft has grown by the equivalent of two wings over the past four years. Over the next five years, we plan to buy 1,284 fighter and attack aircraft for the Air Force and 954 for the Navy and the Marine Corps. This will allow us to reach our goal of 14 carrier air wings by 1987 and about 40 Air Force tactical fighter wings by the early 1990s.

The deployability of Air Force tactical combat aircraft will be increased significantly during the next several years as the recently approved NATO acceleration of European airbase facilities comes to fruition. Additional bases and much-needed concrete shelters will greatly increase the initial effectiveness of our reinforcement aircraft in a European crisis.

Special Operations Forces

The United States must be prepared to respond to low-intensity conflict when it threatens our vital national interests. The Soviets and their surrogates, as a matter of policy, have both encouraged and supported this form of aggression as a way of achieving their objectives without direct confrontation with the Free World. Today, more than 20 insurgencies are threatening peace in the Third World, and one out of every four countries around the globe is engaged in some form of conflict.

Low-level conflict will likely be the most pervasive threat to Free World security for the rest of this century. Special Operations Forces (SOF) provide us the ability to respond to a range of crises in a flexible manner. They contribute to our ability to deter and defeat a major conventional attack by their capability to disrupt the enemy's lines of communication, engage in unconventional warfare, psychological operations, counterterrorism actions, or intelligence missions.

By the end of the decade, the capability of our Special Operations Forces will be enhanced by the addition of a Special Forces Group and a Navy SEAL team. Additionally, mobility will be improved through submarine dry deck shelters, patrol craft, and a significant increase in medium- and long-range SOF-configured aircraft. Readiness and sustainability for these forces will benefit by the emphasis being placed on spare parts procurement, communications equipment, and foreign language training.

Strategic Defense

As previous chapters have shown, the nature of the Soviet military threat has grown during the past quarter-century and will continue to grow during the next. Unless we adapt our response, deterrence will become much less stable and our susceptibility to coercion will increase dramatically. Recognition of these facts is the basis of our strategic and nonstrategic modernization programs and arms control policies. It also is the basis for the Strategic Defense Initiative (SDI) announced by President Reagan in March 1983.

The SDI research program is designed to determine whether advanced defensive technologies could contribute to a future in which nations could live secure in the knowledge that their national security did not rest solely upon the threat of nuclear retaliation but rather on the ability to defend against potential attacks. Specifically, the SDI is examining the possibility of effective defense against ballistic missiles.

At a minimum, the SDI is a prudent response to the very active Soviet efforts in offensive and defensive forces. The Soviets have deployed around Moscow the only operational ABM system in the world. The Soviets also have an active research and development program in both traditional and advanced defenses against ballistic missiles. If they were to have a monopoly on advanced defenses against ballistic missiles, in addition to their large and growing offensive and defensive forces, they might come to believe that they could launch a nuclear first-strike attack against the United States or our allies without fear of effective retaliation.

It is too early in our research program to speculate on the kinds of defensive systems—whether sea-based, ground-based, or space-based and with what capabilities—that might prove feasible and desirable to develop. But we currently see genuine merit in the potential of advanced technologies providing for a layered defense, with the possibility of negating a ballistic missile at various points after launch. Because the security of the United States and that of our allies remains indivisible, we are working on technologies with applications for defense against long-range ballistic missiles and against short-range ballistic missiles that threaten our allies.

Although several years of research will probably be necessary before a determination can be made whether to proceed with development and deployment of defense systems against ballistic missiles, key criteria have been identified by which the results of SDI research will be judged. First, any system to be developed and deployed must be survivable so that the Soviets would not have an incentive in a crisis to strike first. Second, any defensive system to be developed and deployed must be cost-effective relative to offensive forces—meaning that the defensive system must be able to maintain its effectiveness against the possible proliferation of offensive forces or the introduction of offensive countermeasures. Indeed, defenses would provide a significant incentive for deep reductions because they would significantly reduce or even eliminate the military effectiveness of ballistic missiles.

The SDI research program is being conducted in full compliance with the ABM Treaty. If and when our research yields positive results, we will consult with our allies about potential next steps, and we will consult and negotiate, as appropriate, with the Soviet Union pursuant to the terms of the ABM Treaty.

US Strategic Mobility

Our capability to move troops and equipment by air is unmatched by any country in the world. US airlift assets include the transports of the Military Airlift Command (MAC) augmented by the Civil Reserve Air Fleet (CRAF) in time of emergency. Current MAC strategic mobility transports include 70 C-5 and 234 C-141 aircraft. Under the CRAF program, US civilian airlines augment the military with an additional 68 cargo and 237 intercontinental passenger aircraft. The combined cargo-carrying capability of these aircraft is more than twice that of the Soviet Union's military and civilian aircraft. However, when distance to a region of possible conflict is considered, this 2:1 ratio favoring the US changes significantly in terms of maximum number of tons deliverable per day.

In any major overseas deployment, sealift will deliver about 95 percent of all dry cargo and 99 percent of all petroleum products. The US-flag merchant marine's decline necessitates a large pool of government-owned shipping, such as the Ready Reserve Force (RRF), to provide additional tonnage in time of mobilization. The RRF provides the surge shipping needed early for a deployment. The 66 dry-cargo ships and 8 tankers in the RRF are being maintained in a 5-, 10-, or 20-day readiness status at 3 primary anchorages in the US. Another set of government-owned ships, those in the National Defense Reserve Fleet (NDRF), are a valuable but aging asset and are capable of providing approximately 140 ships for sustainment requirements.

The Military Sealift Command (MSC) currently has under charter only enough ships to meet the peacetime needs of our deployed naval forces. Included under MSC long-term charter are the 25 ships of the afloat pre-positioning programs. Afloat pre-positioning programs consist of two parts: the Maritime Pre-positioning Ships (MPS) program and the Pre-positioning (PREPO) ships program (formerly Near-term Pre-positioning Force).

The MPS program is designed to combine the responsiveness of airlifted troops with sealift delivery of pre-positioned equipment. The 13 ships involved in the program will be organized into 3 MPS squadrons that can carry equipment and 30 days of supplies for 3 Marine amphibious brigades. The first MPS squadron has deployed to the US Atlantic Command's area; the second has deployed to Diego Garcia in the Indian Ocean; and the third squadron will deploy to US Pacific Command sometime this year.

The 12 PREPO ships consist of those vessels in the Mediterranean Sea, Pacific Ocean, and Indian Ocean that carry equipment and supplies for the Army, Navy, and Air Force.

Readiness

The capability of US military forces has improved measurably over the past five years and will continue to do so as more new weapons systems and modern equipment are introduced into the operating forces. In absolute terms, we now have the most effective peacetime military force in US history. However, we cannot afford to determine national security requirements on the basis of our military strength alone; we must consider the strength and objectives of our potential adversary. Since ours is fundamentally a defensive strategy, it is essential that we maintain our readiness at or above that of potential aggressors.

Our forces are better prepared to accomplish their warfighting tasks because they are better equipped, trained, and manned with highly motivated people who are confident in their ability to get the job done. Despite the progress made, we cannot lull ourselves into believing that our work is complete; much remains to be done. Readiness quickly becomes a perishable commodity without sustained support and funding.

Sustainability and Logistics

We recognize that our forces, even with a high degree of readiness, might become a "hollow" deterrent if we cannot sustain them in combat. Adequate logistics support for our forces—munitions, fuel, equipment, and repair parts—is necessary for successful deterrence and defense.

Our current level of sustainability is barely adequate for credible deterrence. In Europe, for example, our sustainability remains inferior to that of the Warsaw Pact. We will continue, in conjunction with our allies, to emphasize increases in sustainability to fortify the deterrent value of our forces. Building upon the gains made during the past five years, we seek a level of conventional sustainability to ensure deterrence of the Soviet threat. Besides providing sufficient quantities of stocks to maintain our staying power in combat, we seek forces of superior quality equipped with our most modern and effective conventional munitions.

The pre-positioning of US equipment in Europe began in the 1960s in response to US and European concerns that the forces in the theater were inadequate to meet the Warsaw Pact threat. The Army has pre-positioned in Europe heavy equipment for four divisions and supporting units and is currently pre-positioning equipment for two more divisions. The Air Force pre-positions rapid runway repair equipment, ground support equipment, munitions, fuel, and other consumables. The levels of pre-positioned fuel and munitions, however, continue to fall short of objectives. The US goal is to possess sufficient war reserve stocks to sustain wartime activity until industrial production can provide the required support. Our long-range goal is to correct the NATO-Warsaw Pact sustainability imbalance by the 1990s.

Reserve Forces

The US maintains slightly above one million personnel in the Selected Reserve and about 470,000 Individual Ready Reserves. The Selected Reserve, consisting of National Guard and Reserve units, constitutes approximately 45 percent of the total force structure. Although Selected Reserve manning has improved significantly in recent years, it does not approach the numbers of trained reserves in the USSR. US Selected Reserves include:
- one-third of the Army's combat divisions;
- one-half of the nation's strategic airlift crews;
- one-third of the Military Airlift Command's medical evacuation aircraft; and
- one-fourth of the Marine Corps' infantry divisions, aircraft wings, and force service support groups.

Technology Security

The purpose of the United States' technology security policy is to offset the Soviets' numerical advantages in weapons and manpower by protecting our strong suit—superior high-technology. The Soviet program of acquiring Free World technology is pervasive and aimed at improving the quality and effectiveness of their weapons by using the results of the Free World's research and development. We can maintain our technological superiority only if we continue to strengthen our research and development base and deny Soviet access to our militarily critical technology. The Department of Defense (DoD) is a key player in a government-wide domestic and international effort to safeguard our technological lead.

Participation in the export license application review process, which is governed by the Export Administration Act and the Arms Export Control Act, is the cornerstone of the domestic portion of DoD's Technology Security Program. The Defense Technology Security Administration (DTSA), a newly established DoD field activity, oversees this responsibility. Along with increased automation and other management initiatives, DTSA has greatly improved service to the exporting community while safeguarding our technology. DTSA also has raised the level of public support for the Technology Security Program through industry briefings and industry participation in many vital issues related to technology security.

The Militarily Critical Technologies List,

New Soviet BEAR H bombers, launch plat-forms for the long-range, nuclear-armed AS-15 cruise missile, routinely fly training missions against the United States.

first published in 1980 and continually updated, is used by export license officials as a reference guide to detail the potential military applications of a large number of technologies. The unclassified version of the list enables the business community to see clearly what technology areas DoD has identified as militarily critical. This document also aids business in its own technology security programs.

The effectiveness of our technology security program in the United States is inseparable from similar efforts by other Free World nations. The United States is committed to strengthening the existing multilateral export control organization known as COCOM, or the Coordinating Committee on Export Controls. Based in Paris, COCOM is the only organization through which Japan and the NATO nations (except Iceland) determine what should not be exported to Warsaw Pact countries and a few other destinations. COCOM is much more effective now than it was five years ago owing to a persistent US-led effort to make it a credible technology security force. In the fall of 1985, Spain announced that it would join COCOM, making it the first new member since 1954, when Japan joined at the suggestion of the United States.

Since not all technologically advanced nations are members of COCOM, the United States is negotiating agreements with various governments to establish a COCOM-level of protection for US and for indigenous technology within other countries.

This effort is underway both within and outside the European Theater. And it will grow in importance as the US continues to increase its trade with industrializing countries, particularly in the Far East. Soviet military presence and extension of influence in this part of the world is growing dramatically, making technology security efforts increasingly important.

It is clearly in our national interest to encourage both industry and our research institutions to remain innovative while expanding our rich industrial base. Our Technology Security Program will continue to be focused on protecting the applied technologies that can be incorporated into defense-related systems. Technology security controls are not intended to thwart our traditions of free expression and academic freedom in basic research. Neither are they designed to distance us from our allies and other friendly countries when it is in our national interest, and in the interest of mutual security, to share militarily significant technology.

DoD's Technology Security Program is one of the most cost-effective means of protecting national security. It has had a marked effect on the ability of the Soviets to use our technology for their military benefit. They have been forced to spend more of their resources on military research and development than would have been the case if our improved controls had not been in place. Moreover, our own defense budget reflects a lower level of expenditures than would have been necessary if the Soviets had acquired certain US technical capabilities.

Technology security is a vital component of our national defense effort. Without the West's technological lead, our ability to maintain an effective deterrence would be seriously jeopardized. The institutionalization of the Technology Security Program at DoD builds a strong foundation for the future.

US Industrial Base

The US defense industrial base is comprised of both private sector and government-owned industrial facilities that provide production and maintenance of defense materiel needed to support the armed forces. Government-owned facilities are minimal since public law requires maximum reliance on the private sector for defense goods and services. Consequently, government-owned facilities in most cases are dedicated to the production of unique defense-related materials such as munitions, artillery tubes, and tracked combat vehicles. The current US Government-owned base consists of 72 production and 43 maintenance facilities.

The US has initiated a number of important industrial preparedness measures aimed at preserving, modernizing, and expanding the defense industrial base. "Seed money" concepts and other contract incentive programs have stimulated private sector investment in advancing process technologies and plant-wide capital investments. Production programs are being developed to provide a rapid production surge during crisis situations. Sustained emphasis on vitalizing the defense industrial base is recognized by both Congress and DoD as an integral part of achieving our defense goals.

Alliance Security Structures

The United States has joined with many other Free World nations in alliances designed to deter aggression and provide the ability to defend common interests should deterrence fail. These alliances contribute to deterrence by allowing us to share the burdens without matching the Soviets weapon system for weapon system. Beyond formal alliances, we have established relations with other friendly states to promote common security objectives. The vitality of these alliances and friendships has helped to impede Soviet territorial expansion and thwart the Soviet ambition of becoming the dominant world force.

We and our allies and friends are working together to improve our common security through a variety of programs. Maintaining solidarity among free and independent states—particularly when faced with Soviet efforts to divide and intimidate them—is essential for successful alliances and requires careful attention and willingness to consider each other's views and concerns. Maintaining strong military forces for defense and improving them and our capabilities for coalition warfare in the face of a growing threat remain a top priority. Beyond this, we are pursuing many political-military programs, such as cooperative efforts toward arms control and preventing the USSR and its allies from obtaining our military-related technology.

NATO was established to respond to Soviet expansion in Eastern Europe. A strong NATO is essential to meeting the Soviet and Warsaw Pact challenge. To help meet the threat of Soviet and Warsaw Pact aggression or intimidation, NATO is pursuing new initiatives to improve its conventional forces while it continues to improve its strategic and nonstrategic nuclear forces.

In May 1985, NATO Defense Ministers approved a report that identified critical deficiencies in NATO's conventional defense structure and outlined a plan to overcome those shortcomings. The task remains to carry out this plan. Last December, NATO Defense Ministers endorsed a conceptual military framework for long-term defense planning. Another key program in NATO is to increase the degree of cooperation in research, development, and production of armaments, including exploiting emerging technologies to improve conventional defenses so that the Alliance has the best equipment and makes the best use of resources available.

We have also strengthened our friendship ties in Asia and the Pacific, regions of vital importance for our defense and for the economic well-being of the Free World. We look to Japan to carry out fully its defense missions—including territorial, air, and sealane defense to 1,000 miles—by completing implementation of its 1986-1990 defense program. We are also working with Korea and Thailand to assist them in meeting threats on their borders. In the Philippines, we are encouraging reforms and economic development to strengthen that ally. With regard to the Australia, New Zealand, United States (ANZUS) Pact, are working with our allies to overcome the difficulties caused by New Zealand's port access policy.

We continue to strengthen our relations with nations in the Middle East and Southwest Asia in a continuing effort to deter Soviet aggression and maintain access to that region's resources while promoting the search for a lasting Arab-Israeli peace. Although we have no formal alliances in the Middle East, we are gradually expanding our security relationships with regional states in pursuit of mutual interests. We have expanded our cooperation with Egypt, Jordan, and Pakistan and have moved forward on military cooperation with Israel.

In Africa and Latin America, we have seen the threat that low-intensity conflict and terrorism pose to developing nations that are struggling to build democratic institutions. Since formal alliances are not always practical in these circumstances, security assistance programs have become the basis for ensuring regional security and the stability of friendly nations. Despite the efforts of the Soviets and their proxies to disrupt fragile economies and undermine democratic development, leaders in countries like El Salvador have demonstrated their willingness to resist aggression.

Security Assistance

Security assistance strengthens formal alliances and helps ensure stability in regions where formal alliances are not possible. Our security assistance programs have been instrumental in improving stability in Central America, preventing the spread of the Iran-Iraq war, and strengthening the posture of our friends and allies in Europe, Asia, Africa, and Latin America. The economic burden we bear in providing this assistance to our friends is worthwhile because it is far more effective and less costly for indigenous forces to protect their own freedoms than for the United States to attempt to perform these missions on their behalf.

Our programs are designed to preserve the liberty and independence of the states that receive this assistance.

We develop our security assistance programs from a hierarchy of strategic considerations. Starting with global US strategic objectives, we formulate programs appropriate to each region in which we have major interests. These regional objectives are weighed together with the country-specific threats and military requirements in order to plan, with the country, the details of each country's program. Of special note are the new programs for Pakistan, increased funding for Israel, Egypt, and Turkey, and a vigorous response in Central America.

Security assistance contributes to our foreign policy and defense objectives and to ongoing diplomatic efforts to resolve conflicts in areas such as the Middle East. US security assistance programs also play a crucial role in bilateral and coalition efforts to contain or deter conflicts in areas of concern to the US.

Conclusion

The United States, together with our allies and friends, must maintain the military capabilities required to deter and, if necessary, defeat Soviet aggression against our vital interests. We do not seek to match the Soviet Union in defense spending or in the acquisition of specific armaments. We must, however, continually assess the global military balance in which Soviet forces are a major factor. Realizing that the perceptions of the Soviets, our allies, and other nations are affected by the balance, we cannot accept a position of military inferiority. Maintaining a strong military capability over the long term will require the United States to invest in its defense structure while pursuing genuine, verifiable, and equitable negotiated arms reductions. We and our allies and friends must have a full and precise understanding of the Soviet challenge. The publication of this edition of *Soviet Military Power* is a step in that direction as we pursue our transcending goal of peace and security.